Unwin Education Books: 7

ASSESSMENT AND TESTING:
AN INTRODUCTION

Unwin Education Books

Series Editor: Ivor Morrish, BD, BA, Dip.Ed. (London), BA (Bristol).

Unwin Education Books: 7
Series Editor: Ivor Morrish

Assessment and Testing
An Introduction

HARRY SCHOFIELD
M.A. (Cantab.), M.Ed.
Head of Education Department, St. Katharine's College of Education, Liverpool

London
GEORGE ALLEN AND UNWIN LTD
RUSKIN HOUSE   MUSEUM STREET

ISBN 0 04 370041 1 Hardback
     0 04 370042 X Paper

Printed in Great Britain
in 10 point Times Roman type
by Cox & Wyman Ltd,
London, Fakenham and Reading

To my son, Nigel,
in the hope that his future may be happy

Contents

Acknowledgement

Grateful acknowledgement is due to Messrs. Harper & Row, New York, Evanston, and London, and to Harper International Student Reprints for their permission to quote the passage on p. 87 from *A Practical Introduction to Measurement and Evaluation* by H. H. Remmers, N. L. Gage, and J. Francis Rummel.

Introduction

Lord Kelvin once said:

'When you can measure what you are speaking about and express it in numbers, you know something about it; but when you cannot measure it, when you cannot express it in numbers, your knowledge is of a meagre and unsatisfactory kind.'

We can call this an expression of the scientific attitude. Today, we are better acquainted with the ideas which prompted Kelvin's remarks than people were in his day. In our own age, it is a daily occurrence for large numbers of people all over the world to measure something. Every four years the Olympic Games take place and millions of people become 'record-conscious'. We wait eagerly for people to run faster or jump higher than anyone has run or jumped before.

Such records can be determined only by the most accurate measurement techniques. A new record time may be as little as one-tenth of a second faster than the previous best. Those who watch in the stadium and on television do not ask only, 'Who ran fastest or jumped highest?' They also ask, 'By how much?'

In other areas we are less eager to accept figures or even to accept measurement of any sort. If we apply for a post or a place in an educational institution and we are told that our intelligence is to be measured, we react unfavourably to the suggestion. We fear that the motive behind the measurement is to prove that we are unintelligent. If we submit to the test (or measurement) of intelligence and the score (or measure) is in our favour, we accept it. If it is not in our favour, we reject it on the grounds that the measurement is wrong anyway.

Again, we accept the statement that the optimum age for success in clay-pigeon shooting is thirty-four, because a body of people have studied the ages of all past winners of the event in the Olympic Games, and have produced the evidence of figures to show that their statement is not based on guesswork. But, if the medical profession, also basing its statement on the evidence of figures gathered in a similar way, says that people who smoke thirty-four cigarettes a day run a high risk of dying of lung cancer, we do not believe the figures so readily. We tend to be dogmatic in our rejection of the evidence if we are in the habit of smoking thirty-four cigarettes a day (or about that number), and have no wish to give up the habit. It seems that we are most likely to refuse the evidence of figures and measurements when what is measured involves us personally and the findings are not to our liking.

Assessment and measurement can take many forms. The simplest and probably the best known measure is the teacher's 'mark'. At the other extreme are highly sophisticated tests of intelligence, aptitudes, abilities and personality. For all its simplicity (and for all its defects, as we shall see later) the teacher's mark scheme is rarely questioned except by psychologists. Because of its long history this particular method of measuring is willingly accepted. On the other hand, we are inclined to reject out of hand the sophisticated tests because they are new and unfamiliar. Yet, in other areas, such as clothes and records, we accept what is new with almost alarming alacrity. It seems that we are a curious mixture of the scientific and the unscientific, accepting the teacher's marks but rejecting standard scientific tests. We are also inconsistent, rejecting the old in fashion and records and clinging to the old in assessment and testing.

This is the more surprising when we think about the matter a little further. The teacher's mark is something of a mystery. We do not know how he arrives at that mark. It may be determined by the mood he is in when he awards it, by his state of health at the time, by the impression for good or bad that the person whose work he is marking has made on him in areas outside the work being marked. The reason for the mark may be totally irrational; it may even be the result of downright prejudice.

This is impossible in the case of an intelligence test mark. As we shall see in a later chapter, the marks given for an intelligence test are so designed that they cannot be affected by the mood, bias and prejudices of the marker, or by the impression that the candidate makes on the person administering the test. The mark given is awarded on logical grounds. We prefer the illogical in measurement, just as we prefer the illogical in fashion, for there is no logical reason why we should wear the same type of clothes that everyone else is wearing, especially when such clothes look ridiculous on us.

Moreover, tests of intelligence and personality are designed by experts and carefully tested, as a new aero engine or racing-car is tested before being made generally available. Still we are reluctant to accept them. Yet we will take one look at a person and pronounce him unintelligent or a weak character. If we are asked on what evidence we base these judgments, we reply: 'His eyes are set close together', or 'He has a receding chin'. From these we generalize and say: 'All people whose eyes are set close together are unintelligent', 'All people with receding chins are weak characters'. When we talk about sampling and sampling techniques, we shall see that scientists would never dream of behaving in this way.

The irony is that most people are very concerned with being fair. They would do almost anything to avoid being exposed as unfair, especially to children. Yet there are few things more unfair than the type of sweeping statement that we have just seen. The most famous example of the unfairness of generalizations on irrelevant grounds must be the report of Albert Einstein's Latin master. Commenting on the boy who was to become one of the greatest intellects of our time, he wrote, 'This boy will never make anything'. The evidence for this statement was that the young Einstein's Latin was not up to standard!

Ironically, psychologists who are often criticized, sometimes feared and occasionally even hated, bend over backwards to be fair. Their aim is to eliminate unfairness from all forms of measurement.

This book is not a crusade, however, on behalf of tests of any sort. Crusades are often prompted by the emotions rather than by reason, so that a crusade is often as extreme as the object towards which it is directed. If a crusade is aimed at convincing by rational methods, it is justifiable. If it is merely an attempt to convert some sort of 'unbeliever', whether in the realm of religion or of mental testing, to 'our way of thinking', it is a dangerous undertaking.

This book aims to look at a number of methods of assessing and testing, including the teacher's mark, the interview, the reference and psychological tests. The tests, which cannot be influenced by the person giving them, will be probed for weaknesses and analysed for strengths alongside those methods which can be influenced by the person using them. In this way it is hoped to arrive at a balanced judgment of both methods of measuring.

Statistics are possibly more likely to produce an unfavourable (emotional) reaction than are the tests themselves. In spite of the fact that no scientist would claim that statistics 'prove' anything, the layman says that they can be 'made' to prove whatever you wish them to prove. He believes that statistics merely falsify; the scientist believes that statistics give clearer understanding and eliminate bias and uncertainty and even unfairness. In addition to this suspicion of statistics and the belief that they may be dishonest, many people also fear them and believe that no one but an expert mathematician can hope to understand them. It is true that there are some very complicated statistical techniques such as 'Analysis of Covariance' and 'Factor Analysis'. On the other hand, we do not need to delve into these techniques to obtain a basic understanding of assessment and testing. We shall restrict our study to a number of basic statistical ideas such as 'mean', 'standard deviation', 'normal curve of distribution' and 'correlation', because these are as important in the ordinary everyday marking of the teacher as they are in tests of intelligence.

It is possible to interpret statistics without being able to perform calculations, but in a few places simple examples of basic calculations will be shown. Generally, however, statistical terms will be explained without involving the reader in any form of calculation.

All technical terms will be carefully explained. The first time they appear, and sometimes on later occasions, they will be printed in capitals, to make it easier for those who wish to do so to refer back to a specific term. It is essential to make sure that the basic terms and principles in Part 1 of the book are understood before the reader proceeds to Part 2, since there the principles and terms are related to specific types of tests. Failure to understand the principles in Part 1 will make it more difficult to appreciate the real use made of these tests.

Part 1

BASIC TERMS AND PRINCIPLES USED IN ASSESSMENT AND TESTING

Chapter 1

Basic terms: 'sample', 'chance', 'probability', 'significance'

SAMPLE AND TOTAL POPULATION

The terms SAMPLE and TOTAL POPULATION are basic to testing and research. Total population simply means everyone possessing stated characteristics. Thus, the total population of the world means every man, woman and child in the world. The total population of Great Britain means every man, woman and child in Great Britain. In both cases the term total population means everybody, but, in the second example, the limits have been narrowed from the world to Great Britain. I can narrow the limits even further by talking about the total population of nine-year-olds in Great Britain. I now refer only to every boy and girl who at the present time is nine years old and lives in Great Britain.

A sample is part of the total population. Samples may be of different sizes or of different types according to the requirements of the person taking the sample. A sample is used because very rarely is it possible to test the total population. We hope, from the sample, to be able to generalize findings and say that characteristics or trends, discovered in the sample, are typical of the total population. Sometimes we are entitled to generalize from our sample; at other times, we are not entitled to generalize as we shall see in a moment. A great deal of harm can result from generalizing from a sample to a total population when we are not entitled to do so.

THE IMPORTANCE OF SAMPLE SIZE

The smaller the sample we take, the greater the risk of its not being typical of the total population. We might, for example, aver that people with straight hair are more intelligent than people with curly hair. We might test the intelligence of half a dozen people with straight hair and half a dozen people with curly hair and find that all the straight-haired people were more intelligent than the curly-haired ones. But later we might test another six straight-haired people and six more with curly hair and find that the opposite was true.

Again, we might spin a penny ten times and find that on each occasion it came down 'heads'. We appear to be showing that a penny is more likely to come down 'heads' than 'tails' when spun in the air. But we might toss the penny in the air another ten times and this time every fall is 'tails'. On this evidence we would have to say that, if we toss a penny in the air, it is more likely to come down 'tails' than 'heads'.

In both these instances it would be dangerous to generalize too soon – a most important point. By generalizing too soon we obtain biased results. Moreover, we obtain results which are contradicted when we repeat our experiment. If we generalized about spinning a coin, little harm would be done, except that certain Test Match captains might lose Test Matches by accepting our generalization. We would be more likely to do a great deal of damage if we persuaded people to accept our theory that straight-haired people were more intelligent than those with curly hair. We might, for example, find that an employer would not employ a curly-haired person for a post which required high intelligence.

For this reason we frequently find attached to research reports, especially research reports of small experiments carried out by individuals, such a statement as: 'The following were the findings *for the sample tested.*' This statement is deliberately used to warn the person reading the report that the findings may not be generally true. It also warns the examiner, if the research is submitted for a research degree, that the candidate knows better than to generalize from too small a sample. His findings cannot be stated as facts about the total population. They are only suggestions and indicate only suggested tendencies in the total population.

From what we have written we can say that the only way to be absolutely sure is to test everybody. As this is never possible we must say that the nearer we come to testing everybody the nearer we shall be to absolute certainty. But, unless we do test everybody, we shall never be able to use such words as 'absolutely certain' or 'undeniably right'.

CHANCE

We are now in a position to look at the word CHANCE, which is often used by psychologists. Again, the way the psychologist uses the term is very much the same as our use of the term 'accident', in everyday life. If a man is walking along the street and a tile blows off the roof of a house and kills him, the verdict is 'accidental death'. Death happened by chance. However, if the man is walking along the street and someone who hates him very much deliberately hurls a tile off a roof and kills him, it is not an accident. It did not happen by chance; there is a definite explanation for what happened.

Let us take another example. If we invest money in a sufficiently large number of company shares we are almost bound to pick some shares which will go up in value. In the same way, if we take enough people with straight hair we shall almost certainly obtain some who are more intelligent than those with curly hair. But, another person may make money on almost all the shares he buys. Moreover, he buys less than we do. He buys less shares, yet makes more money. In this case, we are forced to conclude that it is not accidental or by chance that he makes money by buying shares. To say that he does not make money by chance, does not say why he *does* make money. But whatever the reason, it is not accidental. It happens too often to be just coincidence.

This is what the psychologist means when he uses the term SIGNIFI-CANT. He means that something happens too often for chance. Let us take another example. For many years people have thought that there may be something called 'extra-sensory perception'. This covers a number of different ideas, such as being able to see into the future, or to communicate with people who have died, and so on. Because psychologists wish to be scientific in their investigations (to be fair – in this case by not dismissing the idea out of hand because it is difficult to accept), they structure experiments to test the truth of the claims. In such experiments they attempt to find if there are people who can predict with greater-than-chance accuracy. Such experiments belong to that area called parapsychology (1). The Greek word *para* means 'beyond'. Thus parapsychology investigates phenomena which are *beyond* the scope of what we normally refer to as 'psychology'.

One well-known series of experiments in parapsychology was carried out by Dr Rhine of Duke University (2). It is not necessary for our purposes to examine all the details of these experiments. Basically, they tested the hypothesis that certain individuals were able to make predictions with greater-than-chance accuracy. The hypothesis was tested by requiring people to state, without seeing the symbols on the faces of cards, what those symbols were. The cards were rather like playing cards (3), and Rhine found that there were some people who did predict correctly too frequently for chance. Their scores (number of correct predictions) were significant.

Now, this was not *proof* that these people possessed extra-sensory perception. It meant simply that some people, when asked to predict, did so correctly at chance level, while others did so too frequently for chance. The latter might have done so for any one of a number of reasons, one of which *may have been* that they possessed extra-sensory perception.

Psychologists never state that an event is one hundred per cent certain to occur. They estimate only the probability of its occurring. When they do this, they state how often in how many trials the event can be expected to occur by chance. Three levels of probability are commonly quoted: the ·05 level, the ·01 level, and the ·001 level. The ·05 level is the minimum acceptable to the psychologist. It means that the event is likely to occur five times in 100 trials by chance, or once in twenty trials. The ·01 level means that the event will occur once in 100 trials by chance, while the ·001 level means that it will occur once in 1000 trials by chance. Thus, the psychologist has greater confidence in making claims if the event is only likely to occur once in 1000 trials by chance than he has if it is likely to occur by chance once in 100 trials. Similarly, he has greater confidence in his claims if the event is likely to occur once in 100 trials by chance than if it is likely to occur five times in 100 trials. For this reason, we talk about the ·05, ·01 and ·001 LEVELS OF CONFIDENCE.

The CHANCE AVERAGE of correct predictions in the extra-sensory perception experiments is five. If the reader tested his friends, he would find that most of them scored five correct predictions per trial. If he tested them on 150 trials, he would find that the average chance prediction would be 150 times 5, or 750. But, it might happen that one particular friend averaged ten correct predictions per trial, or 10 times 150 (i.e. 1500) correct predictions. This person has predicted correctly twice as often as we would expect by chance. The psychologist wants to know next the probability of anyone predicting correctly twice as often as chance. By applying the appropriate statistical technique he can tell whether this level of correct prediction could be expected once in twenty (five times in 100) trials by chance, once in 100 trials, or once in 1000 trials. He would then be able to say whether he could claim that the person in question possessed extra-sensory perception at the ·05 level of confidence, the ·01 level, or the ·001 level.

SAMPLING, CHANCE AND PROBABILITY

We can now relate to one another the terms we have discussed. The larger the sample tested, the more confidently we can generalize our findings to the total population. The more trials of our experiment we undertake, the greater confidence we have that the expected event does not occur by chance. The PROBABILITY of a coin coming down 'heads' is 50–50 (once in two spins). But we *could* spin it twice and get two 'heads'. We could *not* spin it 10,000 times and get 10,000 'heads'. A small number of spins, like a small sample, produces DISTORTION. If we link this to what we have already said in this chapter about sampling, we can say that, when we carry out experiments, we take large samples to reduce the likelihood of distortion. The larger the number of people tested, the less likely chance is to distort the results. Thus, if certain characteristics appear in a large sample, there is more likelihood that these characteristics are typical of the total population. The technical term in psychology for greater likelihood is GREATER PROBABILITY.

It follows that taking more than one sample and making replications (repeats) of a particular experiment and obtaining similar findings on each occasion increases the probability that the findings can be generalized to the total population. The experiments of Piaget, on which he founded his theory of child development (4), began with observations of his own children (sample of five). One of the criticisms levelled at him in the early stages, was that he was not entitled to generalize from a sample of five to the total population of children of similar age. There was more likelihood, or greater probability, of distortion creeping in if he so generalized.

However, other researchers undertook REPLICATIONS of Piaget's experiments. They not only took larger samples, but also samples from other countries, since another criticism of Piaget had been that children in Wigan and New York were not necessarily the same as children in Geneva. The findings of all the replications of Piaget's researches were in the same direction, thus increasing the probability that Piaget's ideas were correct.

However, bearing in mind what we said a moment ago about chance and extra-sensory perception, we cannot, on the evidence of the replications, say that Piaget's theory is correct and every other theory is wrong; but we are justified in saying that the original criticisms show lack of foundation. The more samples that are taken, the larger the samples and the greater number of areas and countries represented by the samples, the more replications of Piaget point in the same direction, the greater probability there is of his ideas being correct. The greater the probability of his being right, the less justification there is for the claim that his findings resulted from chance.

TYPES OF SAMPLE (METHODS OF SAMPLING)

SAMPLES can be of different types as well as of different size. When we say that samples are of different types, we are really saying that we use different methods of sampling. The method of sampling depends on the reason for taking the sample. This will become clear as we describe the different types of sample and methods of sampling.

RANDOM SAMPLING

'Random' is the opposite of 'purposeful'. There is, therefore, a close connection between the terms 'random' and 'chance'. A simple example will illustrate the meaning of RANDOM SAMPLE and random sampling.

If I require to move some heavy equipment and cannot do it by myself, I decide to obtain some assistance. I go to the students' coffee bar where I find there are 100 students present. I say: 'Will you, and you, and you help me move some heavy equipment?' As I speak, I point to students in various parts of the room. In the end, I may have asked twenty of the hundred to help me. If I choose the twenty students haphazardly, for no specific reason other than a desire to have the equipment moved, and if I select the students with no other idea than this in mind, I obtain a random sample. The twenty individuals are chosen by chance.

However, perhaps unconsciously I make my choice for specific reasons. I may know that the first student whom I ask is the College rugger captain and a tremendously strong fellow. He is admirably suited to moving heavy equipment. The second member of the sample may be known to me as a particularly obliging fellow, who will be pleased to help move the equipment. These specific reasons, called by psychologists SELECTION CRITERIA, prevent the sampling process from being random or chance. Both the men selected were selected because they measured up to the criteria of 'strength' and 'willingness to oblige'. They were not chosen at random, but selected according to particular criteria.

Any form of selection involves criteria. When students apply for admission to colleges of education, they are given interviews, to decide whether they measure up to the criteria of suitability for teaching. The interviewers have decided beforehand on the selection criteria, in the light of their own experience of teaching and teachers. These may include such qualities as a balanced personality, high academic ability, and so on. The applicants who are successful are those who measure up to the selection criteria. In this particular situation, unlike the previous one, selection is very purposeful indeed. In no sense of the word can it be called random.

We have said elsewhere (5) that the human mind is prone to prejudices and bias. We have preconceived ideas which colour our judgment. This is one of the things we must guard against when we are assessing and testing. It is all too easy to make the facts fit these preconceived ideas, instead of keeping an open mind and making decisions in the light of the evidence.

Applying this to the idea of choosing a random sample, we can say that it is extremely difficult for the human mind to choose completely at random. For this reason, we usually determine a random sample by using a TABLE OF RANDOM NUMBERS. Most books on statistics have one of these at the back along with tables of squares and square roots, logarithms, etc. If we wish every pupil in the school to have an equal opportunity of being included in our sample, we simply give each child a number and make our selection by reading off the numbers in the table of random numbers.

SYSTEMATIC SAMPLING

Random sampling, as we have seen, must be entirely unsystematic if it is to be genuinely random. A SYSTEMATIC SAMPLING technique has a large element of randomness in it, but it is not entirely random. Again, simple examples will illustrate the point.

If we wish to choose 1500 people at random, we could obtain an electoral roll and, by using our random number table, obtain the 1500 without difficulty. However, we may wish to have an equal number of upper-class, middle-class and lower-class people in our sample. We thus require 500 from each class. We do not, however, wish to select the people in any of the three classes on any criteria other than class. Consequently, we take our electoral roll, split the names into the three classes required, and then, from each class in turn, we select 500 names on the random number principle.

We must issue a warning here to show just how easy it is to make sampling errors without even realizing that we are making them. A famous public opinion poll concerning an election went badly astray because the list from which the names were selected at random – the telephone directory – was biased. Certain types of people are more likely (again we deliberately use the term) to be on the phone than certain other people. There is a greater probability (note this term again) that middle-class people will have a telephone than working-class people. Those who own their own business are more likely to have a telephone than those who do not. There is a greater probability that people earning a salary will have a telephone than those who are living on a fixed pension.

To return to our electoral roll: if we took 1500 names from the list as it stands, we might not have the three classes equally represented, which might be important or it might not. In most cases, e.g. in testing attitudes, interests, incomes, or possessions, it would matter very much to which of the three groups people belonged. Taking a single random sample of 1500 may appear to remove bias. It may, in fact, cover up a great number of biases.

STRATIFIED SAMPLING AND PROPORTIONAL REPRESENTATION

From time to time we hear people talking about proportional representation in Parliament. It is claimed by some that P.R. is allied to the principles of fairness and justice. Its proponents argue that it is unfair that 50,000 people should return one member while in another area 200,000 people are also represented by only one member. Their argument is that the 200,000 people ought to have four representatives to keep the proportion the same.

This problem is most relevant to sampling. We have already said that the nearer we come to testing the total population, the nearer we come to being able to generalize with certainty. Large samples make generalizations and conclusions more certain than small samples, since it is in small samples that bias is more likely to occur.

Let us assume that we wish to test 'class attitudes' towards something, e.g. the best use of leisure time. We may find that in the total population there are 20,000 upper class, 40,000 middle class, 80,000 working class. The grand total of 140,000 shows that total population refers to a comparatively limited area, such as a county borough. We cannot test all 140,000, so we decide to take a sample. If we take a completely random sample we may get completely disproportionate representation. Even if we decide to split the people into classes and take a random sample from each of the three, we still only take $\frac{1}{80}$ of the lower class compared with $\frac{1}{40}$ of the middle and $\frac{1}{20}$ of the upper class. In other words, we come much closer to testing the total population in the upper class than in either of the other two classes. Or, in terms of what we have already said about bias, our sampling makes bias more probable in the middle and lower classes than in the upper class.

To reduce or eliminate bias, we must take the same proportion from all three classes. That means that we come equally near to testing the total population in all three classes by taking a STRATIFIED SAMPLE, or by representing all three classes proportionately. We are entitled to choose the percentage, in this instance, just as in the random sample we were entitled to choose the number. The only proviso is that we must choose the same percentage for all three classes.

Let us assume that we decide to take a 20% sample from all three classes. This means that from each class we select, by random sampling, one person in five. It is important to note that although we are anxious that the proportion from each of the three classes shall be identical, we do not wish any one person within a given class to have greater probability of being selected than any other person. Consequently the sampling within each class will be random sampling. Twenty per cent from each class would give:

Upper class	4,000
Middle class	8,000
Lower class	16,000

HOMOGENEOUS AND HETEROGENEOUS GROUPINGS

The word *homo*, in Greek, means 'the same'; the Greek word *heteros* means 'other'; and the Greek word *genos*, like the Latin word *genus*, means, 'race, type, or species'. Thus, the reader will see that HOMOGENEOUS GROUPS are composed of the same race, type, or species, while HETERO-GENEOUS GROUPS are composed of people of different or opposite races, types, species. Just as we could select a total population according to certain characteristics, so the sameness of a homogeneous group or the difference of a heterogeneous group can be on one characteristic, or, as we said earlier, on one criterion.

Thus if we take a group of working men, we have a homogeneous group, since the characteristic, or criterion for assessing the group is belonging to the working class. Similarly we can have a group of graduates. This also is a homogeneous or one-type group. The one thing that all members of the group have in common is graduate status.

A group which contains both working-class people and graduates, is a heterogeneous group, since we employ two criteria in forming the group, working-class status and graduate status. Some of the graduates may come from the working class, but they are assessed, for present purposes, against the criterion 'graduate status' not 'working-class origin'.

A school is a HETEROGENEOUS GROUP. On the criterion of age, it contains pupils of different ages, whether it be an infant, primary, or secondary school. It also constitutes a heterogeneous group on the criterion of ability since it contains children of different levels of ability.

But, within any school, there may be homogeneous groups on a number of criteria. In the secondary school, we may have a 'stream'. This is a homogeneous group on the criterion of ability. Some secondary schools have a house system and assign children to a particular house according to the geographical area in which they live. Thus, in this situation, a house would be a homogeneous group on the two criteria of belonging to the same house, e.g. Blogsfield House, and coming from the same geographical area, e.g. Newtown.

The reader will be able to think for himself of many more criteria for homogeneous grouping. Among those which come most readily to mind are religious belief (Catholic and Protestant members, if separated, would form homogeneous groups, if mixed, they would form a heterogeneous group), outside interests and political persuasions.

We shall find homogeneous groups and heterogeneous groups important in Chapter 5, where we shall discuss how heterogeneous and homogeneous groups produce different distribution curves, when measured on some criterion such as intelligence. In a school, to take an obvious example, one would not expect identical ranges of intelligence in a homogeneous group such as the 'A' stream, and in a heterogeneous group such as a mixture of 'A' stream and 'D' stream pupils. This sort of thing must strike the reader as very obvious when it is singled out for particular notice, but it is surprising how frequently in research distortion creeps in, because the researcher (especially the inexperienced researcher) overlooks some obvious factor, such as the difference between homogeneous and hetero-geneous groupings.

NOTES AND REFERENCES FOR CHAPTER 1

1 The reader who is interested in this subject is referred to Pratt, J. Gaither, *Parapsychology; An Insider's View of E.S.P.* (London, W. H. Allen, 1964). Dr Pratt was chief assistant to Dr Rhine in his experiments (see 2 below).

2 The reader is referred to:
 Rhine, J. B., *The Reach of the Mind* (New York, Sloane, 1947);
 Rhine, J. B. and Pratt, J. G., *Parapsychology; Frontier Science of the Mind*
 (Springfield, Illinois, Thomas, 1957);
 Rhine, L. E., *Hidden Channels of the Mind* (New York, Sloane, 1961).
3 Rhine did not use playing-cards in his later experiments. Playing-cards are
 familiar to most people, and just as some people are more likely to give one
 colour than another when asked to choose a colour, so some people are
 more likely to choose one card than another when asked to choose a card
 from a pack of conventional playing-cards. Such a choice increases the
 subjectivity of the experiment and, to eliminate this, Rhine invented the
 Zener Cards in packs of twenty-five. These bear symbols which differ from
 those of the four suits of conventional playing-cards. It can be argued that
 eventually subjects will be more likely to choose some Zener symbols than
 others, but this would not apply at first.
4 Jean Piaget (born Neuchâtel, 1896) is a biologist, psychologist, philosopher
 and prolific writer. He systematized the stages of mental evolution of the
 individual from birth to adulthood. In addition, he founded the famous
 Centre of Genetic Epistemology in Geneva. A good account of the mental
 development of the child is found in Peel, E. A., *The Pupil's Thinking*
 (Oldbourne, 1960). The account requires very careful reading by the
 inexperienced student and will not necessarily become clear at the first
 reading. However, the knowledge contained in this book is most important.
 The works of Piaget, even in translation, are often extremely hard going.
5 Schofield, H., *The Philosophy of Education: an Introduction* (London,
 Allen & Unwin, 1972). This book is a companion volume to the present
 work, applying the same simple approach to philosophy as is applied to
 psychology in this book.

Chapter 2

The Teacher's Mark

NUMERICAL AND LITERAL MARKS. SCALES AND SCALE POINTS

One of the most commonly used and best-known methods of assessment and testing is the teacher's mark. This may take the form of a number – NUMERICAL MARK or a letter – LITERAL MARK. It is possible, as we shall see in a moment, to give literal marks numerical equivalents.

Both numerical and literal marks are always points on a MARK SCALE. Mark scales are always defined in terms of the number of points on them. This, again, is apparently simple, but rarely fully appreciated by those who use mark scales. For example, if we mark out of ten, we may be using a ten-point scale or an eleven-point scale. If we intend to assign 0 to the worst piece of work, we use an eleven-point scale, but if we argue that no piece of work ever merits 0, and assign 1 to the worst piece of work, then we use a ten-point scale. However, as we shall see later in this chapter, we often claim to be using a ten- or eleven-point scale, although in reality we reduce this to something like a five- or six-point scale through failure to use the marks at the upper and lower ends.

Sometimes, especially in the sixth form and in higher education, we do not use numerical marks. Instead we use literal marks, which also form parts of a scale. If we award A, B, or C to all pieces of work, we use a three-point literal scale. It cannot be a four-point scale, since we cannot combine 0 with literal marks. If we award A, B, C, D, or E, we are using a five-point literal scale. We can extend this to a twelve-point literal scale, by adding pluses and minuses to the letters as follows:

A, A−, B+, B, B−, C+, C, C−, D+, D, D−, E

If we include E+ and E− (which we rarely do) we make the twelve-point into a fourteen-point scale. Adding A+ (again a rare symbol), we make a fifteen-point scale.

A literal grading is not usually so precise as a numerical grading. We may say that, in a five-point scale, each letter represents a fifth of a mark scale. Thus, if we use a five-point literal scale instead of a 100-point numerical scale, we can show the equivalence as follows:

$$A = 81{-}100$$
$$B = 61{-}80$$
$$C = 41{-}60$$
$$D = 21{-}40$$
$$E = 0(1){-}20$$

We often use the literal scale when we wish to assign students to large categories. In this way we could make the equivalence as follows:

$$A = \text{Distinction} \quad (81\text{--}100)$$
$$B = \text{Credit} \quad (61\text{--}80)$$
$$C = \text{Pass} \quad (41\text{--}60)$$
$$D = \text{Weak pass} \quad (21\text{--}40)$$
$$E = \text{Failure} \quad (0(1)\text{--}20)$$

On the other hand, we could make the literal scale exactly equivalent to a numerical scale. In the example below, the literal scale is made equal to a fifteen-point numerical scale:

$$A+ = 15$$
$$A \ = 14$$
$$A- = 13$$
$$B+ = 12$$
$$B \ = 11$$
$$B- = 10$$
$$C+ = \ 9$$
$$C \ = \ 8$$
$$C- = \ 7$$
$$D+ = \ 6$$
$$D \ = \ 5$$
$$D- = \ 4$$
$$E+ = \ 3$$
$$E \ = \ 2$$
$$E- = \ 1$$

In this case, there is little point in using the literal scale. If precise marking is required, it is better to use a numerical scale.

WAYS IN WHICH MARKS AND MARK SCALES ARE USED

There are different reasons for using mark scales, whether these are numerical or literal.

    i. For evaluation. This use of marks indicates progress to the child and the teacher. It shows the child whether he is mastering the knowledge on which he is tested; it shows the teacher how effectively he is tested; it shows the teacher how effectively he is teaching each individual child.

    However, it must be realized that we do not only teach facts, we also teach attitudes. Whenever we say that marks indicate progress or the effectiveness of teaching, we think of teaching *facts*. If we teach attitudes, it is also important to know how successful we are· But, in such cases, it is more difficult to devise a system of marking than it is when we are testing factual information.

Finally, we can evaluate individuals, classes, schools, or total populations (e.g. all nine-year-olds).

ii. For rank-order placing. Using this technique, the measurer assesses each individual, not against himself, but against the other individuals in the group. In evaluation we would say that if John's marks over a given period were:

$$4, 4, 5, 4, 6, 5, 7, 7, 8, 7, 8, 9, 8, 9 \text{ (out of 10)}$$

he is improving steadily. The criterion (standard of judgment) is John's initial performance. At the beginning of the teaching he was scoring 4 or 5 out of 10. At the end of the teaching, after more practice, he is scoring 8 and 9 out of 10.

In rank-order placing, we assess John's standard against that of every other individual in the sample or total population. In this form of marking, we are looking for average, above-average and below-average performance by John in relation to the others.

We are, therefore, often concerned with two things in rank order placing: (*a*) pass or fail; (*b*) the grade of pass. We must remember that the pass mark can vary from one sample to another or from one population to another. The pass mark for the old School Certificate Examination was $33\frac{1}{3}$ per cent, while the pass mark for the 'O' level of the G.C.E. is 45 per cent. In the School Certificate examination, there was a 'credit grade' (45%) and 'distinction grade' ($66\frac{2}{3}$ per cent).

iii. For prognostication. We shall come across the term 'prognostication' again in Chapter 5, when we talk about the uses of intelligence tests. If we use marks to prognosticate, or predict, we use present performance as a criterion for predicting future performance. Thus if a pupil obtains grade 1 in seven 'O'-level subjects and grade 3 in two more, we prognosticate (or predict) that the boy is 'university material'. His present performance leads us to believe that he has sufficient ability to go to university later on.

This is prognostication for external use. Prognostication for internal use is the use of marks in the first (unstreamed) year of a secondary school, to prognosticate into which stream pupils will go in the second (streamed) year. We often use 'French marks' to prognosticate which pupils are likely to succeed with Latin which is begun one year later. When we later talk about 'correlation', we shall see why French marks are used in this way.

iv. For diagnosis. We shall also meet this term in Chapter 5 when we talk about intelligence tests. Its use is the same as in a doctor's

a

diagnosis. The doctor looks at a patient's symptoms and diagnoses what is wrong with him. The teacher, using marks diagnostically, looks at the marks (symptoms) and diagnoses the area of performance where the child is 'weak' or 'poor'. The diagnostic use of marks may be to determine whether a child ought to remain in the 'A' stream, receive special teaching in mathematics because he is below average in that subject, or, more seriously, whether he shall be placed in a remedial stream because he is below average in the basic subjects such as English and arithmetic.

v. For survey. This evaluates the progress of all children in a given population on some criterion. We may wish to find how nine-year-old working-class children compare in concept formation with nine-year-old middle-class children.

In the five categories above, we have mentioned some uses of marks, where tests of a particular construction could be used instead. We shall say more about this when we talk about the terms 'subjective' and 'objective'. For the moment, we must realize that, although it is possible to use marks and even impressions, these are not always as accurate as specially designed tests. The teacher's mark is only the teacher's interpretation of how well a child has done on that teacher's test. It may well be that there is a much better method of measuring the same thing which will give much more accurate information. One example of a diagnostic test replacing the diagnostic use of marks is the Binet test (1), which was devised as a scientific method of determining whether the right children were being diagnosed as mentally defective by teachers' marks and assessments.

SCALE POINTS AND ASSESSMENT

Teachers are often asked such questions as, 'Is John Smith reliable?' This is a simple question, apparently requiring no more than a simple 'Yes' or 'No' answer. If we answer 'Yes' or 'No', we are really assessing John Smith's reliability on a two-point scale. But such characteristics as 'reliability' and 'honesty' vary from one situation to another, as Hartshorne and May (2) discovered. Because of this, we frequently wish to qualify our Yes/No answer. We then say, 'He is reliable generally, but . . .'

The phrasing of our answer gives a hint of how to make a more accurate assessment of such qualities as 'reliability'. By using a three-point scale, or a five-point scale, we can ask:

'Is John Smith reliable? –

ALWAYS SOMETIMES NEVER (three-point-scale).
ALWAYS GENERALLY SOMETIMES RARELY NEVER (five point scale).

Alternatively we could rate or assess John Smith's reliability on a three-point or a five-point literal scale. In this case, we would substitute the letters A, B, C for always, sometimes, never; and the letters A, B, C, D, E for the terms always, generally, sometimes, rarely, never. Whichever method we use, the principle remains the same. But, just as we saw that numbers are sometimes clearer or more accurate than letters, so we can see that, for some people, the words would be more meaningful, clear and accurate than the letters. The words tell more precisely what is required.

Because, as we said in the introduction, the human mind is full of biases, it is always more desirable to use demanding criteria for assessment. We can illustrate this by using a simple, everyday example. John Smith was once asked by his teacher to post a letter for him. It was most important that the letter be posted that day. One week later, John Smith admitted to the teacher that he had forgotten to post the letter. Yet, in every other respect, that teacher had found John Smith completely reliable. But, human nature being what it is, any time that teacher is asked, 'Is John Smith reliable?', he will remember the time when he relied on him to post an important letter and was let down and, if asked to give a 'Yes' or 'No' answer to the question, he is likely to say 'No'. Even if he is presented with the five-point scale, shown above, his prejudice, arising from this one failure by John Smith, may cause him to tick 'Never'. However, he is less likely to tick 'Never', as one choice out of five, than he is to say 'No', as one choice out of two. What he ought to tick, if he is genuinely unbiased, is 'Generally'.

GLOBAL ASSESSMENT: 'HALO EFFECT'

Even worse than the bias, which makes the teacher say that John Smith is never reliable, because of one lapse from reliability, is that prejudice which spreads to other areas. In such a case the same master is asked if John Smith is clever and his answer is 'No'. On another occasion, he is asked if John Smith is sociable and again his answer is 'No'. The unfavourable impression, which one mistake by John Smith made on that teacher, colours his impression of John Smith *in every area*. He condemns him, whatever quality is under discussion.

This is known as GLOBAL ASSESSMENT or the HALO EFFECT, both terms meaning the same thing. Global, as in children's thinking (3), is the opposite of analytical. The entire judgment is based on a single factor or incident. The term 'Halo' is used because all the qualities are enveloped by the impression made in one particular area. Prejudice spreads to cover every area.

SCALES; HISTOGRAMS; THE NORMAL CURVE OF DISTRIBUTION

We have already suggested that a teacher may say that he is using an *x*-point scale, but, in reality is using something different. We suggested that one instance of this was not using 0 (zero) in a given scale. But, more serious is the omission of marks which are not 0 (zero). We illustrate this in Figs. 1 and 2 below. In both cases, we assess thirty-six children by marking out of ten. (Psychologists denote the number in a sample by $N = x$. Here we would write $N = 36$.) For each child awarded a particular mark an *x* is placed above that mark on the scale

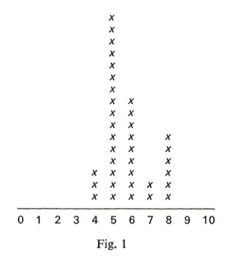

Fig. 1

Because only five of the ten points (or five of the eleven points, if 0 is included) have been used, the teacher has reduced the scale to a five-point scale. In Fig. 2 we give a different distribution of marks. In this case, all eleven points on the scale have been used in marking the work of the same thirty-six children.

$N = 36$

```
                                      x
                        x   x   x
                        x   x   x
                        x   x   x   x
                    x   x   x   x   x
            x   x   x   x   x   x   x   x
    x   x   x   x   x   x   x   x   x   x
    ─────────────────────────────────────
    0   1   2   3   4   5   6   7   8   9   10
```

Fig. 2

In Fig. 2, all the points on the scale have been used, but those nearer the upper end of the scale have been used much more frequently than those near the lower end. Although the complete scale has been used in Fig. 2, and only five points in Fig. 1, marks above 5 in both figures are much more numerous than marks below 5.

The distribution of marks on the eleven-point scale shown in Figs. 1 and 2 should be compared with the distribution of marks in Fig. 3 below. Again, the same eleven-point scale has been used.

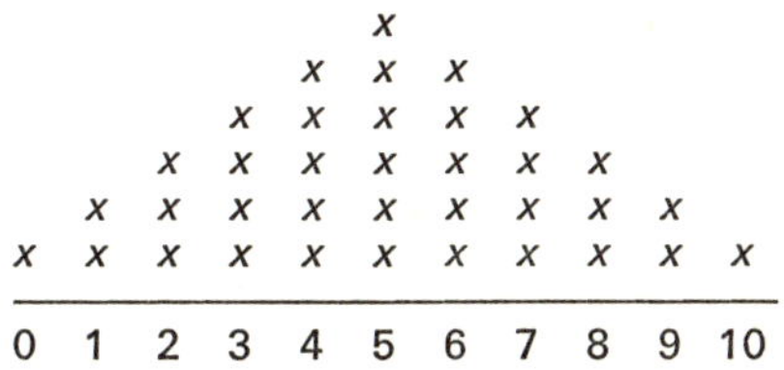

```
                  x
              x   x   x
          x   x   x   x   x
      x   x   x   x   x   x   x
      x   x   x   x   x   x   x   x   x
  x   x   x   x   x   x   x   x   x   x   x
 ─────────────────────────────────────────
  0   1   2   3   4   5   6   7   8   9  10
```

Fig. 3

The distribution of marks in Fig. 3 is much more regular than in Figs. 1 and 2. The highest column of *x*'s is at the middle point of the scale, i.e. 5. From there they taper down gradually to 0 on one side and 10 on the other side of the middle point. For every child with a score of 0, there is one with 10. For every child with a score of 0, there are two with a score of 1, three with a score of 2, and so on. The number of children obtaining any given mark is directly related to the number of children obtaining one mark lower or one mark higher. This does not apply in the mark distributions in Figs. 1 and 2. There is a clearly visible pattern of scores in Fig. 3, which is not present in Figs. 1 and 2.

One conventional way of representing scores like those in Figs. 1 to 3 is by using a HISTOGRAM, which consists of a number of columns built of bricks, or blocks, of identical size. Each person obtaining any given mark on the scale is represented by one block. The blocks are placed on top of one another (as in Figs. 4 to 6) to form columns. Thus, if two people obtain a score of 5, and one a score of 4, the '4' column will be one block high while the '5' column will be two blocks high. Like the symbols in Figs. 1 to 3, the histogram is a pictorial presentation but in a more striking form. Much more can be seen at a glance in the histogram. The three mark distributions used above are used for the histograms below.

The histograms in Figs. 4 to 6 are another way of showing the information given in Figs. 1 to 3. After seeing both for himself, the reader will observe at once that the histograms give the clearer presentation. For the moment our main concern is with Fig. 6, and with the even tapering-off of the marks from the middle column (5) to the extreme points on the scale, 0 to the left and 10 to the right. The marks are evenly distributed about THE MEAN (which is always represented symbolically by M). Because of this, the number of children scoring 0 is the same as the number scoring 10.

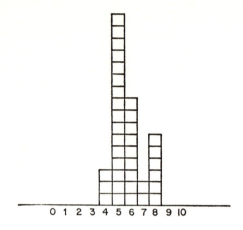

Fig. 4

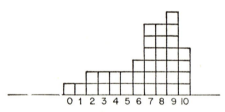

Fig. 5

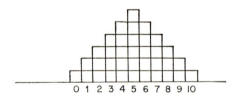

Fig. 6

Similarly the numbers in the columns for 4 and 6; 3 and 7; 2 and 8; 1 and 9 are identical. Having been shown one half of the histogram 0–5, we can complete the other half without any further information.

A third method of presenting marks is by a GRAPH. A graph may be a straight line or a curve. If we take the mark distribution shown in Fig. 3

and by the histogram in Fig. 6 and plot a graph, we obtain the shape in Fig. 7 below.

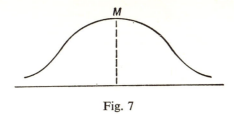

Fig. 7

The dotted line M is the middle point of the scale. In the normal curve (but in no other curve) the middle point of the scale is also the mean. We can show this from our example in Fig. 6; the middle point of the scale is 5. We obtain the mean by adding up all the marks and dividing by the number in the sample (i.e. 36). This gives us:

Pupils		Mark		Mark Total
2	×	1	=	2
3	×	2	=	6
4	×	3	=	12
5	×	4	=	20
6	×	5	=	30
5	×	6	=	30
4	×	7	=	28
3	×	8	=	24
2	×	9	=	18
1	×	10	=	10
36				180

$$M = \frac{180}{36} = 5$$

If we were to cut out the curve and fold it down the dotted line, the right-hand half would exactly cover the left-hand half. We call this type of curve a SYMMETRICAL CURVE, meaning that it has the same shape on either side of the mean. This symmetrical curve is called by statisticians the NORMAL CURVE OF DISTRIBUTION. By combining the form of mark presentation in Figs. 3 and 6 with the normal curve in Fig. 7, we can illustrate another vital feature of the normal curve of distribution (Fig. 8).

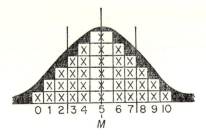

Fig. 8

STANDARD DEVIATION FROM THE MEAN

We recall that there were thirty-six children (N = 36) in the sample tested. We can now see that two out of every three of these children obtained a mark between 3 and 7 out of 10. If we draw vertical lines before the 3 and after the 7 and count the number of *x*'s or histogram squares between these vertical lines, we find that there are twenty-four of each. The vertical lines represent 1 STANDARD DEVIATION FROM THE MEAN. We call the standard deviation to the left of the mean 1 standard deviation below the mean, and that to the right of the mean 1 standard deviation above the mean. They are also called MINUS 1 and PLUS 1 standard deviations from the mean.

There are two ways of expressing this symbolically: -1 SD and $+1$ SD; or -1σ and $+1\sigma$ (σ is the Greek letter *sigma*). Whenever we see the normal curve of distribution (as in Chapter 4), we shall always look for the mean and 1 SD (Standard Deviation) below the mean, and 1 SD above the mean. This is shown in Fig. 9.

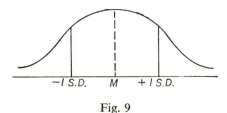

Fig. 9

What we must always remember is that, if we measure a sample or a population, and the spread of scores results in a normal curve of distribution, two out of three people tested lie between one standard deviation below and one standard deviation above the mean. When (in Chapter 4) we examine intelligence test scores and the normal curve of distribution, we shall see that the two-thirds of the total population, lying between -1 SD and +1 SD form the group which we call normal or average in terms of intelligence.

However, when we mark the work of the people we teach, we rarely, if ever, obtain a normal curve of distribution of marks. Later in this chapter we shall see that there are a number of reasons for this. We can, however, discuss one of the reasons at this point because it relates to what we have said already about sample size and total populations.

In Chapter 1 we saw that, if we test or measure the total population on any criterion we obtain an accurate picture of whatever characteristic is represented by that criterion, e.g. height, weight, or ability. However, the smaller the sample, the greater probability there is of distortion. Exactly the same distortion occurs in the distribution of scores, when we test a small sample. An example will show what form the distortion will take.

Let us suppose that the thirty-six pupils whose marks we made produce a normal curve of distribution. For illustrative purposes, let us assume that they are a homogeneous group of 'A' stream pupils in a secondary school taking an end-of-the-year Maths examination. Let us suppose, too, that in the 'D' stream of the same school, there are another thirty-six pupils taking the same examination. Again, we have a homogeneous group. In the 'A' stream the children are homogeneous because they are all very bright; in the 'D' stream they are homogeneous because they are all dull.

When we come to mark the examination papers out of, say, 100, we find that most of the children in the 'A' stream obtain the correct answers to most of the problems. We also find that most of the children in the 'D' stream cases fail to obtain the correct answers. It is possible that the average (or mean) score for the 'A' stream in this examination is 75% while that for the 'D' stream is 25%. We say that the 'A' stream marks are distributed about a mean of 75, while the 'D' stream marks are distributed about a mean of 25. The standard deviation tells us how widely or how narrowly the marks are distributed about the mean of 75 in the 'A' stream and 25 in the 'D' stream. If the standard deviation is small, the distribution of marks about the mean is narrow. The marks are not well spread. If the reader returns for a moment to Fig. 1 (p. 22), he will see an example of a small standard deviation. The marks are not well spread, since the lowest out of 10 is 4 and the highest 8.

On the other hand, if the standard deviation is large, the marks have a wider spread. Large standard deviations produce wide distributions of marks. Reference to Fig. 2 (p. 22) will show that the marks here have a wider distribution than do those in Fig. 1, because every point of marks on the scale is used.

A small standard deviation produces a narrow distribution which, when presented in the form of a graph, gives a LEPTOKURTIC CURVE (*leptos* is

Greek for 'narrow'). A large standard deviation produces a broad distribution which, when presented in the form of a graph, gives a PLATYKURTIC CURVE (the Greek word *platus* means 'broad'). Examples of the two types of curve are given in Fig. 10.

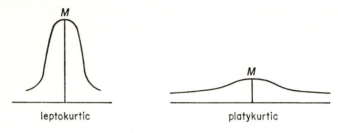

leptokurtic   platykurtic

Fig. 10

If we return for a moment to our Maths examination marks in our imaginary 'A' and 'D' stream, we see that the 'A' stream mean is above the middle point of the scale (50·50). In the normal curve of distribution, the mean and the middle point coincide. In our 'D' stream the mean is below the middle point of 50·50. These two features, a mean above the middle point, and a mean below the middle point, produce two specific types of curve. The 'A' stream mean of 75 produces a NEGATIVELY-SKEWED CURVE (Fig. 11).

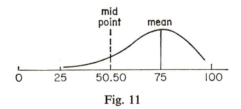

Fig. 11

The 'D' stream mean of 25 produces a POSITIVELY-SKEWED CURVE (Fig. 12).

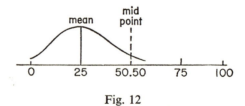

Fig. 12

We can now see that both these curves are distortions of the norma curvel of distribution. If we set the same Maths examination to the 'A', 'B', 'C' and 'D' streams, and plotted their scores on a single curve, the result would be a curve much more like the normal curve than either of the curves in Figs. 11 and 12.

We can illustrate these two types of distortion of the normal curve with the actual marks obtained by the writer from two samples, N = 40 and N = 37. Both sets of marks were awarded for pieces of Latin translated into English. Before we examine the actual marks, however, we must look at two useful ways of presenting marks, in addition to the conventional mark list. These two forms are the MARK TALLY and the CLASS INTERVAL presentations.

MARK TALLY

Let us assume that we wish to mark a test out of 35, as we shall actually do in the first example below. If we wish to keep a MARK TALLY, as we mark the scripts, we first of all make a list of the marks from 0 to 35. Then, each time a pupil obtains a mark between 0 and 35, we place an oblique stroke (/) against the mark obtained. After we have recorded four such strokes, we draw a line through them to show that a fifth child has obtained that score. This representation makes for easier recognition of the number of pupils obtaining any given mark. From the above symbols, we can see at a glance how many pupils have obtained any given mark. This is the mark tally for the pupils used in Example 1:

0	9	18	27 ++++ /
1	10	19 /	28 ++++ /
2	11	20	29 / / /
3	12	21	30 / / /
4	13	22 / /	31 /
5	14	23 / / / /	32 /
6	15 /	24 /	33
7	16	25 / / /	34
8	17 /	26 ++++ / /	35

It will be seen that the mean is higher than the mid-point of the scale (17.50), and that, when plotted on a graph, the marks would produce a negatively-skewed curve.

CLASS INTERVAL: FREQUENCY DISTRIBUTION

The CLASS INTERVAL divides the mark scale into a number of smaller sections of equal size. A common class interval is 5. When we use a class interval of 5 and keep a mark tally, we do not have separate tallies for those scoring 1, 2, 3, 4 and 5, but a single tally of those scoring some mark between 1 and 5. The class interval can be any number which the user thinks feasible. Below we give the marks from the example used in our mark tally. The mark scale 1–35 is divided into class intervals of 5. The numbers in the second column show how often a mark is scored in each class interval. The number of times the mark is obtained is known as the FREQUENCY of that mark, and Column 2 is known as the FREQUENCY DISTRIBUTION of the marks.

Class Interval	Frequency
1–5	0
6–10	0
11–15	1
16–20	2
21–25	10
26–30	25
31–35	2

In Examples 1 and 2, the marks will be presented as in the conventional mark list so that the reader can look down the list at every score obtained. Readers who wish to show the marks by a mark tally or by a class interval can make a scale for themselves, using the scores in Examples 2. In both examples, we shall use the symbols learned in this chapter: N (number in sample), M (mean), SD (standard deviation). The SD has been calculated for the reader, for the important point is not how it was obtained, but the size of the deviation. In addition the mid-point of the scale is given in both examples.

Example 1

N = 40. Maximum mark possible: 35.

31	25	29	26	32	22	24	23
27	25	26	27	28	28	27	23
29	29	28	28	27	26	28	26
26	27	30	26	30	17	25	30
26	23	23	22	28	19	27	15

Total = 1039. Mean = $\dfrac{1039}{40}$ = 25·79. Mid-point = 17·50. SD = 3·50.

(For readers who are interested in how the SD is calculated, a brief example is given in the notes for Chapter 2, Section 4.)

Example 2

N = 37. Maximum mark possible: 100.

23	15	53	39
30	22	49	55
37	33	40	28
20	36	33	46
59	16	37	50
36	29	48	44
30	67	40	46
58	33	22	37
32	48	36	35
38			

Total = 1400. Mean = $\dfrac{1400}{37}$ = 37·84. Mid-point = 50·50. SD = 12·03.

The two samples were from 'A' stream Latin classes in two schools. They were, thus, homogeneous groups, selected according to two criteria: general brightness and ability to do Latin. In Example 1, the marks clustered narrowly round the mean. Thus they were similar to our hypothetical 'A' stream marks in the Maths. examination. The piece for translation was well within the capabilities of the pupils in the sample, and a mark was awarded for each Latin phrase correctly translated. Most of the pupils translated most of the phrases correctly, so that the mean of 25·79 was well above the mid-point of 17·50. No pupil translated every phrase correctly, so that no pupil obtained full marks. On the other hand, no pupil translated every phrase incorrectly. The marks would produce a negatively-skewed curve.

In the second example, the marks were spread more widely about the mean than those in Example 1. Again the group was homogeneous, and again the mark scheme gave one mark for each phrase correctly translated. No pupil gained full marks; no pupil obtained 0. But the passage was too difficult for the average pupil of the age of the sample tested. Consequently the average (or mean) was lower than the mid-point, 37·84 instead of 50·50. The very able pupils found that the passage enabled them to show just how good they were; the weak pupils found their weakness glaringly exposed. The spread of marks was similar to that of our hypothetical 'D' stream. They would produce a positively-skewed curve.

No mark in isolation has any meaning. If a child comes home and tells his father: 'I got 73 in my Maths. examination', he is usually congratulated, since it is assumed that he has done well. On the other hand, if he comes home and says: 'I obtained 51 in my Maths. examination', he is criticized, because it is assumed that he has done badly. What we have seen in this chapter shows us that in neither instance is the praise or blame necessarily justified. In both instances, we need to know what was the maximum mark possible for the examination. If, in the case of the child who obtained 73, the maximum mark possible was 100, and, in the case of the child who obtained 51, only 60, the second child has obtained a higher percentage than the first.

Even when we know the maximum mark possible, we need to have further information. What marks were obtained by the other children? Was the standard deviation small, as in our first example, or was it large, as in our second example? Unless we have this information, we cannot tell whether either child has done well or not. There may be a large number of children in the sample with an equally high (or even higher) mark. The child in question may have a high mark but not an equally high rank-order position. If we wish to know whether either boy's mark is higher, or lower than his mark in a previous Maths. examination, we are using the marks for evaluation.

RAW SCORES: DERIVED SCORES

A RAW SCORE is the mark awarded out of a maximum mark possible on any given test. Thus, the points on the mark scale, with which we began this chapter, were raw scores.

As the chapter has progressed, we have become increasingly aware of how meaningless a single raw score is. When two boys came home with raw scores of 73 and 51 in an examination, the information which these single scores gave was so little that we had to ask several questions in order to make them meaningful.

A child might come home and say that his marks in three subjects were:

Algebra   52
English   116
Science   163

Only by applying some of the techniques discussed in this chapter can we make a meaningful comparison between the three raw scores given. When we apply such techniques to raw scores, we obtain DERIVED SCORES. The simplest instance of derived scores in this chapter was the frequency distribution which we obtained after splitting up our mark scale into class intervals (p. 30). Another common type of derived score is the Z-SCORE or STANDARD SCORE. Below we show how the marks in the three subjects are converted from raw scores into derived scores (in this case, Z scores).

Z-SCORE

To obtain a Z-score, we use only terms which we have learned in this chapter: M (mean), SD (standard deviation) and raw score, which we can represent by x. The formula for obtaining the Z-score (or standard score) is:

$$Z = \frac{x-M}{SD}$$

If we apply this formula to our three raw scores, we obtain the following table:

	x	M for group	$x-M$	SD	Z
Algebra	52	47·92	+4·08	10·00	+0·41
English	116	120·26	−4·26	21·02	−0·20
Science	163	163·00	0·00	23·19	0·00

Note that the SD for Science is much greater than that for Algebra. The reader should ask himself what this information tells him about the spread of scores in Algebra and Science. From the table above, we can see that our pupil is exactly average in Science, well above average in Algebra, and slightly below average in English. Four marks above average with an SD of 10 is much more important than four marks below average with an SD of 21. In the former case, four marks could mean a difference of many rank-order places, whereas, in the latter case, it might mean as little as one rank-order place. In the same way, when seven football teams at the top of the First Division have almost the same number of points, one defeat for one team when all the others win can send that team tumbling down the rank-order.

NOTES AND REFERENCES FOR CHAPTER 2

1 Alfred Binet was a Frenchman, who, in 1905, produced a test at the request of the Paris authorities to see whether the right children were being recommended for special education, because their teachers' reports suggested that they were mentally defective. The authorities were seeking a more reliable guide than the teachers' marks and assessment. This point will be better understood after the reader has studied Chapter 3, especially the sections on subjectivity, objectivity, and standardization. The characteristic term of measurement associated with the Binet test, mental age, is fully explained in Chapter 4.

2 Hartshorne and May carried out a massive and famous research in the USA in the 1920s. The purpose of the investigation was to discover whether there were certain personality characteristics such as honesty. Can we say that So-and-so is honest, or should we say that in certain situations So-and-so is honest and in others dishonest? Does 'honesty' have the same meaning in children and adults? The findings of the investigation and other ideas of the two researchers can be found in Hartshorne, H. and May, M. A., *Studies in Deceit* (New York, Macmillan, 1928), and *Studies in Service and Self-Control* by the same authors (New York, Macmillan, 1929).

3 Jean Piaget is one of the most famous contemporary names in psychology.

It is virtually impossible to take a course in teacher training without hearing his name. He is a biologist, philosopher, psychologist, and genetic episto-mologist, and a prolific writer. His best-known works deal with the process of thought development in the child. He divides this evolutionary develop-ment into the following stages:

Sensori-motor	(birth–18 months/2 years)
Pre-conceptual	(2–4 years)
Intuitive (global)	(4–7 years)
Concrete operational	(7/8–11/12 years)
Formal operational	(11/12 years onwards)

At the intuitive, or global stage of development, the child is capable of thinking in terms of only one factor at once. For example, if we take two identical beakers full of coloured liquid, each containing identical amounts, and pour the contents of one into a tall, thin cylinder and the contents of the other into a broad, flat dish, the child will say that there is more liquid in the tall cylinder. When asked the reason for this, he will answer: 'Because it is taller'. He is unable to work in terms of the two concepts, 'height' *and* 'width'. One factor dominates his perception, and consequently his thinking, which, at this stage, is based on his perception.

4 The following example of how to calculate the SD is extremely short and simple. It is designed solely to show the mechanics of calculation.

Pupils	*Mark*	*Deviation from Mean*	*Deviation squared*
A	15	+5	25
B	14	+4	16
C	11	+1	1
D	10	—	—
E	9	−1	1
F	7	−3	9
G	4	−6	36
—	—	—	—
7	70	0	88

$$\text{Mean} = \frac{70}{7} = 10. \qquad \text{SD} = \sqrt{\frac{88}{7}} = \sqrt{12\cdot57} = 3\cdot55.$$

Step 1. Add up number of pupils = 7

Step 2. Add up the marks = 70

Step 3. Find the mean $= \dfrac{\text{Total of marks}}{\text{No. of pupils}} = \dfrac{70}{7} = 10$

Step 4. Calculate how much above or below 10 each mark is. Those above the mean are plus, those below are minus.

Step 5. Square the deviation to get rid of the minus signs.

Step 6. Add up the squared deviation = 88.

Step 7. Find the mean deviation $= \dfrac{88}{7} = 12\cdot57$.

Step 8. SD = square root of 12·57 = 3·55.

Chapter 3

More key terms in assessment and testing

SUBJECTIVE

Subjective means 'coloured by personal preference, preconceived ideas, or bias' (1). What is subjective cannot be proved scientifically. If I say, 'Woolley was more graceful than Hammond', I am making a subjective statement, since there is no scientific measure of gracefulness, and my statement cannot be checked. My statement is based, not on fact, but on the impression which each batsman made on me.

The reference or confidential report is an example of subjective assessment. In the reference, one person is asked to express an opinion about another. He bases that opinion on the impression which the person makes on him. Thus, if I am asked to give a reference stating the suitability of a person for teaching, I can use two criteria, both of which are impressions. The first is my impression of the candidate, the second is my impression, which becomes an opinion (even a well-informed opinion), about the qualities required for a success in teaching.

We have already seen how dangerous the impressions which one person makes on another can be. Equally dangerous is the wrong opinion of what is required in terms of abilities and personal qualities for a particular job. The less well-acquainted the referee is with the job in question, the less meaningful will be his reference. A referee may recommend a person as suitable for teaching, because of high academic ability, but the candidate may turn out to be totally unsuitable on personality grounds.

Moreover, Iliffe (2) found that head teachers, when recommending students as suitable for university, tended to stress things which were self-evident to the interviewer. For instance, one might say: 'Mr X is a tall man, who speaks with a soft, West Country accent, and has an impressive academic career to date.' The first two facts would be apparent the moment the candidate entered the room and spoke; the third would be stated on his application form.

In an attempt to guide the referee, employers and college interviewers often send out a form with headings under which the referee can make comments. The headings are really criteria, which the person asking for the reference knows are relevant to the job or college place for which the individual is applying. This does not lessen the subjectivity of the referee's comments, but it does save a good deal of comment on irrelevant points.

We have already suggested that teachers' marks can be subjective.

Indeed, they can be greatly influenced by personal feelings and preferences. Faced with two essays apparently equally lacking in merit, I look about for a way of distinguishing between them. I recall that A is a pleasant fellow and cooperative, and that his father has had a long spell off work through illness. This fact must have had some effect on the boy. By contrast, I have found, from past experience, that B is an unpleasant fellow, that he is able but idle, and that one of my colleagues describes him as an inveterate bully. As a result, I award A a higher mark than B. The grounds on which I make the awards are quite irrelevant, since the characteristics mentioned have nothing whatever to do with essay-writing. I assess both essays on irrelevant criteria and all my mark does is to reflect my personal bias.

There are two main methods of marking essay-type answers in any subject. One is called IMPRESSION MARKING, the second ANALYTICAL MARKING, because it represents an attempt to be less subjective and more objective.

In impression marking, I read an essay, and, as I read it, it makes an overall impression on me. At the end of my reading, I *feel* that the essay is good or bad. On the strength of this *feeling*, I award the essay a mark or raw score. At first sight, it may appear that the method is satisfactory. But, if we think back for a moment to what we said about Woolley being a more graceful batsman than Hammond, we realize that, although this was the impression made on me, other people may have got the opposite impression. If this can apply when two people compare two cricketers, it may also happen, when two teachers mark two essays. I may be so favourably impressed by A's essay, even discounting the irrelevant criteria, that I award it 17 out of 20. Again, discounting the irrelevant criteria, when I mark B's essay, it impresses me so little that I award it 7 out of 20. Yet another marker, reading both essays, might award 11 out of 20 to A and 16 out of 20 to B.

Unfortunately, in this situation, there is no easy solution. We can only bring in a third marker and see whether his marks are nearer to mine than to those of my colleague. But, if we think what happened when we said that people with curly hair were more intelligent than people with straight hair, and tested a small sample, or what happened when we tossed a coin ten times and found that it came down 'heads' on nine occasions, we feel that a fourth marker and a fifth might confirm one set of marks rather than another, but that a twenty-fourth and twenty-fifth might begin to reverse the trend.

OBJECTIVE

When we are objective, we attempt to eliminate subjectivity. We attempt to be more scientific in our approach to whatever task we undertake. We attempt to rid the situation of personal prejudices and preferences and to justify actions on rational grounds. In marking essays, we attempt to remove some, if not all, of the arbitrariness with which marks may be awarded.

We noted one way of attempting to reduce subjectivity when we said that analytical marking was sometimes used as an alternative to impression marking of essays. When we mark analytically, we award a number of marks for certain characteristics of the essay. For example, if I mark a history essay, I may decide on a mark out of twenty. This total consists of five marks for factual accuracy; five for originality of ideas; five for correctness of spelling and grammar; and five for neatness of presentation.

Immediately, I encounter difficulties. How many spelling errors do I allow, before I deduct a mark from the five allocated to correctness of grammar and spelling? If a boy spells 'Napoleon' incorrectly five times, do I deduct all five marks or only one? is it fairer to ignore this, and penalize some other incorrect spelling, e.g. 'priviledge'? Do I deduct a mark, because he puts the date of Waterloo as 1806? This was the date of Jena, and he has previously been discussing Jena. I am sure that he knows that Waterloo was fought in 1815 and that his 1806 was nothing more than a slip of the pen, caused by 'examination nerves'. Immediately, we are back to our irrelevant criteria, which played an unjustified part in our subjective, impression marking.

OBJECTIVITY AND OBJECTIVE TESTS

But there is a more serious objection to my so-called objective system of marking by the analytical technique. There is a school of thought that argues that awarding marks for spelling and grammar and for neatness of presentation, in a history essay, is as irrelevant as awarding A marks because his father has been ill for a long time. Its proponents claim that we are awarding marks for English, not for History. If we accept their argument, only ten out of our twenty marks are awarded on relevant grounds.

We shall refer to this again, when we consider what is meant by the term 'validity'. For the moment we must realize that the objection just mentioned has led to the introduction of objective tests, not only in History, but also in other subjects.

The philosophy behind objective tests is that marks are awarded only on relevant grounds, and that the marks are awarded in such a way that they cannot be influenced by the personal preferences and prejudices of the marker.

The type of test referred to as an objective test, is usually the MULTIPLE-CHOICE test. These tests do not require the candidate to give the answers in essay form, but require him to underline the correct answer, delete the wrong answer, or place the answer in a blank space. They are sometimes referred to as 'one-word-answer tests'.

The simplest form of such test is not strictly multiple-choice at all: the true/false test. The examinee is confronted with a series of statements followed by the words 'true/false', and he is required to delete the wrong alternative, e.g.

Eskimos live in Africa   True/False.

This is a somewhat naïve type of test and is little used, generally in primary schools. A multiple-choice test is a test with a number of questions followed by x alternative answers. The candidate is required to underline the correct answer, e.g.

The Battle of Waterloo was fought in   1914
1066
1815
1588
1806.

In this case the number of choices is five. This is the commonest number, although the alternatives are sometimes reduced to three.

In a later section, we shall discuss the advantages and disadvantages of objective tests, but there are a number of features of such tests which must be mentioned here. First, if any choice is so ridiculous as to be virtually eliminated as an answer by almost all candidates, we reduce a five-alternative test to four alternatives and a three-alternative test to two alternatives for that particular question. If, in the example above, we omitted the date 1806 and put in 55 BC, we should be most surprised if any candidate selected this as his answer. In the first place, it is totally unlike the others in the number of digits that it has and in its overall appearance. Because of this, candidates would suspect that it was a trap. In the second place, all the five dates in the original question are dates of famous battles. There is thus logical justification for the inclusion of all of them. The date, 55 BC, does not fall into this category.

Secondly, there are features common to a number of the alternatives. The third and fifth are very close together in time. The third and fourth contain the same digits. Psychologists tell us that the more similar two objects are, the more difficult it is to discriminate between them, a fact which Pavlov (3) demonstrated this with his Alsatian dog. Consequently, if the alternatives are well chosen, the candidate has to exercise considerable care in selecting the correct answer.

Thirdly, the correct answer must not appear in the same rank-order place every time. In this question, it appears in third place; in the question before and the question after, it must appear in a different place. Nor should there be a pattern which the examinee can spot; such a detectable pattern might be 3, 2, 1, 4, 5, 1, 3, 2, 1, 4, 5, 1.

When the alternative answers are shown to the candidate, the test is classified as a RECOGNITION TEST. He sees the answer among possible alternatives, and has to recognize it as the correct one. There is another variation of the objective test known as a RECALL TEST. Here, the candidate is not given alternative answers but has to fill in a blank at a particular point in the statement. Two alternative forms of the question might be:

The Battle of Waterloo was fought in - - - -.

The Battle of - - - - - - - - was fought in 1815.

If we deliberately point a dash for every digit in the date and for every letter of the word 'Waterloo' we are using a device taken from programmed instruction known as CUEING, by which we give the candidate a certain amount of assistance with his answer.

Both types of test are marked objectively. In the multiple-choice test, the marker is supplied with a MARKING KEY. This consists of a card in which a certain number of holes have been cut, in this case down the right-hand side. The card is the same size as the test paper, and is placed over it to cover it exactly. The holes on the right-hand side then fall over the correct answer. Each time an answer underlined by the candidate appears in the hole, one mark is awarded. The marker is not allowed to interpret the marks in any way, unless he is instructed to produce some sort of derived score (see Chapter 2) from the raw score. Even in this situation, he treats all the raw scores in exactly the same way. In the section on subjective marking, we saw that we could overlook in an essay the error of placing Waterloo in 1806. This cannot happen in the objective test. Nor can the marker lift the card whenever 1815 does not appear in the hole and award, say, a half mark to those candidates who put 1806 because they gave the nearest to the correct answer.

GUESSING AND THE CORRECTION FORMULA

Although, in the last section, we stressed that every care is taken to deprive the candidate, in a multiple-choice test, of the opportunity to guess the answers without looking at the questions, guessing can still occur. Because guessing reduces objectivity, psychologists have developed a CORRECTION FORMULA. They assume that everybody who takes the test, has guessed and, consequently, they deduct marks from everybody. It will be seen that the score which is obtained by applying the correction formula is a derived score. The actual number of marks scored on the test before the correction formula is applied is the raw score for that candidate on that test.

THE 'NUMBER-RIGHT' FORMULA

The chances of guessing the correct answer in a multiple-choice recognition test depend on the number of alternative answers given for each question. In the true/false test the chances of guessing correctly are 1 in 2. In a three-alternative test they are 1 in 3, in a five-alternative test they are 1 in 5. The formula used to correct the raw score is known as the NUMBER-RIGHT FORMULA, and is simply:

$$R \text{ (right answers)} = \frac{W \text{ (wrong answers)}}{N \text{ (number of alternatives} - 1)}.$$

We can illustrate the use of the number-right formula by simple examples. Suppose we set an objective test of 100 questions in history. Each question has five alternative answers. Thus, $N = 5$ and $(N-1) = 4$. The number of wrong answers given by all candidates is divided by 4.

Candidate A has a raw score of 69 right answers. His wrong answers are therefore 31. Applying the formula to him, $R = 69$; $W = 31$. We are now ready to calculate the derived score:

$$R - \frac{W}{N-1} = 69 - \frac{31}{4} = 69 - 7 \cdot 75 = 61 \cdot 25.$$

A's derived score is 61·25, obtained, after correction for guessing, from a raw score of 69.

Candidate B, on the other hand, obtains a raw score of only 20. We apply the formula in the same way to him:

$$R - \frac{W}{N-1} = 20 - \frac{80}{4} = 20 - 20 = 0.$$

B's derived score is 0, obtained, after correction for guessing, from a raw score of 20. At first sight, this seems highly unfair. But if we think back to what we said about the chances of obtaining the correct answer by guessing, we recall that, in tests where there are five alternative answers, there is a 1 in 5 chance of obtaining the correct answer by guessing. In this way, B could have obtained all his 20 marks by guesswork. He is therefore justly penalized by the application of the formula.

SUBJECTIVE AND OBJECTIVE COMPARED

We are now in a position to compare subjective and objective methods of marking, and to consider the relative merits of essay-type answers and the recognition or recall answers of multiple-choice tests.

If we begin with a comparison of impression marking and analytical marking, it is easy to see that the two methods are by no means as different as they appear at first sight. We said that the impression marker reads the essay and awards a mark based on the overall impression that it makes on him. But this overall impression is made up of a number of factors. Bad spelling, untidy handwriting, poor expression, and lack of originality all contribute to a poor impression. If we have been teaching only for a short while, we cannot avoid noticing the faults just mentioned. Although we may not consciously decide to deduct marks for each of these faults, we do in fact deduct marks as a result of the bad impression which these faults make on us.

Whenever researchers (4) have investigated the marks awarded to particular essays by impression markers and analytical markers, they have found that there is no significant difference between the two sets of marks. The reader will recall that, if the difference is not significant, it must be the result of chance. If it is the result of chance, it cannot be the result of the particular marking technique used. The available evidence suggests that it makes little difference which technique we use, since they are basically the same.

A question which is more important for those who are training to teach or who are just beginning to teach is whether the essay-type answer is superior to the objective test. Before attempting to answer the question we must examine the evidence briefly. This can best be done by giving the credit and debit sides of each method.

THE ESSAY

On the debit side it must be said that:

i. The essay is one question; to answer it takes a large amount of time, in which many smaller questions could be asked and answered.
ii. The area of knowledge which can be tested in the essay is limited.
iii. Degrees of merit (or grading) have to be accepted instead of hard and fast scores.
iv. One essay marked once does not give an acceptable measure of the ability of the writer to write essays; this is shown more clearly if seven essays are marked twice, which is very time-consuming.

On the credit side it can be said that:

i. The essay is a good measure of expression; the writer is given scope to develop ideas and is free to compose the answer to the question in any way he wishes.
ii. The essay does not consist of a number of single responses, all of

which can be marked right or wrong; there is therefore more than one way open to the candidate to make a favourable impression.
iii. Experiments have shown that the essay and objective tests of English are not measuring the same thing.

MULTIPLE-CHOICE TESTS

On the debit side it must be stated that:

i. It is very easy to construct a poor multiple-choice test; a bad multiple-choice test may be much worse than other methods of testing the same area of learning.
ii. It takes a short time to mark a multiple-choice test but a very considerable time to construct one, a point which is relevant only if the teacher decides to construct his own test.
iii. The multiple-choice test does not demand coherence of expression, which in some areas may well be of paramount importance. The candidate is required only to perform a simple act of recognition or recall; he is not required to formulate ideas.
iv. Because all questions follow a well-defined form, any chance of the candidate not understanding the question is reduced; but, if the candidate becomes too familiar with the method, he may do less well than he would when confronted by other types of test.

On the credit side it can be said that:

i. Multiple-choice tests can be completed in a reasonably short space of time and cover a good deal of ground in that time.
ii. Multiple-choice tests are easily marked.
iii. The marking is objective, since every answer is either completely right or completely wrong.
iv. When standardized objective tests can provide a good deal of comparative information, which should be compared with the extra information which is obtained when a mark is derived from a raw score.

It is not difficult to see, in the light of this evidence, that there are occasions when the teacher would find the essay a useful method of testing, and others when he would find the multiple-choice method more useful.

There is another type of test, which falls half way between the two. This is the SHORT-ANSWER TEST, which can be summarized; on the debit side:

i. The short-answer test may penalize the better pupils unduly and unduly help the weaker ones. The former have insufficient scope to show their abilities, while the latter have insufficient opportunity to display their weaknesses. In Chapter 2, we saw that an over-difficult piece of Latin translation had the opposite effect: it gave the best pupils a chance to show their real strengths and mercilessly exposed all the weaknesses of the poorer ones.

ii. Although the short-answer test requires the candidate to sustain his effort for longer than the multiple-choice test on any given question, it still makes less demands of concentration and application than does the essay-type test.

iii. Certain answers may not be possible in short-answer form – for example, answers to questions on literary appreciation.

On the credit side:

i. The short-answer test requires more than mere recognition or recall.

ii. The short-answer test demands more than a simple response; it requires a certain amount of 'coherence' in the presentation of the answer.

iii. The short-answer test can be marked more objectively than the essay-type test but less objectively than can the multiple-choice test.

iv. In the short-answer test a greater area of the material which has been taught, can be tested than by means of the essay. The multiple-choice test covers more material than either the essay or the short-answer test, but at the price of not requiring coherence of expression.

v. The short-answer test can be marked more quickly than the essay but less quickly than the multiple-choice test. It is less time-consuming, however, to construct a good short-answer test than a good multiple-choice test.

vi. The short-answer test, like the essay, does not provide opportunities for guessing. The equivalent fault in short-answers tests and essays is padding and irrelevant material, both of which are easily detectable.

In the light of all the evidence we have presented, it would appear that only very rarely can we ask ourselves simply which type of test we should use on a particular day, as we might ask ourselves which of three ties we shall wear. The three types of test make three different types of demand on the person constructing them, on the person marking them, and above all on the person who is subjected to them. Any teacher must make the decision which test to use in the light of his reason for testing a given area of knowledge.

There will be many occasions when it will be profitable to use all three types of test. A combination of several types of test is called a TEST BATTERY. In the eleven-plus examination the test battery consisted of tests of English, arithmetic, and intelligence. The combination of the essay, the short-answer test, and the multiple-choice test might well have been an interesting and useful test battery for such an examination.

It is always helpful to know the findings of acknowledged experts in a given field; but it is also both useful and satisfying to experiment for oneself. Teachers who use all three types of test subject not only their pupils, but also themselves, to three separate types of discipline. In the process, it is not impossible that they will become better teachers of their own particular subjects.

POINTS TO REMEMBER IN CONSTRUCTING TEACHER-MADE TESTS

Every teacher will, at some time in his or her career, set questions which will require an essay-type answer. Many will doubtless try to construct short-answer tests and multiple-choice tests. Because of this, it may be salutary to set out briefly at this point some ideas which should always be borne in mind, if the test is to be effective. We shall deal with the three types of test already discussed.

ESSAY

    i. The essay should not be used merely because it is familiar and generally accepted. The teacher must use the essay, only where he feels that the short-answer test or the multiple-choice test would be a less suitable means of measuring learning.

    ii. Determine precisely *why* you are setting the essay and word the question accordingly. An essay

        a. may aim to test factual information, given to the learner over a period of time;

        b. may require the pupil to assess, interpret, and evaluate facts. (To do this, the pupil will need not only to know the facts but to appreciate their significance. He will have to develop an argument, take a stand on certain issues, and present ideas of his own);

        c. may be a means of obtaining information (asking children to write essays on someone they like or dislike or on things which make them happy and sad can often reveal the sources of problems which prevent the child being as successful in school as he could be);

        d. should be on interesting topics. (No child of fifteen will find it interesting to be asked to write an essay on 'Water'. Because he has no interest in the topic and no ideas about it, his essay will be poor, but this does not mean that he is a poor essay-writer. If asked to write an essay on 'The Beatles', he might well write a good one).

Ways of making marking more effective

i. If possible, mark all essays without knowing whose work is in front of you. This becomes difficult as one comes to recognize the pupils' handwriting. It is important to attempt to preserve the writer's anonymity, so that the sort of prejudice which we discussed in earlier parts of this book will not affect the marking. This difficulty is not present, of course, when marking scripts for public examinations.

ii. If essays are written by all the pupils on a number of topics, mark one question *throughout the sample*, and then mark each of the other topics throughout the sample. If this is done, the teacher will develop an idea of the group standard. Each child's essay is not then marked in isolation. Some teachers prefer to read all the essays first without assigning a mark to any of them. In this way, they avoid unfairness to the first few candidates. Until the marker has developed some idea of the group standard, he may be too generous or insufficiently generous in awarding marks to the early scripts.

iii. If possible, and certainly in an important examination, make sure that the essay is marked by more than one person.

iv. Decide at the outset whether you are going to penalize errors of spelling, grammar, punctuation, etc. If you are not, it will require a deliberate and sustained effort not to allow such errors to influence the mark given. This applies especially in the case of markers who are particularly sensitive to such errors.

SHORT-ANSWER TESTS

The following points should be observed by teachers constructing short-answer tests.

i. Decide precisely what knowledge, ideas, or skills are to be tested. It is advisable to make a list of these so that there is no doubt what they are.

ii. Divide the list above into areas, rather in the way we divided a mark scale into class intervals. For example, a natural division of areas to be tested in physics is HEAT : LIGHT : SOUND.

iii. Decide what sections are to be tested within each of the major areas. If each of the three major areas above contains four smaller areas, the examination paper must consist of twelve short-answer questions.

iv. Spend considerable time wording the instructions at the top of the paper. This is especially important if the pupils examined have never been subjected to this type of test before. At the same time, make out a careful mark scheme, and, where appropriate, provide yourself with a marking key.

MULTIPLE-CHOICE TESTS

The following points should be observed in constructing multiple-choice tests.

   i. Decide the total area of knowledge, ideas, or skills to be tested.
  ii. Sub-divide the main area into smaller sub-areas.
 iii. Decide the number of questions necessary for each sub-area.
 iv. Decide whether the test is to be a recognition test or a recall test.
  v. If it is to be a recognition test, decide on the number of alternative answers for each question.
 vi. If it is to be a recall test, decide on the layout of the questions. Consider such problems as whether the answer will always be a single word, whether it will always be given in a space at the end of the statement, or whether some answers will be given in the middle of the statements, and how much, and what sort of cueing is to be given.
 vii. Give clear instructions to the students, especially if they are meeting this sort of test for the first time.
viii. Avoid making all the answers so obvious that the test will produce a narrow spread of marks and fail to separate clearly the best pupils from the worst.
 ix. Avoid trivial items and meaningless terms. Avoid ambiguous terms and catch questions.
  x. Avoid distractions, especially those which may appear as irrelevant clues. A simple example of this is:

> Man is a animal
>   plant
>   fish
>   quadruped
>   monster

The answer is 'animal', but the indefinite article 'a' is appropriate for all the wrong answers, and inappropriate for the correct one.

 xi. Determine whether all the items (questions) are intended to be of equal difficulty, or whether they are intended to become gradually harder as the test progresses.
xii. Make certain that each question examines a separate piece of knowledge, skill, or idea. Avoid questions where the answer forms part of the answer to a question already answered, or to a question still to come. Such overlap of items reduces the number of items in exactly the same way as an impossible alternative answer reduces the number of choices.

xiii. Make sure that the correct answer does not appear in the same rank order every time. Ensure also that there is no regular pattern of correct answer placing.

xiv. Decide whether you wish the pupils to have a 'warm-up' test. This consists of a short practice test, in which the pupils answer a number of questions of the sort which appear in the main test. Warm-up tests are most valuable with pupils who have never seen multiple-choice tests before. Do not allow too long a warm-up period. If you do, the bright pupils become bored. They see what is required of them but, at the same time, realize that their answers will not obtain any marks for them. On the other hand, you must allow sufficient time for all pupils to understand exactly how they must answer the questions in the main test or examination.

STANDARDIZED TESTS

The term STANDARDIZED TESTS is an important one, and possibly strange to those who are beginning a study of psychology. However, in attempting to explain what the term means, we shall use some of the ideas which we have already dealt with.

First of all, 'standardized' has close connections with the term, 'objective'. We would therefore assume, and rightly so, that it has no connections with the term 'subjective'. Earlier in the present chapter we noted that when I said that Woolley was a more graceful batsman than Hammond, I was unable to prove the statement. The reason is that there is no standard measure which is universally accepted as applying to gracefulness of batting.

On the other hand, when I estimate that Edward is heavier and longer in the leg than George, I can test my impression by the use of two standard measures, the stone and the foot. Moreover, I can compare the weight and length of leg of Edward and George in Bognor Regis, with the weight and length of leg of Charles and William in Glasgow. The reason I can do this is that my standard measure remains the same wherever I use it. Thus, if I say that George weighs 15 stones and has a leg measurement of 33 inches, and that William weighs 12 stones and has a leg measurement of 31 inches, I know that George is both heavier and longer in the leg than William.

However, if I write to a friend in Glasgow and tell him that George weighs 290 apples, and that his leg measurement is $4\frac{1}{2}$ pieces of elastic, my friend may write back and say that William is heavier and longer in the leg than George, for he weighs 342 apples and his leg measures 6 pieces of elastic. We would never attempt to make such comparisons of the height and weight of people in different parts of the country, because we know that apples can vary in size, and that pieces of elastic are not only different in length, but may also be used stretched.

Yet, we do make this sort of comparison with school marks. A friend of mine has a child, who has just taken his first French examination and obtained a mark of 83 per cent. He tells me that his son has done much better than his nephew who lives 180 miles away. The nephew, in his first French examination scored only 73 per cent. The statement is meaningless, just as it is meaningless to compare W. G. Grace's batting average with that of Bradman to decide which was the greater batsman. They lived in different ages and battled on different types of wicket against different bowlers. Similarly my friend's son and nephew took examinations set by different teachers, possibly using different French syllabuses, different teaching methods, and very possibly using the 100-point mark-scale in different ways.

Standardized tests are designed, as foot-rules are designed, to give standard measurements, wherever they are used. One such test is a standardized reading test, which gives the READING AGE of each child tested. In the next chapter, we shall see that the Binet test similarly gives a mental age for each child. Because the tests are standardized, they will give meaningful differences. If a child, living in Birmingham, has a physical age of eight and a reading age of six and a half, while a child, in Penzance, has a physical age of eight and a reading age of nine and a half, both measured by the same test, we know that the child in Penzance is a more able reader than the child in Birmingham. Because the test is standardized, the difference between the two children is due to differences of reading ability, and not to differences in the measuring device or to differences arising by chance.

When a test is constructed, it is tested by being given to a large sample, which as we have seen will, in such circumstances, give much more reliable results than a small sample. Thus, when Binet constructed his famous test, he decided what questions he thought average children of given ages ought to be able to answer. He formulated thousands of questions which he thought the average nine-year-old, for example, ought to be able to answer. Having constructed the questions, he put them to thousands of nine-year-olds and then examined their answers. Questions which 80 per cent of the children answered correctly were rejected because they were too easy. From our study of the normal curve of distribution (Chapter 2), we found that only about 67 per cent children are average, that, 80 per cent of the children chosen by Binet when he tested his test answered any given question correctly, it was too easy. Some children of below-average intelligence would be likely to be able to answer that question when the test was completed, published and regularly used.

If any question was answered by, say only 20 per cent of the sample tested, that question was thought to be too difficult. If the question appeared in the final version of the test, only children of well-above-average intelligence would be able to answer it correctly. Binet was looking for questions which roughly 60 per cent of the sample tested could answer correctly.

While he was testing the test, Binet was taking the first step to establishing norms or standards. At the end of Chapter 2, we talked about standard scores. These form part of a series of TEST NORMS. For example, in the Pidgeon Non-verbal test, the handbook gives conversion tables for boys and girls between the ages of 8 years and 9 years 11 months. Using this table, any teacher, in any part of the country, can convert the raw score obtained by any child on the test, to a standard score. After this has been done, the individual score has a meaning in relation to the scores of other children.

Every standardized test has norms. Our discussion of the Binet and the Pidgeon tests shows immediately that one of these norms is always age. We would not use an 11+ test on adult samples. Nor would we use an adult test to determine the intelligence test of eleven-year-old children. There are some tests which give population norms for two different age-groups, but such tests are really two tests in one. There is a separate set of test items for each of the populations, for which norms are provided; a test might, therefore, give information through two sets of norms about populations of secondary modern boys and girls and male and female undergraduates.

Consequently, when we consult the norms of a particular test, to decide whether it is suitable for our purposes or not, we are looking for ideas which we have met already in this book:

i. The age and composition of the sample tested to establish the norms. The sample might be regional, national, or international.
ii. The mean score for the sample tested.
iii. The standard deviation from the mean for the sample tested.
iv. The number used in the sample tested to determine norms.
v. Conversion tables showing standard scores derived from the raw scores obtained by the sample tested.

Every test has its own set of norms and these must be analysed separately for every test used.

This use of standardized tests is yet another example of relating the performance of an individual child to that of other children.

STANDARDIZED TESTS AND TEACHER-MADE TESTS

As we saw, when we compared essay-type tests with multiple-choice tests, there is no simple answer to the question whether to use standardized or teacher-made tests. The most effective way of approaching the problem is to consider the distinctive features of both types of test and see when each can be used with maximum effectiveness. The distinctive features of standardized tests are:

i. They are based on general features, content, and objectives common to many schools throughout the country. However, such things cannot be modified to suit particular requirements in particular schools or individual classes without invalidating the standardization.

ii. They deal with large segments of knowledge or skill; teacher-made tests are often designed for a much smaller area of knowledge or skill, or even for a single topic.

iii. They are constructed and developed by experts with ample resources at their disposal. Such people often devote their entire careers to developing tests. By comparison, teacher-made tests depend on the limited skill and slender resources of one or two teachers.

iv. They provide norms for various groups often on a national scale.

Standardized tests should be used when teachers wish:

a. to compare the present achievement of their pupils with their potentiality (we have already seen that a standardized reading test is used in this way);

b. to compare achievement in different subject areas;

c. to evaluate the status of pupils from different schools on a common basis (this is most helpful when pupils transfer from one school to another and have to be placed in the most suitable year, stream, or form);

d. to make comparisons between different classes in different schools, e.g. to compare the performance of fourteen-year-old pupils in the Latin class of Direct Grant and local authority schools;

e. to study the development of individual pupils over a period of time, to determine whether their performance is improving or declining; unless standardized tests are used in such cases, improvement or decline may be attributable to different difficulty levels in the tests.

Teacher-made tests are useful:

a. to determine how well pupils have mastered a certain limited amount of instruction;

b. to determine the extent to which the teacher has achieved the aims of his teaching;

c. to provide a basis for assigning marks to pupils.

It is an obvious but frequently overlooked fact that the better the teacher is at compiling teacher-made tests, the better the tests themselves will be and the more useful the results obtained. There is no short-cut to acquiring skill in this direction. Such skill depends on a thorough knowledge of the fundamentals.

VALIDITY

In the chapters in Part 2 of this book, we shall be referring to a large number of standardized tests. In assessing the effectiveness of these tests, there are two terms which must be taken into account – VALIDITY and RELIABILITY.

Very simply, a valid test measures what it claims to measure and nothing else. So, if we use a valid test of intelligence, we know that we are measuring intelligence, and not something else such as personality. A valid test possesses relevance for a particular kind of measurement.

When we discussed analytical marking we saw that some teachers claimed that, to deduct marks from a total for a history essay because of poor spelling and untidy presentation, was irrelevant, since neither of these factors is relevant to ability in history, whereas, in assessing English essays, they might well be relevant factors.

What such teachers are saying, in terms of validity, is that a marks scheme for history essays, which takes account of incorrect spelling and untidy presentation, is invalid for testing ability in history. With a standardized test, we are assured of its validity. A valid test of intelligence does not measure personality, a valid test of non-verbal reasoning, does not measure verbal reasoning. In other words, we can say simply that, if a test is valid, it is doing the job it was designed to do. For this reason, we must not ask whether a test is valid, but whether it is *valid for x*. In the same way we must not ask if a man is trained, but whether he is *trained for x*.

Another important use of the term validity is in the expression PRE-DICTIVE VALIDITY. Many tests are used to predict future performance, perhaps the most famous of which was the 'eleven plus' test. This attempted to predict, at the age of eleven, which pupils would benefit from the academic education provided by the grammar school. Bearing in mind our basic definition of validity, namely, that a valid test performs only the task for which it was designed, we realize that the 'eleven plus' test would not be a good predictor of, for example, success as a power-station operative. If it were, it would probably be invalid as a predictor of grammar school success. Similarly, a test for power-station operatives would have predictive validity, only if it selected those applicants who subsequently proved to be efficient in their job.

E

PREDICTIVE VALIDITY AND EXTERNAL CRITERIA

In what we have said above we have suggested a way in which we can test the predictive validity of any given test. In the case of the 'eleven plus', we are concerned to select only those pupils who are likely to benefit from a grammar school education. It is accepted that this, in terms of our present educational system, means acquiring 'O'-level passes in five or more subjects. Those who obtain these passes have been correctly assigned to grammar school, as the result of the predictions of the 'eleven plus' test.

To determine the predictive validity of the 'eleven plus', we perform what psychologists call a FOLLOW-UP TEST. We note the children selected by the test in a given year, say 1960, and calculate that they will take their 'O'-level examination in 1965. In 1965 we find the number of children who obtain five or more 'O'-level passes, and calculate what percentage this is of the number assigned to grammar school five years earlier. If we follow the same procedure in 1966, 1967 and 1968, we shall, because we have examined more samples, be more justified in generalizing our findings. In 1965, we would be able to talk of the predictive validity of the 'eleven plus' in 1960, but if 1965 was the twentieth follow-up test, that we had performed, we might be justified in making statements about the 'eleven plus' in general. We would certainly be more likely to make justifiable statements about it than we would after only one follow-up test.

But suppose that we do not wish to wait so long to obtain some idea of the predictive validity of our test for power-station operatives. Industry is keenly competitive, and those who run it are very profit-conscious. They want to be able to see a quick return for money expended, and to wait five years would be unthinkable. In such circumstances, a technique called CONCURRENT VALIDATION can be used as some sort of guide to the effectiveness or otherwise of the test as a predictor.

A test for power-station operatives would be prepared by industrial psychologists. They would analyse the jobs which power-station operatives perform and base their tests on the skills involved. To validate the completed test concurrently would require two things: (1) the managers of the power-station would have to grade their present employees on, say, a five-point scale (excellent; very good; good; satisfactory; poor), and (2) the operatives at present employed in the power-station would themselves be required to take the test. Their performances would be measured and, according to this measurement, they would be graded as excellent, very good, good, satisfactory, or poor. If there was a high level of agreement between the gradings of present employees by the managers and the grading of such employees by the test, there would be a reasonable suggestion that the power-station test had a high predictive validity.

In the last section, we talked of two ideas without giving them their technical names. The terms are EXTERNAL CRITERION and CORRELATION. We have already learnt that a criterion is a standard against which we compare someone or something, to see if that person or thing measures up to our requirements. When we attempted to determine the predictive validity of the 'eleven plus', we used the degree of success achieved by the pupils at 'O' level to help us. Success at 'O' level, in other words, became our criterion, and because it was a standard external to the test itself, it is called the EXTERNAL CRITERION.

CORRELATION

This is a very important term (5). Earlier we avoided using the term 'correlation' only by substituting the much longer term 'degree of overlap', so we can define CORRELATION as the degree of overlap or similarity between two persons or things. The symbol used for correlation is r.

Perfect correlation, if it existed, would be complete identity, and would be represented by the symbol $+1.0$, and perfect oppositeness (such as the proverbial difference between chalk and cheese) would be represented, if it existed, by the symbol -1.0. If there was no correlation (no point of similarity between two persons or objects) we would express this by the symbol 0 (zero). Thus, we can have degrees of similarity moving towards identity. We call this POSITIVE CORRELATION. We can also have degrees of oppositeness moving towards perfect oppositeness, which we call NEGATIVE CORRELATION. Correlation is, therefore, always between $+1$ and -1; positive correlation between 0 and $+1$; and negative correlation between 0 and -1, as shown in Fig. 13.

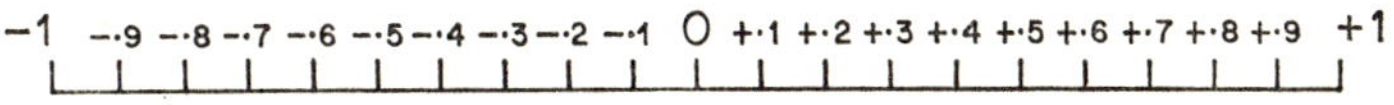

$$-1 \quad -{\cdot}9 \ -{\cdot}8 \ -{\cdot}7 \ -{\cdot}6 \ -{\cdot}5 \ -{\cdot}4 \ -{\cdot}3 \ -{\cdot}2 \ -{\cdot}1 \quad 0 \quad +{\cdot}1 \ +{\cdot}2 \ +{\cdot}3 \ +{\cdot}4 \ +{\cdot}5 \ +{\cdot}6 \ +{\cdot}7 \ +{\cdot}8 \ +{\cdot}9 \quad +1$$

Fig. 13

For our test for power-station operatives to be a valid predictor, we needed a high positive correlation between the test scores of the employees and the managers' ratings of their employees. The nearer to $+1$ the correlation, the more valid a predictor the test is. Correlation of $+{\cdot}90$ would be better than correlation of $+{\cdot}65$. The correlation of intelligence test scores of so-called 'identical twins' is over $+{\cdot}90$; that for other brothers and sisters is about $+{\cdot}65$.

A high degree of positive correlation between two criteria, however, means that it is immaterial which we use. We can either use identical twin A's score as a guide to B's intelligence or vice versa. Similarly, if there is a correlation of +·90 between the managers' ratings of their employees in the power-station, and the expensively produced test of efficiency, the managers are entitled to feel that they would be justified in continuing to use their rating in selecting employees. This can be put in the form of a generalization: If there is a high correlation between two types of selection procedure, one can be used as effectively as the other.

We can now use a familiar example from school marks as a further illustration of what is meant by correlation and why we are entitled to use either of two predictors which correlate highly. Below is a table of correlations for five school subjects:

	Classics	*French*	*English*	*Maths*	*Music*
Classics	—	·83	·78	·70	·63
French	·83	—	·67	·67	·57
English	·78	·67	—	·64	·61
Maths	·70	·67	·64	—	·51
Music	·63	·57	·51	·51	—

(Note that a dash is used to show that a subject cannot correlate with itself.)

This table is a useful illustration of correlation and also has implications for intelligence, which we shall discuss in the next chapter. We can see at once that Classics and French correlate very highly (·83). Readers will recall that, when schools select pupils to study Latin in the second year of Grammar School, ability in French is often the selection criterion used; the table above appears to justify this choice. Without a doubt, the best test of ability to do Latin is to make the pupils do some Latin, but, in the absence of such evidence, it appears that the next best thing is to use ability in French. The high correlation suggests that, whatever type of ability is required to succeed in one of the two subjects is required in the other. If information about the pupils' ability in French were not available, the table suggests that the English mark is the next best guide, followed by the Maths mark. The Music mark would be the worst guide of all, suggesting that the ability to do well in music is different from the ability required to do well in Latin. Alternatively, we could use the Latin mark to predict ability in French, English, or Maths, but not in Music.

If we return to 'eleven plus' examination and the testing of the predictive validity against the external criterion of success at 'O' level, we can now see that, if the 'eleven plus' examination has high predictive validity, it will correlate highly with the external criterion.

RELIABILITY

The last term with which we must concern ourselves in this chapter is RELIABILITY. When we use a standardized test, we know that it is reliable as well as valid. When we use teacher-made tests and essays this guarantee is not available.

Once again, the technical use of reliability is not far removed from its meaning in everyday life. If a watch is reliable, it always tells the correct time. A test which is reliable gives the same results every time. This does not mean that identical scores will be given every time. What it does mean is that there is a high correlation between scores for successive attempts on the same test.

The essay is a notoriously unreliable form of assessing, as we saw when we discussed the strengths and weaknesses of the essay. We said then that seven essays marked twice are much better than one essay marked once as a basis for assessing the essay-writing ability of any individual. We saw, too, that the subject can have a marked effect on the quality of the essay. A stimulating subject, of which the writer possesses considerable knowledge, will produce a better essay than will a subject of which the writer has little knowledge.

Thus, when we say that a standardized test is valid and reliable, we are saying that it measures what it claims to measure (and nothing else), and that there will be a high correlation between the scores obtained by a candidate making successive attempts at the test. If we use a test of reading ability, that is valid and reliable, we know that it tests reading ability and nothing else. We also know that, if it gives a reading age for a particular child, of seven years and six months today, it will not give a reading age of nine years and six months tomorrow and five years three months hence. There will be some variation in the ages produced, but the variation will be within predictable limits.

MARKER RELIABILITY

Markers of tests can be unreliable, just as the tests themselves can. Marker X is given an essay to mark. He awarded it 17 out of 20. A month later, he is asked to mark the same essay again, without realizing that he has marked it previously. This time he awards it 9 out of 20. Later still, he is given the essay a third time and now awards it 13 out of 20. These are wild variations in the mark which he awards the essay, much wilder than the swings in reading age which we would obtain by using the standardized test of reading ability already mentioned.

Because markers, whether using the impression method or the analytical method of marking, are so unreliable, it is sometimes found necessary to establish norms for a particular marker. This is done by calculating MARKER ERROR, that is, the wildness of swing in marks awarded by a particular individual. Once this is known, any marks which he awards subsequently can be adjusted in terms of his own error. By this process, those who check on his error are really deriving a mark from the raw score, which this particular marker awards to an essay.

It will be realized that it is quite impossible to calculate the 'marker error' for all those who mark essays. This is one piece of ammunition regularly used by those who attack the essay-type test, and suggest that it be replaced by objective tests.

NOTES AND REFERENCES FOR CHAPTER 3

1 Further discussion of preconceptions and prejudices, and the way in which they govern everyone's thinking to a greater or lesser extent, is undertaken in Schofield, H., *The Philosophy of Education: an Introduction* (Allen & Unwin, 1972).
2 'The Foundation Year in the University of Keele', an unpublished report by A. H. Iliffe, Research Fellow, 1962–4.
3 The Russian physiologist, Pavlov, performed experiments to condition the reflex of an Alsatian dog. In one experiment, he starved the dog, and then showed it food. The dog salivated at the sight of the food. After a few trials, Pavlov shone a circle of light on the wall at the same time as the dog was given the food. Eventually, the dog was conditioned to salivate at the sight of the circle of light. Pavlov also conditioned the dog not to salivate when an ellipse of light appeared on the wall. After teaching the dog to salivate to the circle of light by shining it at the same time as he provided the food, he shone the ellipse of light without giving the dog food. The fact that the dog continued to salivate when the circle of light appeared, and failed to salivate when the ellipse appeared, showed that the dog was able to discriminate between the two shapes. Finally, Pavlov so altered the shape of the circle and the ellipse that they became almost identical (there was a high degree of correlation between their shapes). At this point, the dog, unable to distinguish one shape from the other, never knew whether the light hearlded food or not. The result was that he exhibited all the symptoms of a nervous breakdown. The impression that the experience made on the dog was such that, for a long time afterwards, it showed signs of terror each time Pavlov attempted to return it to the laboratory, where it had received its unpleasant experiences.
4 Classic works in this area are: Hartog, P. J. and Rhodes, E. C., *The Marks of Examiners* and *An Examination of Examinations* (both published by Macmillan, 1935).
    Rhodes and Burt found that markers differed in standard, whether they used the impression or the analytical method. Thus, neither method eliminated 'marker error'. Even when the same marker used both methods, his standard varied in both cases. When ten markers marked the same essay by the impression method, the result was a higher average mark for that

essay. When the same essay was marked by the analytical method, there was no noticeable rise in the average mark for the essay. Finally, markers using the impression method tended to spread their marks more. The marks were more widely distributed about the mean, tending to produce a larger standard deviation (SD) and a platykurtic curve.

5 Two technical terms have been used in this chapter, namely 'test battery' and 'correlation'. In Chapter 1, we discussed teachers' ratings of pupils. One piece of research was carried out with the aim of determining the degree of correlation between the items in the test battery. The figures obtained were:

Essay correlated with Moray House intelligence test   ·690
Essay correlated with achievement in English/Arithmetic ·755
Essay correlated with combined teacher estimates   ·776

The reader should, in the light of what he has read about correlation in this chapter attempt to interpret these correlations and ask himself what the correlations tell him. It should also be noted that the correlation figure here is taken to three decimal places. For simplicity in the chapter only two decimal places were used.

GENERAL NOTE

In this chapter we have dealt with a number of technical terms essential to users and constructors of tests. To show their interconnection and importance, we give below the main points dealt with in the manual for a group-reading test designed by Dennis Young:

Raw Scores
Reading-age norms
Educational gains
Test construction:
  (a) item construction and selection
  (b) standardization
  (c) validity
  (d) reliability
  (e) practice effects.
Norms: (1) reading quotients for ages 6 : 6 to 8 : 11 (i.e. 6 yrs 6 mths – 8 yrs 11 mths).
       (2) reading quotients for ages 9 : 0 to 12 : 11.
       (3) reading ages on the Young Test and equivalent scores or reading ages on Neale, NFER, Schonell Tests, Burt Tests.
(Note that 3 is possible only because all the tests mentioned are standardized.)

Part 2

METHODS OF ASSESSMENT AND TESTING;
TYPES OF TESTS; THE APPLICATION
THROUGH TESTS OF THE PRINCIPLES OF
ASSESSMENT AND TESTING DISCUSSED IN
PART 1

Chapter 4

Intelligence Tests I

The term INTELLIGENCE TEST is an omnibus term. It has no single, simple, precise meaning, but embraces a number of different ideas or concepts. During the present century, our knowledge of intelligence, though still limited, has increased, and has resulted in more numerous and different types of intelligence tests.

If we use the term 'intelligence test' meaningfully, today, we are really referring to a test of general ability (1), or general intelligence, since we no longer accept that intelligence is one thing and one thing only. The term is also used, though not with strict appreciation of its meaning, to cover tests of SPECIAL ABILITIES. The reason why the term can be used so loosely will become clear as the chapter progresses.

However, all accepted intelligence tests have certain features in common. They are objective, they all possess norms, and they are valid and reliable. From the raw scores obtained by those who take the tests we can obtain derived scores, and thus compare the individual tested with the total population. For this reason, if I administer a test of arithmetical ability (and we shall see, in a moment, that this comes within the term 'intelligence') to John Smith, aged 8 years and 6 months (8:6), I can, from the derived scores, obtain his ARITHMETICAL AGE. Once I have obtained his arithmetical age, I can compare John Smith's ability in arithmetic with the scores of the total population to decide whether he is average, above average, or below average for his age. (For this idea see also Z-scores on pp. 32–3.) Because the test is standardized, I know that it enables me to make a realistic comparison of John Smith with other children; because the test is valid, I know that it is measuring arithmetical ability and not some other ability; because the test is reliable, I know that, if I apply it to John Smith today, next week, and three months hence, there will be no wild and unaccountable variations in the results obtained. I could not have this degree of certainty if I used tests of my own devising, which had not been standardized and for which norms had not been established.

THE BINET TEST

We have referred to the BINET TEST (2) in previous chapters. It was devised by the Frenchmen, Binet and Simon, and developed between 1905 and 1908, to provide a more scientific measurement of a child's intelligence than that provided by teachers' marks and assessment. It is still used as a test of general intelligence. Subsequently, it underwent two revisions, the first at Stanford University, in the United States, because of which this particular edition is known as the STANFORD-BINET TEST. The second revision was also undertaken in the United States, by Terman and Merrill in 1960. Just as the first revision resulted in a modified title, so the test which developed from the second revision is commonly referred to as the TERMAN MERRILL TEST (3).

The Binet Test takes about two hours to complete and provides a single score of ability. The range of the test (and the range of any test is vitally important) is from two years to 'superior adult', and it consists of a number of sub-tests. For the two to five years age-group, the sub-tests are for half-year intervals in the scale of ages. For the age range five to fourteen, the sub-tests are spaced at one-year intervals.

The aim of the test is to estimate the probable rate of progress of the child in school. It also aims to pick out those who are unlikely to benefit from formal instruction in school. It must be remembered that the original Binet test was compiled as a scientific measurement of mental deficiency, or what we now call 'educational subnormality'. A child who is E.S.N. (educationally subnormal) will be unable to profit from the ordinary, conventional schooling.

The Binet test is described as a verbal test, which simply means that the asking of the questions and the answering of them involves the use of words. We shall see later that there are also non-verbal tests of intelligence, which are known as PERFORMANCE TESTS. They require the child tested to do something, rather than to write or say something. Here are some examples, taken from the Stanford-Binet Test, of what the child tested is required to do:

Age 2:6   Child points to toy object: 'We drink out of . . .'
           Child points to 'doll's hair'.
           Child names 'chair', 'key'.
           Child repeats numbers 4, 5, 6, 7.

We recall that the test is designed to measure what the child of average intelligence of a given age *ought* to be able to do. While it may seem that any child could achieve the tasks listed above at the age of two and a half, the reader is asked to think of any children he knows who cannot do so. The number of mentally, physically, and emotionally handicapped children who cannot perform such simple tasks at this age is surprisingly large.

It is also important to note that, although the first two tasks involve 'motor-activity' (or 'muscular' activity), words are involved. The third question is obviously verbal, while the fourth is numerical. We shall see later that there is a connection between numerical and verbal ability.

Since someone has to administer the test to the young child in a fairly intimate way, the effect that the tester has on the child is most important. It is not uncommon for some people to be described as 'having a way with children'. Testers lacking this quality would probably adversely affect the child's score.

At the age of six, the child is required to define an orange and an envelope, hand nine blocks to the person administering the test, work through a puzzle maze, and complete a 'verbal relationship', e.g. 'An inch is short; a mile is . . .'. Again it will be seen that the first question is purely verbal, while the second demands a response to verbal instructions and involves motor movement. The third task calls for motor activity, while the fourth question is again verbal. (This last question, by the way, reminds us that intelligence is often defined as 'seeing relationships'. The type of question: 'Hand is to arm as foot is to . . .' is a very common one in verbal intelligence tests.

Children in the higher age groups are asked to supply definitions of increasingly difficult terms, such as 'juggler', and 'skill', to compare words of similar meaning like 'laziness' and 'idleness' (4), to explain proverbs, to detect absurdities in statements and pictures, and so on. It is interesting to note that the child required to define the abstract term 'skill', would be an average child of twelve, the age at which, says Piaget, the ability to think in abstract terms begins (5). Before this age, the child's thinking is centred on concrete objects, and his vocabulary, which expresses his experience, is also concrete.

THE BINET TEST AND MENTAL AGE

Eysenck (6) tells us that the difficulty of defining and measuring intelligence is that intelligence is not a thing but a concept or an idea. We saw that, if I wanted to compare the weight and height of two people living far apart, I could do so because there are generally accepted standard measures to enable the comparison to be made. When, however, we seek to measure intelligence, we cannot use the methods we use when dealing with tangible objects. Consequently, we have to devise a special measure, or a number of measures.

The measure of intelligence characteristic of the Binet Test is MENTAL AGE. Although we know that a child's mental age may be the same as, less than, or greater than his physical age, we continue, as a general rule, to assign children to classes in school according to physical age. We are most reluctant, for example, to stream children in the junior school. But to assume that all children of a given physical age have the same mental ability is naïve and fallacious.

The idea of mental age is not only important; it is also easy to understand. A simple example will demonstrate how to derive a child's mental age from the Binet Test, and also how we convert a mental age to the more familiar measure of intelligence, the I.Q. (or intelligence quotient).

Let us assume that there are three children, Smith, Brown, and Robinson, each of whom is ten years old, and that to discover their mental ages we give them the Binet Test. Because they are ten years old, we use part of the test which applies to children between the ages of five and fourteen, for we know that, if Smith, Brown, and Robinson, are of average intelligence, they ought to be able to answer the questions in the sub-test for ten-year-olds.

Before we start the actual test, we give the children a 'warm-up' (often referred to as 'practice'). Because the children to be tested are ten-year-olds, it is convenient to use for a warm-up the sub-test for nine-year-olds. (Whatever the age-group to be tested, the sub-test one below that age-group is used for warm-up purposes.)

Smith successfully completes the warm-up questions and completes the sub-test for ten-year-olds. He is then given the opportunity to answer the questions in the eleven-year-old sub-test, to see if his mental age is higher than his physical age. He fails to answer these questions, and is given a mental age of ten.

Brown, like Smith, completes the warm-up sub-test successfully. He also completes the sub-tests for ten, eleven, twelve, thirteen, and fourteen years, and is therefore given a mental age of fourteen or four years in advance of his physical age.

Robinson, however, is unable to complete the questions in the warm-up section, and he is set to work on the seven-year-olds' sub-test. This is done because, having failed to answer the nine-year-olds' sub-test, his mental age will at the highest be only eight. It is therefore only fair to allow him to warm up on material for a child one year younger. He completes this sub-test, and with difficulty, completes the sub-test for eight-year-olds. He is assigned a mental age of eight, or two years below his physical age.

Thus, we can list our three children, giving their physical and mental ages as follows:

Name	Physical age	Mental age
Smith	10	10
Brown	10	14
Robinson	10	8

This information tells us that one of our three children thinks like a ten-year-old, one like a fourteen-year-old, and one like an eight-year-old. It is absurd to think that these children should be in the same junior school class, would benefit equally from the teaching they received, and would have similar career prospects in the future. By deriving their INTELLI-GENCE QUOTIENTS from their mental ages, and by relating these derived scores to the norms for the total population, predict what they are likely to achieve in the future.

First, however, we must calculate their I.Q.'s.

$$\text{I.Q.} = \frac{\text{Mental age}}{\text{Physical age}} \times 100.$$

Applying the formula to each of the three children in turn, we obtain the following results:

$$\text{Smith:} \quad \text{I.Q.} = \frac{10}{10} \times 100 = 100$$

$$\text{Brown:} \quad \text{I.Q.} = \frac{14}{10} \times 100 = 140$$

$$\text{Robinson:} \quad \text{I.Q.} = \frac{8}{10} \times 100 = 80.$$

We have stressed that any score in isolation is meaningless. From these I.Q. scores, we can say that Smith is of average intelligence, Brown is above average, while Robinson is below average. We can also say that Smith is cleverer, or brighter, than Robinson, and that Brown is cleverer, or brighter, than both Smith and Robinson. But this is only a sample of three. The figures as they stand do not tell us anything about these three in relation to all others in the total population.

If we tested the intelligence of the total population of ten-year-olds in Great Britain, we could obtain for each a mental age and from this an I.Q. score. If we plotted all these I.Q. scores on a graph, we should obtain the normal curve of distribution, shown in Fig. 14.

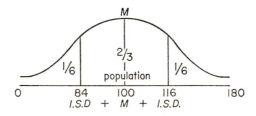

Fig. 14

The mean of 100 and the SD of 16 are the norms for the Binet test. Recalling what we said in Chapter 2 about the normal curve of distribution, we can deduce the following facts about the curve of distribution of intelligence.

1. With the mean of 100 and a SD of 16, one standard deviation below the mean (−1 SD) will give an I.Q. score of 84.
2. With a mean of 100 and a SD of 16, one standard deviation above the mean (+1 SD) will give an I.Q. score of 116.
3. Two out of every three children will fall between −1 SD and +1 SD. This means that two out of every three children will have an I.Q. somewhat between 84 and 116.
4. Because the normal curve of distribution is symmetrical, there will be as many children with an I.Q. of below 84 as there are children with an I.Q. above 116. Since two-thirds lie between 84 and 116, one-sixth have an I.Q. greater than 116, and one-sixth an I.Q. less than 84.

It will be observed that the range of 84–116, described as the range of normal, or average, intelligence, is very great. If we sub-divide at 100, we can call 84–100 lower-average, and 100–116 upper-average. The important fact for us, in the light of our three hypothetical pupils, is that Smith is absolutely average, Brown lies outside the average range at the upper end of the scale, and Robinson outside the average range at the lower end. Brown is in the top sixth of the total population, while Robinson is in the bottom sixth of the total population.

In fact, we can discriminate more finely than one-sixth above average and one-sixth below, as the following figures will show. It is not necesasry, however, for the reader to concern himself at this stage with the mechanics of this discrimination. In the table of figures below, we see the results of testing a sample, N = 2904:

I.Q.	% in sample
140+	1·3
130—139	3·1
120–129	8·2
110–119	18·1
100–109	23·5
90–99	23·5
80–89	14·5
70–79	5·6
below 70	2·6

Notice that the class interval for this scale is ten, because the total range of scores has been divided into units of ten, and that the curve is not the normal curve of distribution. This is because of the comparative smallness of the sample tested compared with the total population. The curve will be positively skewed.

Brown is in the very top group on this scale. One researcher in the United States found that the mean I.Q. for all persons receiving a Ph.D. was 130 (7). If we take the level of educational subnormality as 70, and the lower level of average intelligence as 84, we can see that Robinson lies somewhere between the two. He would not be sent to an E.S.N. school, but would be described as 'backward'. This would mean that he was below the average level of performance in school subjects for children of his age. He would be assigned to a remedial stream, where children are taught in smaller groups and the teacher has the opportunity to come to know the needs of each child and to teach him as an individual needing special attention.

Before we leave this section, it is interesting to note some figures provided by Eysenck (8) which give the following correlations between first and second attempts (test-retest is the technical term for two consecutive attempts) on the Stanford-Binet tests:

Time interval (test/retest)	correlation (test/retest)
1 week	·95
1 year	·91
2 years	·87
3 years	·83.

TESTS OF SPECIAL ABILITIES

The idea that intelligence consists of general ability (represented in the text-books by the symbol g) and special, or specific abilities (represented in the text-books by the symbol s) began with Spearman. He stated that different tasks require general and specific (or special) abilities in different proportions. Thus, to be good at Classics would require a high level of general ability, while to be a good draughtsman would require a high level of special (or specific) ability.

If we refer to the table of correlations on page 54, we see that there is a high degree of correlation between Classics, French, English, and Mathematics, but a low degree of correlation between any of these subjects and Music. This suggests some sort of common ability required for success in Classics, French, English, and Mathematics. It is reasonable to assume that this common factor is general ability. The four subjects contain like elements and require like ability if a pupil is to study them successfully.

But it appears that, whatever this general ability is, it is not required to the same extent for an individual to be good at music. Music, it appears, requires a greater proportion of special ability. It is not difficult to accept

F

this, since we have already suggested that there is a connection between verbal and numerical concepts, and the four subjects where marks correlate highly have a high verbal or numerical content. Music, on the other hand, requires a sense of rhythm, and this is possibly a special ability. Some books refer to general and specific abilities as the general and specific factors of intelligence. There is a connection between the correlations on page 54, and the special abilities, which Spearman distinguished from general ability. An ability is isolated when a number of responses, or performances, within tests correlate with one another but not with other responses. For example, we may find, after setting certain tests for people wishing to obtain clerical jobs, that responses to clerical questions or performance on clerical tests correlate with one another. After testing these same people on Arithmetic and English, we may well find that the clerical responses and performance do not correlate with the arithmetical and English responses. This would show that there is a CLERICAL ABILITY (10) (or as we shall see later, a clerical aptitude). For the moment, the important point is to remember that an ability is revealed when responses correlate positively.

In Fig. 15, we illustrate in diagrammatic form Spearman's distinction between general ability and special abilities. Responses for ability A would correlate with one another, but not with responses for abilities B and C. Likewise, responses within ability B would correlate with one another but not with those within A and C.

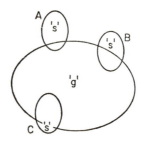

Fig. 15

Thomson, working like Spearman in the field of abilities, modified the idea which Spearman put forward. While he accepted a general ability *g*, and special abilities *s*, he thought that there were some performances which could not be assigned to *g* or *s*. For this reason, he developed the idea of GROUP FACTORS. According to Thomson, intelligence consisted of a general factor, group factors and special factors. Presenting this idea, in diagrammatic form, we would have the following modification of the material shown in Fig. 15:

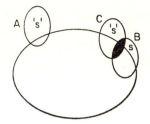

shaded area = group factor

Fig. 16

THE SEVEN PRIMARY MENTAL ABILITIES

In the 1930s the American, Thurstone, developed the idea of particular abilities at the expense of the general ability of Spearman and Thomson, when he stated that intelligence was an omnibus term used to describe seven primary mental abilities. These he called:

Verbal Ability
Verbal Fluency
Numerical Ability
Spatial Ability
Perceptual Speed
Associative Memory
Reasoning.

VERBAL ABILITY is the ability to derive sense and meaning from spoken and written language. VERBAL FLUENCY is the ability to utter a large number of words quickly. The words *may* make sense, but not necessarily. Verbal fluency is what the layman often refers to as 'the gift of the gab'. The reader will appreciate that it is very desirable to have high ratings on both these abilities, especially for teachers.

NUMERICAL ABILITY means the ability to understand and to manipulate numbers. A word of warning is not out of place here. To test numerical ability we must *not* use problem arithmetic. The reader should pause for a moment at this point and ask himself, in the light of what he has read in this book about test validity, why we make this statement.

Many people do not appreciate the subtle difference between mechanical arithmetic and problem arithmetic. The present writer has often been approached by parents who ask, 'Why can my child get all his sums right but never his problems?' The answer is simply that the ability required for sums, i.e. for mechanical arithmetic, is numerical ability, while verbal ability plays a large part in problem arithmetic. The relationship between the numbers in mechanical arithmetic is shown by the numbers themselves and by a small number of symbols such as $+$ and $-$, with which the child is perfectly familiar. But in problem arithmetic, the relationship between the numbers is indicated by words. If the child cannot understand the words, he cannot grasp the relationships.

The parents who ask the question are often offended when one's answer to their question is, 'Because your child cannot read'. They indignantly retort that his report says that his reading is good, not realizing that such reports often mean little more than that the child can recognize words and utter them. In this sense, anyone who has learned his native language can 'read' anything. A navvy can 'read' a book on symbolic logic, if, by 'read', we mean that he can utter the words which appear on the printed page. But real reading consists of two parts: recognition of the words and derivation of meaning from the words in combination. And for this verbal ability is required.

SPATIAL ABILITY is the ability to perceive spatial relationships and to manipulate what one perceives mentally. For instance, we may show a person a diagram of a piece of machinery and ask him to visualize it working. If he is able to manipulate mentally the moving parts of the machinery and envisage what happens, he has high spatial ability. If his spatial ability is low, he will not be able to visualize the machinery in in operation. To understand the process, he needs to have a working model and make the parts move manually.

MEMORY, perhaps surprisingly for some readers, correlates with intelligence. The more intelligent we are, the better our memory should be. For this reason, a very good memory in children of pre-school age is a suggestion of high intelligence, although not infallible proof. In terms of correlation, there is a higher correlation between a test of memory and a test of intelligence than there is between two tests of memory.

PERCEPTUAL SPEED is the ability to recognize similarities and differences quickly. The reader will no doubt have seen the popular test of perceptual speed consisting of a row of faces in outline. The candidate has to spot the 'odd man out'. A person with high perceptual speed can spot a large number of 'odd ones out' in a very short time.

REASONING can be measured by a variety of test types. It includes verbal reasoning (reasoning with words) and non-verbal reasoning (reasoning from pictures). It is sometimes tested by having to deduce the third line of a syllogism:

All men are mortal
All Greeks are men
Therefore.................

The candidate must write down the deduction to be made from the first two lines, namely, that all Greeks are mortal. Reasoning can also be tested by requiring the candidate to complete a letter series, such as: aabccdeefgg–. (The candidate has to write down 'h'.)

By accepting Thurstone's idea of what we mean by intelligence, we are bound to set tests which examine all the seven primary mental abilities when we measure intelligence. If we do not do this, Thurstone would argue, we are being unfair to the candidate. A test of general ability is not a valid measure of intelligence in this case.

Thomson had begun to suspect this. Examining the place of origin of those children, who obtained scholarship places in grammar schools (the pre-war equivalent of passing the 'eleven plus'), he discovered that urban children obtained grammar school places more frequently than rural children. Further investigation showed that the rural child had less command of vocabulary than the urban child. In some cases, rural children were unable to derive meaning from the verbal instructions at the top of the test. This was the beginning of the idea of CULTURE BIAS in intelligence tests (see p. 77). It also culminated in the discoveries and writings of Bernstein (11).

From the seven primary mental abilities of Thurstone, the Americans have derived many others. There are tests of finger-dexterity, and even an appropriate test for those who apply for posts as junior clerks. We need, however, to ask how much more information we derive from tests of such minor abilities as finger-dexterity than we derive from the more familiar tests of the seven primary mental abilities. If we are to go to the trouble of constructing, applying, marking, and interpreting the scores of a large number of tests, does the extra knowledge which we gain justify the time, labour, and expense involved?

HIERARCHY OF ABILITIES

As a first step to answering this question, we need to consider the combined ideas of Spearman and Thomson, shown in Fig. 17. This is a diagram of the HIERARCHY OF ABILITIES.

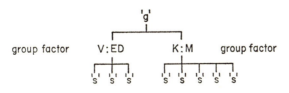

Fig. 17

The symbols V:ED and K:M stand for VERBAL EDUCABILITY and KINESTHETIC/MECHANICAL ABILITY, ideas which can better be understood as ACADEMIC ABILITY and PRACTICAL ABILITY. The diagram also shows the connection between verbal and numerical ability (see p. 69), since both appear on the academic side of the diagram.

Statistical analysis will show to what extent the general factor, g, the group factor, and the special factor, s contribute to a person's final score on a test. Again, we need not know how the calculation is done; only the results need concern us. Let us assume that we wish to discover whether a test of general intelligence or a test of spelling ability itself is a more valid and reliable measure of spelling ability.

What we are really asking ourselves is which factor in this situation makes the greatest contribution to the final test score – g, group factor, or s factor. If we discover that the largest contribution comes from s, then the best test to use is a test of spelling ability. However, if we find that the greatest percentage of the score does not come from s, then a test of spelling is not necessarily the best way of determining a person's ability to spell. Suppose that such a test has been given to measure, g, group factor, and special ability (12), and the following result obtained:

g	Group factor (V)	Special factor s
64%	25%	11%

The conclusion to be drawn from these figures is that a test of general ability is a better indication of a person's ability to spell than a test of spelling. Again, as in the case of memory, it appears that there is a high correlation between high intelligence and ability to spell correctly.

However, a form-board test gives a different picture. All readers will have seen the equivalent of a form-board test in the guise of a well-known educational toy for very young children. The child is given a board from which various shapes – apple, pear, etc. – have been cut. He is also given shaped pieces representing apple, pear, etc., and has to put the apple shape in the apple space and so on. The results for this test were as follows:

g	Group factor (K)	Special factor (s)
16%	25%	59%

We can now see that there appears to be no single answer to our original question. It appears that, in the academic type of test, the special ability plays little part in providing the total score, whereas in the practical tests, it plays a considerable part, while the g factor plays a much smaller part.

In terms of the technical expressions which we have learned so far, we can make a tentative generalization. It appears that, in tests for V:ED, tests of general ability may be more valid predictors than tests of special (and small) areas of ability. On the other hand, it appears that, in tests for K:M, tests of specific abilities may be more valid predictors than tests of general ability. We could back this statement up with another one, relating to the seven primary mental abilities, namely that, on the V:ED side, it is better to measure the larger abilities than to measure minor abilities derived from these larger abilities. However, on the K:M side, even the larger abilities (e.g. spatial, perceptual) are more specific and localized than their counterparts on the V:ED side. Finally, some abilities, derived from the larger ones on the K:M side, are so specific that the only valid predictor of possession of these abilities in high measure is a test of that particular ability. Thus, while a test of verbal ability might tell us more about a person's level of vocabulary than a vocabulary test, a test of finger-dexterity, might tell us more about his level of finger dexterity than would a test of spatial ability.

We can now relate the present findings to what we have already said about test validity, reminding ourselves again that a valid test measures what it claims to measure and nothing else. Relating this to tests of special ability, a test which is a valid measure of special ability A must not be thought to be a valid measure of special ability B. A test of finger-dexterity, if it measures only finger-dexterity, is a valid test. It would not, however, be a valid test of aiming.

We can relate what we have been saying to what we have learned about correlation. If there is a great deal of common content in verbal and numerical ability, there will be a high degree of correlation between the two abilities. If there is a high degree of correlation between two tests or methods of assessment, we can use either as a predictor of the other. In view of this, we would expect very little common content in two specific abilities. Consequently, we would expect a low degree of correlation between them, which means that one is not a guide to the other.

PROFILES OF PERSONS TESTED ON THE SEVEN PRIMARY MENTAL ABILITIES

We said, earlier, that everyone possesses the seven primary mental abilities, but that each has a higher score, or weighting, on some than on others. Consequently, by testing the total population, we can find the mean score on each of the abilities. We can represent this on a histogram, and then, by measuring the scores of individuals on the seven abilities, produce a histogram for them, and compare each with the score for the average member of the total population. Figure 18 is for the total population, while Figs. 19 and 20 represent two hypothetical individuals.

Mean Score per Ability (Total Population) for Seven Primary Mental Abilities

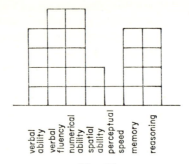

Fig. 18

Person A

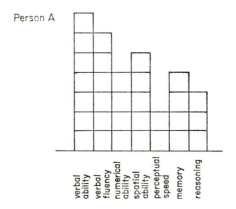

Fig. 19

Person B

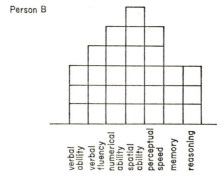

Fig. 20

We can assess persons A and B, in relation to the total population as follows:

Person A	Factor/Ability	Comparison with total population
	Verbal ability	above average
	Verbal fluency	above average
	Numerical ability	below average
	Spatial ability	above average
	Perceptual speed	above average
	Memory	average
	Reasoning	below average
Person B	Verbal ability	below average
	Verbal fluency	below average
	Numerical ability	average
	Spatial ability	above average
	Perceptual ability	above average
	Memory	below average
	Reasoning	below average

It must be appreciated that these profiles are purely for illustration; they must not be taken as accurate representations either of the total population or of individuals.

INTELLIGENCE A AND INTELLIGENCE B

The Russian physiologist, Pavlov, experimented with the conditioning of reflexes in Alsatian dogs. By studying intelligence from the physiological angle, D. O. Hebb (13) developed his ideas of INTELLIGENCE A and INTELLIGENCE B. We shall see later what is the distinction between the two ideas, but first we must say something about the heredity *v.* environment problem of intelligence (sometimes called the 'nature/nurture problem') (14).

Very simply the problem is this: over the years, some have argued that intelligence is something which we inherit, while others have claimed that it is something resulting from the environment. If we accept the former view, we accept a sort of 'Calvinism' of ability (some are born to intellectual salvation, others to intellectual damnation) and there is nothing that can be done about it. If we accept the latter idea completely, we are asserting that we have only to provide the right environment for every individual to make him intelligent.

Not unexpectedly, neither extreme interpretation is correct. Our intelligence is partly due to our physical inheritance (and this comes from distant ancestors as well as from parents) and partly the result of our environment.

If 'intelligence' were entirely the product of heredity, then identical twins (15) would have identical (or almost identical) intelligence, whatever their environment. It is true that, if identical twins take an intelligence test, their scores correlate very highly (above ·90), and this is a powerful piece of evidence in support of the hereditary theory. On the other hand, if identical twins are separated, and one is kept in a good environment and the other in a poor environment, the correlation between their subsequent intelligence tests scores falls considerably to about ·65/·70.

If the environmental theory of intelligence were true, we would expect children separated from their parents and placed in a common environment to have intelligence test scores with high intercorrelation. The best example of such a common environment is an orphanage. Yet, if we measure the intelligence of children in an orphanage, we find the same spread of intelligence test scores which we find in children outside the orphanage.

We are now in a position to understand Hebb's Intelligence A and Intelligence B. He calls the former 'genetic potential' and the latter 'present mental efficiency'. The first type is the inherited potential which we are capable of achieving if all the factors in our environment are favourable. Intelligence B is the level of efficiency which we maintain after being subjected to a certain environment. It is Intelligence B that we measure when we use intelligence tests.

If the reader thinks back to the seven primary mental abilities, he will recall that they are abilities which are exercised and trained in school. We know that some children come from good homes and see these abilities exercised in the home. They are given books and psychological toys. They frequently have stories read to them, and the emotional atmosphere of the home makes them feel secure. We also know that there are many children who come from poor homes. They are not necessarily 'poor' in the material sense (though they are often this as well); but there is little conversation for the child to hear, no stories are read to him, no educational toys provided, and there is no emotionally satisfying atmosphere.

By sending the children from good and bad homes to school together, we ensure that, at least for a certain period of time, they are subjected to a common environment. Unfortunately, however, it does not follow that children in a common environment will all benefit equally from it. It has been said (16) that one of the most significant discoveries of the last fifty years in education is that the children from certain types of deprived homes are almost incapable of benefiting from formal schooling.

Thus, when we measure Intelligence B, we are really measuring the extent to which a child has benefited from his schooling. A child who produces a low score on the test may be dull, i.e. he may have a low Intelligence A or a low genetic potential. In this case, however good his home and his school, he will never achieve great things. On the other hand, his low score may be indicative of an average or even above-average genetic potential, which has not been fulfilled because of adverse environmental factors.

CULTURE BIAS IN INTELLIGENCE TESTS; PERFORMANCE TESTS

We referred earlier in this chapter to the work of Thomson and Bernstein, which suggested that certain children were unable to benefit from their schooling because the language of the teacher (a middle-class language) was one that they had never heard before they started school and never heard subsequently outside the school. The teacher was, to all intents and purposes, speaking a foreign language. Thus, the child was unable to understand the content of instruction, because he could not understand the language of instruction.

The term CULTURE BIAS is directly connected with this. The culture bias of an intelligence test is the degree to which it favours some children who take it and penalizes others. It is not surprising to learn that verbal intelligence tests are particularly biased culturally. They favour the middle-class child and penalize the child from the poorer homes. For this reason we ought not to be surprised that the Binet test is culturally biased, a fact which Davis (17) deals with at some length. She also found that some of the most famous of all American intelligence tests have tremendous culture bias. One instance she gives is of a question, which few children could answer, because the correct answer depended on the knowledge of what the word 'sonata' meant. Most children would not be familiar with the term.

We can now see why it is fairer to test Thurstone's seven primary mental abilities, than to measure intelligence by applying the Binet test. Another problem is how to measure the intelligence of immigrant children. These fall into two categories, those who have learned to speak English before they arrive in England, and those who have not. It is a very difficult task indeed to test the intelligence of the latter group. However, even supposing that we can communicate with those who do speak English and are able to explain the test to them, there still remains the fact that an English test is culturally biased in favour of English children, and against immigrant children. The more their culture differs from our own, the greater the handicap under which they take the test.

There are also deaf children, and children handicapped or deprived in other ways, who are not immigrants. In all these cases it is impossible to use a verbal test, but we can use a non-verbal test, or performance test. Such tests dispense with the verbal element and use either pictures or apparatus, such as wooden blocks or cubes.

NOTES AND REFERENCES FOR CHAPTER 4

1 See Burt, Sir Cyril & Durant, P., 'Early Researches on General Ability', *British Journal of Statistical Psychology*, VII (1954), pp. 114–24.

2 For an expert assessment of the Binet test soon after its introduction, see Burt, C., 'The Measurement of Intelligence by the Binet Tests', *Eugenics Review*, VI (1914), pp. 36–50, 140–52.

3 See Burt, C., 'The Latest Revision of the Binet Tests', *Eugenics Review*, XXX (1938), pp. 255–60; and Burt, C., 'The Revision of the Stanford-Binet Scale', *Occupational Psychology*, XVII (1943), pp. 42–5.

4 The difficulty of distinguishing between objects and ideas which contain considerable degrees of similarity is further discussed in Scholfield, H., *The Philosophy of Education: an Introduction* (Allen & Unwin, 1971).

5 Piaget refers to this stage of development in the child's thinking as the 'formal operational' stage. At this stage, the child is capable of thinking in terms of ideas without the assistance of concrete objects to guide his logical processes which he used at the 'concrete operational' stage. He is able to formulate hypotheses and test them against the available data. Thinking of this type is sometimes referred to as 'hypothetico-deductive'. Because of the different characteristics of the concrete operational and formal operational thinking, it is demanded of the child in the pre-eleven sub-tests, that he defines concrete objects. In the older groups he is required to define abstract terms such as 'skill'.

6 Eysenck, H. J., *Uses and Abuses of Psychology* (Pelican, 1953).

7 Cronbach, Lee J., *Essentials of Psychological Testing* (Harper International, 2nd ed., 1964). (London, Harper & Row, 1960.)

8 See 6 above.

9 See Burt, C., 'The Two-Factor Theory', *British Journal of Psychology* (Statistical Section), II (1949), pp. 151–79.

10 See Burt, Sir Cyril, 'Tests for Clerical Occupations', *Journal of the National Institute of Industrial Psychology* (1922).

11 Bernstein, B., 'Social Class and Linguistic Development; A Theory of Social Learning' in Halsey, A. H., Floud, J. and Arnold, C. (eds), *Education, Economy, and Society* (Anderson, Free Press, 1961) Chapter 24. (London, Collier-Macmillan, 1961.)

12 See Vernon, P. E., *The Structure of Human Abilities* (Methuen, 2nd ed., 1965). Beginners are advised to approach this book carefully, since it is not easy to understand. It is, however, an excellent book for those who have mastered the technical language of psychology.

13 Hebb, D. O., *The Organization of Behaviour* (John Wiley, 1949). This is an extremely difficult book and the beginner is advised to do no more than read pp. 294–6 ('The Two Meanings of Intelligence'), and pp. 299–303 ('The Nature and Nurture of Intelligence') as an introduction to Hebb. As with the previous book, once the reader has gained some basic knowledge and wishes to explore more deeply, he may feel inclined to dip further into this book. For those who can cope with its contents it makes fascinating reading.

14 See Burt, C., and Howard, M., 'The Relative Influence of Heredity and Environment on Assessments of Intelligence', *British Journal of Statistical Psychology*, X (1957), pp. 99–104.

15 Technically known as 'monozygotic' from the Greek words for 'single' and 'joining'. The twins are the product of a single cell. See Burt, C., 'The Genetic Determination of Differences in Intelligence: A Study of Monozygotic Twins Reared Together and Apart', *British Journal of Psychology* (1966), pp. 137–53.
16 Jarrett, James L., 'American Teacher Education; Caricature and Promise' in 'Education for Teaching', *Journal of the Association of Teachers in Colleges and Departments of Education*, Number 77, Autumn 1968.
17 Davis, Allison, *Social Class Influences upon Learning* (Harvard University Press, 1948). This little book is excellent. It is easy to understand, yet full of the most useful information, much of which is directly useful to teachers in the classroom at all levels of education.

GENERAL NOTE

The Association of Educational Psychologists produced a *Journal and Newsletter* entitled: *Modern Concepts of Intelligence*, the contents of which are:

'The Concept of Intelligence'	Sir Cyril Burt
'Education and the Concept of Intelligence'	Douglas Pidgeon
'The Relation between Ability and Attainment Tests'	Conrad Graham
'The Development of Current Ideas About Intelligence Tests'	Philip E. Vernon

Details can be obtained from:
The Editor, *Journal and Newsletter*, 94 Chatsworth Road, Croydon.

Chapter 5

Intelligence Tests II

There is an important interconnection between the terms PROGNOSTIC TEST and GROUP TEST, on the one hand, and DIAGNOSTIC TEST and INDIVIDUAL TEST on the other hand.

PROGNOSTIC TESTS; GROUP TESTS

We saw something of the prognostic or predictive use of intelligence tests when we considered the 'eleven plus' test and the test for selecting power-station operatives. A prognostic test, using present performance as the criterion, attempts to predict future success in a specific field. Thus the 'eleven plus' seeks, on the evidence of the child's school performance at the age of eleven years to predict how successfully that child will cope with the academic curriculum of the grammar school. In the test for power-station operatives, those applying the test attempt, by using the candidate's score on the test (his present performance or efficiency in executing the movements necessary for working power-station machinery), to predict how efficient a power-station operative that candidate will turn out to be.

We suggested earlier that, in cases such as these, a precise score for any given candidate is less essential than his rank-order position in relation to other candidates. We want to know whether he is near the top, in the middle, or near the bottom of the rank-order. This is a further reminder that a raw score in isolation is of little use. If Joe Brown scores 77 on the power-station operative tests, what does this mean? Is he potentially a very good power-station operative? Only by obtaining a score for all the applicants and placing them in a rank-order determined by these scores, can we derive any real meaning from the scores.

Because we are concerned with rank-order placing, and not with a precise score, we use a GROUP TEST. Group tests originated with the American army in the First World War. In selecting its recruits for war service, the American government used two relevant criteria – age and physical fitness. These are relevant criteria, because neither old men nor those who are physically unfit are useful in war.

However, fitness for war not only demands men who are young and fit. War requires that some men lead while others follow, that some make crucial decisions, possibly affecting the lives of tens of thousands of other men. War demands an efficient intelligence service, to discover as much as possible about the enemy's planning and strategy. In addition to youth and fitness, war demands intelligence.

Now, the Americans found that, among those who were young and fit enough to satisfy the basic selection criteria, there were illiterate and literate conscripts. The potentially dangerous consequences of this situation soon became apparent, and the army command was faced with a dilemma similar to that which faced the French authorities when they retained Binet to devise an intelligence test. In addition, in the case of the American army, speed was essential. Wars do not stop while the combatants decide which of their soldiers are bright and which are not.

From this situation developed the ARMY ALPHA tests. To comply with the demand for a rapid appraisal of the intelligence of all conscripts, these were group tests, so that large numbers of men could be tested simultaneously and norms rapidly established.

The reader should ask himself at this point what sort of curve would be produced by graphing the scores of the following groups of conscripts:

1. All enlisted men
2. All literate enlisted men
3. All illiterate enlisted men
4. All commissioned officers
5. All non-commissioned officers.

Without representing exact scores from the tests, the five graphs (Figs. 21–25) show the shape and type of curve produced by graphing the scores obtained by each of the five groups.

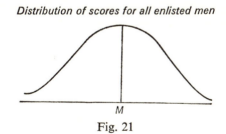

Distribution of scores for all enlisted men

M

Fig. 21

Distribution of scores for all 'literate' enlisted men

M

Fig. 22

Distribution of scores for all 'illiterate' enlisted men

Fig. 23

Distribution of scores for all commissioned officers

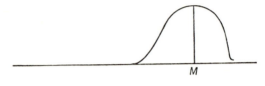

Fig. 24

Distribution of scores for all non-commissioned officers

Fig. 25

Not surprisingly, the curve which would provide the normal curve of distribution, or that which approximates most closely to the normal curve, would be that for all enlisted men. This group is the most heterogeneous of the five. In view of our previous findings, it is not surprising to discover that the curve for all literate enlisted men (Fig. 22) is negatively skewed. One would expect the scores of this homogeneous group (on the criterion of literacy) to produce a mean score above the mid-point of the scale. The positively skewed (Fig. 23) curve results from scores for a homogeneous group (on the criterion of illiteracy) with the mean score below the mid-point of the scale. Finally, in Figs. 24 and 25, we have two negatively skewed curves. We would expect the mean for both non-commissioned and commissioned officers to be above the mid-point of the scale, with that for commissioned officers higher than the non-commissioned officers. We would expect the scores for the commissioned officers to be more narrowly distributed about their mean. In other words, we would expect a low standard deviation (SD) in the case of scores for commissioned officers.

From these beginnings have developed many types of group tests, all having standardization in common. All such tests are standardized for procedure and possess standardized scoring systems and norms of their own. Because of this, it is most important, when making tests and retests of intelligence, to use the same test. This sounds obvious, but there have been errors of children being tested with test A and retested with test B. It might appear, in such cases, that the intelligence of the people tested has increased in the time which has elapsed between the test and the retest. In fact it merely means that the scores are not strictly comparable, because the mean scores and standard deviations of the two tests are not identical. The Binet test, as we have seen, has an M of 100 and an SD of 16, and the range of normality or average intelligence is 84–116. If we have a test with a mean of 100 and a SD of 25, the corresponding range of scores for average intelligence would be 75–125, and if we used test A and retest B, we would show (quite wrongly) that the I.Q. score of the average group – 2 out of every 3 – had increased with time and further teaching. On the other hand, if we used test B and retest A, we would show (again quite wrongly) that the I.Q. of the average group had fallen with time and further teaching. What we would be entitled to look for in the scores of two tests with different means and different standard deviations is whether the pupils tested appeared in the same rank-order on both tests. Thus if we were using a standardized test of known validity and a non-standardized test of unknown validity, we would obtain concurrent validation of the non-standardized test if the rank-order were very similar for both tests.

By collecting data from many researches involving testing, we are able to obtain information against which to compare the results of subsequent tests. For example, the following data has been recorded from tests in the United States of America:

I.Q.	Capability of person obtaining this I.Q.
130	Mean score of persons receiving the degree of Ph.D.
120	Mean score of all college graduates
115	Mean score of freshmen in typical four-year colleges; mean score of children from white collar and skilled manual worker homes
110	Mean score of all high school graduates
100	Mean score of total population
90	Mean score of children from low-income city or rural homes

In 1946, in this country, the following figures were obtained for the seven classes in the general classification scale (1).

Mean I.Q.	Group on General classification Scale
116	Group 1. Professional and higher administrative
112	Group 2. Managerial/executive
108	Group 3. Inspectorial/supervisory (Higher grade)
104	Group 4. Inspectorial/supervisory (Lower grade)
95	Group 5. Skilled manual. Routine grade non-manual
94	Group 6. Semi-skilled manual
91	Group 7. Unskilled manual

G

A comparison of mean I.Q. scores, in the two sets of data, suggests that different tests were used by the respective researchers.

It is also possible to show what percentage of the total population has a particular I.Q. Some typical figures are:

I.Q.	Percentage with this I.Q. in total population
145+	0·20
130–144	1·80
115–129	10·00
100–114	38·00
85–99	38·00
70–84	10·00
55–69	1·80
below 55	0·20

It will be seen that this data would give a normal curve of distribution. Thus, in the total population, there are roughly as many geniuses as there are idiots, as many very bright as there are educationally subnormal, showing some sort of balance of nature in mental abilities. The reader may be puzzled to know why 76 per cent of the total population falls between what we have come to accept as the limits of normality or average intelligence, whereas we said that roughly two out of three people fell within these limits. The answer is that there is always some blurring at the borderline between categories, and that, in calculations of this nature, we could not expect an exact 2:3 ratio nor expect one in every six to fit neatly into a compartment above the upper limit of the average group and one in every six to fit into a compartment below the lower limit.

DIAGNOSTIC TESTS; INDIVIDUAL TESTS

The word 'diagnostic' has the same meaning in the area of mental testing as in the area of physical examination. If we go to the doctor and report certain symptoms to him, he gives us a diagnostic examination. Similarly, there are certain children in school, who show symptoms of not benefiting as well as other children from the education they are receiving. Their work, related to the norms for the age-group, is always below standard, or below average. At one time, such children would have been labelled 'unintelligent' or 'mentally defective' and left severely alone. In the same way, a less enlightened age abandoned physically weak babies to die on mountainsides. It was thought, in both instances, that those who were subnormal were not worth caring for.

Even after we abandoned the idea that subnormality deserved such callous treatment, we continued to use the term 'mentally defective' in an omnibus way, and still condemned children as 'unintelligent'. If the reader casts his mind back to Chapter 4, he will realize that to call anyone unintelligent is not really meaningful. Nor will he be surprised to find that Ballard gave, as a sort of motto to all who diagnosed backwardness in their pupils: RUN THE GOOSE DOWN. He was warning teachers of the importance of diagnosing accurately the precise area and cause of backwardness. When we discussed the seven primary mental abilities, we suggested that many children who fail to perform well in problem arithmetic, do so because they are unable to read, not because they are unable to do mechanical arithmetic. There is a low correlation between their scores in problem arithmetic and mechanical arithmetic, simply because the same ability is not required in both. But, unless we do 'run the goose down' in this particular example, we shall not realize that the cause is inability to read, not inability to manipulate numbers.

Such mistakes are serious enough, but what of the cases involving the transfer of children from the school for normal children, to schools for the educationally subnormal? Here, the most tragic mistakes could result from failure to diagnose accurately. It was this danger which resulted in the construction of the Binet test.

When I visit the doctor with the symptoms of my illness, I am not seen by the doctor along with a group of patients all suffering from different ailments, manifesting themselves through different symptoms. I am seen by the doctor individually. He tests me diagnostically by individual examination, so that he can concentrate all his attention on *my* weakness, quite distinct from other people's ill-health.

For the same reason, diagnostic tests of mental ability are individual tests. We do not find a rank-order placing sufficient for our purposes; we require an accurate score from individual tests. Furthermore, a doctor, before recommending any form of drastic treatment, would want a second opinion. He would not recommend a major surgical operation on the evidence of one examination. Similarly, no child would be recommended to an E.S.N. school on the evidence of one test alone. Even in 'eleven plus' selection, the child has, in more recent times, been given a series of tests, spaced out over a period of weeks, or even months, in an attempt to be fair to the child and to eliminate such chance factors as illness or emotional upset on one given day. In the same way, a very careful testing programme, involving a series of individual tests, is given to a child suspected of being educationally subnormal.

Finally, when we go to the doctor, we make sure to go to a qualified medical practitioner. Because of his training and professional expertise, he is capable of administering the appropriate test or examination, and of interpreting the results. Again, a doctor should have a good 'bedside manner'; his manner and method of approach must inspire confidence in his patients. A poor bedside manner builds a barrier between doctor and patient making effective communication impossible.

There is again a direct parallel between physical and mental testing. The average qualified teacher is capable of administering group tests and of deriving a rank-order of performance from the raw scores, but only a qualified educational psychologist is allowed to administer individual diagnostic tests. Such people must develop a special skill in dealing with intellectually weak and emotionally disturbed children. The scores of normal children on group tests can be affected adversely by such things as late arrival for the test, fear of failure and incurring parental displeasure, or a quarrel with another child just before taking the test. With the subnormal child, or the child suspected of being subnormal, the situation is even more critical. Such a child comes to be tested with a long history of failure behind him, which builds up frustration within. Moreover, meeting a stranger who again confronts him with a test, thus reminding him of previous failures, is not the situation best calculated to make the candidate feel at ease. For such reasons as these, it will be appreciated that special expertise is required and a good deal of time is necessary for administering individual diagnostic tests. Even if the average teacher acquired the necessary expertise, he or she would not have the time required to administer the tests in the best possible interests of the children tested.

ACHIEVEMENT TESTS

We have already seen that the term 'intelligence test' is frequently used when the person using it does not mean a test of general intelligence or general ability. We have so far, for the sake of convenience, implied that the group tests and individual tests, which we have considered, are tests of intelligence in every case. In fact, many of the tests to which we have referred, especially in the diagnostic field, are more accurately called ACHIEVEMENT TESTS. Thus, after we tested our hypothetical child, Robinson, by administering the Binet test (p. 64) and discovered that his mental age was two years behind his physical age, it would become necessary to follow Ballard's advice and 'run the goose down' by applying certain diagnostic scholastic achievement tests. These would cover the major areas of literacy and numerical dexterity, and, because they are standardized and have their own sets of norms, we can compare Robinson accurately, not only with children of his own age, but with younger children. We can obtain his reading age and his arithmetical age. We may also wish to test his perception, to see if any defect here is preventing Robinson from benefiting from his schooling. In this case, we might well wish to use the comparatively recent Frostig Programme (2). Remmers,

Gage, and Rummell (3) describe the nature and uses of scholastic achievement tests as follows:

'Achievement measures appraise a pupil's educational growth. As previously mentioned, tests of intelligence or scholastic aptitude purport to predict a student's performance; tests of achievement assess what he has learned in school or other situations where learning and teaching are intended to go on. But scores on achievement tests are also excellent bases for predicting future educational success in areas measured by the tests. For example, the student high in verbal ability and perceptual aspects of intelligence tests usually shows high reading achievement, and the student low in the quantitative aspects of intelligence tests is usually low in mathematical achievement. Thus, the tests of achievement, probably, should form the core of a systematic program in every school that hopes to do a thorough job of evaluation.

'Achievement tests are designed to measure relative accomplishments in specific areas of work. They are of two main types; general and diagnostic. These are closely related; there is no fine line of demarcation between them. The general achievement test may be defined as one designed to express, in a single score, a pupil's relative achievement in a given field of work. The diagnostic achievement test is designed to reveal a person's strengths and weaknesses in one or more areas of the field being tested.'

This passage is excellent for our present purposes, since it makes a number of important points and reminds us of points made in previous chapters, which can be summarized as follows:

1. There is a definite and important connection between the terms 'intelligence', 'abilities', and 'achievement'. These relationships stem from the 'seven primary mental ability concept' of intelligence and the development of tests of these abilities and of other smaller abilities within each of the seven major areas.
2. A test of achievement, called a general achievement test, may be administered as a group test to produce a rank-order containing the scores of all the pupils tested. At the same time, the scores may indicate that certain students or pupils are weak in one specific area or more. Further, individual and diagnostic tests in these areas can be administered by the teacher. If it still appears that the child cannot benefit from teaching in a normal school, he would be referred to an educational psychologist for a diagnostic test to determine whether it is intellectual weakness which makes this child incapable of benefiting from the teaching which he receives in school.
3. We have another instance of the importance of accurate diagnosis of

weakness. The passage quoted suggests that children, who score high on verbal and perceptual tests, are generally good at reading. This suggests that poor readers ought to receive diagnostic tests of perception as part of their examination, to diagnose whether the poor reading performance stems from inability to perceive letters accurately, as for example, from such defects as dyslexia.

It is worth stressing again that achievement tests, like any other tests based on school work, may be teacher-made or standardized. In certain circumstances the teacher may wish to make the tests himself. However, it must be stressed also that in many cases the object of testing achievement is to determine the degree of normality or abnormality in the pupil's performance. This can be done only by administering a standardized test with norms, which allow us to relate this pupil to the total population on this particular criterion.

APTITUDE TESTS

The Education Act of 1944 laid down three criteria against which children were to be measured, when they were assigned to a particular type of secondary education. The criteria were age, aptitude, and ability (4). We have already seen the importance of age in testing and assessing, and we shall say more about this when we consider later at what age we can reliably test intelligence. We also discussed the meaning of the term 'abilities' and, when we talked about the seven primary mental abilities we were already entering the field of aptitudes and aptitude testing.

The Greek adjective *aptos* means 'fitted for', so that the results of APTITUDE TESTS tell us what type of schooling or occupation any given individual is fitted for. Aptitude tests can, therefore, have both a diagnostic and a prognostic use. We are immediately reminded of the term 'career guidance' and of Youth Employment Officers and Careers Guidance Officers. We would not expect the aspiring clerk to require the same aptitude as the potential engineer, or the potential teacher to possess the same aptitudes as the aspiring dentist. Nor, in view of what we have said about abilities so far, is it sufficient to use broad general advice, when children ask what job they should apply for or say which career they wish to pursue. When a child says: 'I want to be a surveyor', he is told he must have reached 'O' level in Mathematics and Physics. These are qualifications which the student must have if he is to be accepted on to a course of training for surveyors. But an aptitude test, designed for a specific purpose like our test for power-station operatives, would give even more information, both to the teacher and to the pupil about his suitability for surveying. Many children choose a job for no better reason than that they have a fancy for it. If they are given the appropriate aptitude tests they may feel that they would like to proceed with their ambition. On the other hand, the extra knowledge that they obtain about the nature of the job in question may cause them to change their minds. There is no guarantee that possessing a particular aptitude for a particular job will ensure that the person likes the job. But, we are more likely to like a job for which we are fitted, than a job for which we lack the necessary aptitude.

Nor are aptitude tests only useful in job selection. They are useful in schools and, particularly, in colleges of further education, for assigning students to courses which best suit their abilities, aptitudes, and requirements.

It was Thurstone's intention that the tests of the seven primary mental abilities should be used in guidance, so that it is not surprising that tests of aptitude developed out of his tests. They were a logical extension and refinement of the original ability tests. One well-known group (or battery) of tests, in this area, is the GENERAL APTITUDE TEST BATTERY, known by the abbreviation GATB. It is the result of thirty years research into and analysis of job performance (as we suggested when we saw how a test for power-station operatives might be constructed). A number of the tests, in the current battery, are the direct descendants of a series of tests, which became famous in the 1920s under the name of the Minnesota Tests of Vocational Aptitude. The GATB is used by the American Employment Service (AES), which makes the tests available to secondary school pupils who wish to have further knowledge of the type of job for which they are suited. America makes much greater use of such tests than we do in this country. Areas of work studied by those who constructed the tests include:

dry-cell battery assembly	cooking
aircraft electrical assembly	spot-welding
teaching	comptometer operating
X-ray technician work	operating corn-husking machinery
work of nursing aids	operating knitting-machines
sheet metal-working	fruit packing
baking	

It involves a tremendous amount of work to devise such tests, and the time and expense involved in analysing skills necessary for every job or profession would be prohibitive. Consequently, certain jobs have been assembled into 'job families'. Now there are a number of diversified tests, given to everyone, which can be used in different combinations to predict suitability in any given area or situation. The present GATB consists of eight pencil-and-paper tests and four performance tests. It is helpful at this juncture to note that, when tests are used to test the K:M (or practical) side of the hierarchy of abilities (see diagram on p. 71) they fall into the two types, paper-and-pencil and performance. These on the V:Ed (or academic side, testing verbal and numerical ability, are all of the paper-and-pencil type. The ability factors, which GATB is designed to measure, and the tests used in the process are presented below.

Ability factor	Tested by
G. General reasoning ability	vocabulary test
	3D spatial test
	arithmetical reasoning test
V. Verbal aptitude	vocabulary test
N. Numerical aptitude	computation test
	arithmetical reasoning test
S. Spatial aptitude	3D spatial test
P. Form perception	tool-matching test
	form-matching test
Q. Clerical perception	name comparison test
K. Motor coordination	mark-making test
F. Finger dexterity	assembly tests
	dissembly tests
M. Manual dexterity	place tests
	turn tests

In 1947 a battery known as DIFFERENTIAL APTITUDE TESTS (DATS) was introduced. The main aim of this battery was high school counselling. The tests aim to isolate, not pure abilities, but rather complex abilities relating to families of occupations and the curriculum content of the American high school. The battery consists of:

> Verbal reasoning tests
> Numerical reasoning tests
> Abstract reasoning tests
> Spatial reasoning tests
> Mechanical reasoning tests
> Clerical speed and accuracy tests
> Spelling tests
> Sentence tests.

Again, the reader should note the similarity between the component tests in the DAT battery and those used to test the seven primary mental abilities (5). Thus aptitude tests are not separate from tests of intelligence and abilities, but are designed to bring greater precision into measuring people's suitability in specific directions.

To derive maximum benefit from the information supplied by aptitude tests, a PROFILE should be drawn up. (Profiles will be discussed further in the next chapter on measuring personality.) An individual may be given, say, nine aptitude tests and have his score for each recorded. If X, for example, is an engineer, we can plot his profile on the nine aptitudes tested. We can, also, obtain a profile of the total population, showing the mean scores on each of the nine aptitudes. Finally, we can plot a profile of all engineers in the total population. We can then compare X with all engineers in the total population and with the total population. The reader will recall that we used this profile technique when we constructed the histograms on page 74.

PSYCHOMOTOR TESTS

Psychomotor tests are those which measure areas of manipulative performance, as distinct from intellectual behaviour. We have already seen that the intellectual performance on the V:Ed side of intelligence is measured by paper-and-pencil tests of words and numbers, and that the K:M (or practical side) can be measured by tests involving pencil and paper, as well as by performance tests. We also saw that there were speed and dexterity measures in GATB. The psychomotor test is used when a pencil-and-paper test would not be a valid predictor because of the nature of the aptitude itself. Let us return yet again to our power-station operatives. Each of them might do well on a psychomotor test, which required them to do certain things which occur in power-station work. But, if they were asked to describe these actions in a pencil-and-paper test, they might fare very badly. Such poor results would be no guarantee that they would be poor operatives, since their job would involve doing, not thinking, writing and explaining. Their job is practical, not theoretical.

One well-known, and sophisticated, form of psychomotor test is the flight simulator used to train pilots. This resulted from a tremendous research programme undertaken by the US Air Force between 1942 and 1955. One of the key names in psychomotor testing is that of Fleishman. It has been estimated that Fleishman and his collaborators have brought psychomotor testing to a level comparable with that of intellectual testing in 1940, immediately after Thurstone's initial report on the seven primary mental abilities. Fleishman's tests are designed to measure:

> arm/hand steadiness
> arm movement rate
> finger dexterity
> response rate
> manual dexterity
> fine psychomotor coordination
> multiple limb coordination
> postural discrimination
> response orientation
> response integration.

However, there is a most important point to note about psychomotor testing. We saw that pencil-and-paper tests must have both identical marking schemes and identical procedures of administration. Anything which interferes with either of these, interferes with the objectivity of the test. The US Air Force found that it was extremely difficult, if not impossible, to obtain the same degree of objectivity with performance apparatus, since even apparatus made in the same workshop rarely produced identity from one piece to another.

We have mentioned mean and SD very frequently in this book, and have learned how important these two terms are in supplying the tester with information. Those who fully understand the implications of these two pieces of information will appreciate just how much the objectivity of a particular psychomotor test was undermined, when scores obtained by an operator on four successive pieces of apparently identical apparatus produced means of 227, 230, 260, and 291. We can appreciate that the variation between the first and second scores would be within the expected limits of variation and the other scores would not. The difference between the first score and the third and fourth is reminiscent of the different I.Q.s obtained on tests A and B (see p. 83). There the difference resulted from the fact that two tests were used with different means and standard deviations, whereas the same test should have been used twice, thus ensuring the same mean and standard deviation on both occasions.

Before closing this section it is necessary to say something about the relationship between aptitude tests and achievement tests. An aptitude test is prospective (or forward looking). It attempts to assess the suitability of a given individual for some future activity and to answer such questions as: 'Will Smith make a good bank clerk?' and 'Is Jones a suitable person for a career as a salesman?' To use a term that we have used on many occasions, the aptitude test is used 'prognostically', basing its decisions on the individual's present level of competence in a specific area.

The achievement test is retrospective (or backward looking). It attempts to measure progress or educational gains. Because of this, it is interested in the present level of competence in relation to the original level of competence in the same area. If we think of a prospective bank clerk, and for a moment assume that there is a test of banking aptitude, such a test looks forward to the future, to assess the suitability of the candidate for a career in banking. However, after the individual has worked in the bank for some time, and has gained experience of the ways of banking, and has learned more about the way in which the bank system works, he takes an examination of the Institute of Bankers, and later takes a more difficult examination of the same institute. The results of these examinations can be used as achievement tests. The first examination measures the clerk's progress after a given amount of experience. The second examination is a further achievement test comparing his present level of efficiency with the level of efficiency after the first examination.

We sometimes hear of proficiency tests. These can be used prospectively and retrospectively, to prognosticate and to diagnose. The driving test and the test for advanced motorists are excellent examples. If we take a driving test, we are taking an initial examination in the skill of driving a car. In one sense, it is used prognostically – i.e. it seeks to determine whether X will be a suitable person to take a car out alone on a busy road. If a person passes the test, he is deemed a suitable person to drive a car, just as a child who passed the 'eleven plus' was deemed suitable to proceed to grammar school.

However, if a person fails his initial driving test, the instructor uses the test diagnostically. He has failed the candidate, because he was weak in certain necessary skills. His hill start and his three-point turn were not up to the required standard, or his knowledge of the Highway Code was insufficient. After such diagnosis, specific areas of weakness are exposed.

If the motorist passes the driving test and subsequently takes the test of advanced motoring, he is really submitting himself to an achievement test. He seeks to discover whether he has made progress or gains in driving skill. His level of competence or efficiency, after x years' driving experience, is compared with his initial level of competence.

AT WHAT AGE CAN WE RELIABLY MEASURE INTELLIGENCE?

Remarks made in various parts of the present chapter have provided some material for answering this important question. However, the crucial word in the question as phrased above is 'reliably'. We can use intelligence tests with people of most ages and obtain a score. But to what extent is this score meaningful?

If we look at the factors we have studied already, and see how they contribute to the answer, it will be a useful form of revision and a useful test of logical thinking and ability to assemble relevant information.

In the first place, it is clear that aptitude tests can be used only with older children, say from the age of ten years onwards. We have said that aptitude tests are closely connected with tests of the seven primary mental abilities. The numerical ability, for instance, can develop satisfactorily only in the context of the infants and junior schools.

Moreover, we saw that certain children enter school underprivileged compared with other children; they come from homes where there is some sort of deprivation. Even if we could measure intelligence or abilities at the age of five and obtain reliable results, it would, as a general rule, be manifestly unfair to compare the results of the average child and the privileged child with those of the underprivileged.

We do not suggest that merely by subjecting the underprivileged children to schooling, we remove their initial handicap. If this were so, there would be no reason for such publications as the Plowden Report (6). What we are saying is that, when children were tested at eleven years of age, they were tested after all of them had been subjected to five years' schooling. During that five years, they experienced material which was designed to develop their mental abilities.

We also saw that the Binet test had an age-range of two years to that of average adult. This means that, in theory, we can test the intelligence of a child at the age of two years. We saw, too, that the test took account of the abilities possessed by the average two-year-old, and had motor elements in it as well as verbal elements. However, if we look at a wide range of intelligence tests, we shall find that very few of them are designed to test the intelligence of the pre-school child, that is, the child below the age of five years.

At the other end of the age-range there is the problem of measuring adult intelligence. Again, we can note that the Binet test claims to do this, and there are on the market a number of other tests purporting to do this. The difficulty with adult intelligence tests is that, after the adult has ceased to receive formal education, it is difficult to determine whether we are measuring intelligence or experience. At the primary and secondary school level, we try to ensure that all children obtain a common educational experience. However, once the adolescent leaves school, he may acquire vastly different experience from other adolescents. By the time he reaches adulthood, the variation between the experience he has gained outside formal schooling and that of other adults may be tremendous. What we can say, in the light of our knowledge of validity, is that we must be very careful in our choice of test which we apply to adults. A popular Sunday newspaper once ran a feature entitled 'Millionaires fail eleven plus examination'. This could have been taken to mean that it was beneficial to fail the examination, since a number of people, in spite of such failure, had become millionaires. But some of the millionaires tested were fifty years of age. Thus a test designed for children of eleven was given to adults with ages as high as fifty.

If we turn for a moment to achievement tests, we realize that teacher-made tests of achievement can be used soon after the child begins to learn at school. The reason for stressing that they should be teacher-made is that, when such a small amount of material is to be tested, the test must reflect exactly what has been taught, and nothing else. If this is done, any teacher, at any time, can set some sort of test which will answer the questions: 'Has such-and-such a child made educational gains?', 'Have I succeeded in making them learn what I set out to teach them?'

It seems then, that the answer to our question involves a closer look at the younger and older ends of the age-range. It is fitting to begin with the measuring of intelligence of the younger child.

MEASURING THE INTELLIGENCE OF THE UNDER-FIVES

The weight of evidence available suggests that one *can* measure intelligence at a relatively early point in the pre-school years, but that one must not regard the results obtained as an infallible guide to the future. So many parents observe what they take to be signs of precocity in their pre-school children, and are disappointed in later years when these children turn out to be no more than average.

We have already suggested that, since memory and intelligence correlate, a good memory in the young child is a very rough and ready guide to intelligence. Nor is there any harm in such assessment, provided that we do not twist the statement into the form: 'My child has a good memory at the age of three and a half years, therefore, he must be above average in intelligence.' In testing and assessing, there is a world of difference between what may be the case and what is the case in fact. In the case of our $3\frac{1}{2}$-year-old above, we can only hypothesize that, on the evidence of his good memory, his intelligence is above average. The next few years will be experimental, and we shall collect data, which will either substantiate or refute the hypothesis.

Nor must it be thought that we are saying that the child with the good memory at three and a half will not be above average in intelligence. All that we are saying about this particular child, and about the testing of intelligence in general, is that intelligence can be measured much less reliably before the age of six than it can after the age of ten.

SOME TESTS OF INTELLIGENCE FOR VERY YOUNG CHILDREN

The Binet test was designed to test the intelligence of children from the age of two onwards. One of the best-known of all tests of intelligence for pre-school children, the Goodenough Draw-a-man Test, designed in 1926, claims to measure intelligence from the age of one year. The test, which has a complicated scoring system, is basically simple. It merely requires the child to draw the best man he can. Points are awarded for the accuracy of representation, such as the number of fingers on the hand. What the test is really measuring is the child's ability to perceive and to represent his perceptions on paper. We have seen that perception is an important element and one which can affect reading ability. If one wished to compile a small test battery for the under-fives, one could use the Goodenough Test, a test of memory, a vocabulary test, and one called the 'House, Tree, Person' test, which measures personality rather than intellectual ability (see p. 143).

What we are really doing, when we use intelligence tests with very young children, is assessing how an individual child compares with the average child of the same age according to the norms of certain selected tests. Every parent knows that some children develop more quickly than others. The psychologist talks about 'maturation', which means roughly the same thing. It means that all children are ready to do certain things at certain ages without being taught to do them. Thus, at a certain age, baby *x* is ready to climb the stairs; baby *y* may not be ready until a week or two later. Experiments with identical twins have shown that trying to make the child perform feats, before he is ready, is detrimental. A twin taught for six weeks to climb stairs before he was ready to do so, climbed less well than the other twin, who only began stair-climbing, when he was ready, when he was able to do so through maturation. Research has also shown that, in the case of intelligence tests in the junior school, three to five coaching sessions are likely to be beneficial, although more than five may be detrimental. Therefore, to eliminate any unfairness which may result from coaching, many schools allow all their pupils three practice/coaching sessions.

Another test for pre-school children is the Columbia Mental Maturity Scale, designed by Burgomeister, Blum, and Lorge. The age-range for the test is 3–12 years, and a correlation of ·75 with the Stanford-Binet test has been recorded. There is also the Leitner International Performance Scale for the age-range 2–18 (the same as for the Binet test), the items of which require no language. The reader who recalls what we said about culture bias, will see that the elimination of items requiring language to answer them is one justification for designating the test international. The compilers of the test envisaged that it would be excellent for use with handicapped children, but Cronbach (7) makes the point that the I.Q. conversions are of questionable accuracy at the pre-school level.

Distinct from the tests which claim to measure the intelligence of very young children, are those which test whether the child is capable of performing certain natural acts at specific age-levels. The norms for these tests are related to the average age of maturation. Again, it must be stressed that, if the child tested is not able to perform a given act at a given age, it is not absolutely certain that there is something wrong with him. Defects have usually manifested themselves in some much more obvious form by the time the child is tested. It is as dangerous to assume defect at this early age on the evidence of tests as it is to assume brilliance, unless the tests are clinical diagnostic tests given on the advice of a medical practitioner.

The advantage of these tests of natural acts performed by the child is that they are not testing an adult interpretation of the meaning of intelligence. Thurstone claims that intelligence consists of seven primary mental abilities, and to measure these the appropriate tests have been devised. But the measure is based on Thurstone's interpretation of the meaning of intelligence. If future research shows that intelligence does *not* consist of seven primary mental abilities, we shall need to devise new measures in keeping with this new interpretation. One well-known test of natural actions of children was devised by Gesell. The achievements and the average age for performing these achievements are presented below:

lateral head movement, lying down	2 weeks
vertical eye coordination	6 weeks
reaching for object	3 months
discrimination of strangers	$5\frac{1}{2}$ months
lift cup by handle	$6\frac{1}{2}$ months
say 'da-da' (8)	$8\frac{1}{2}$ months
finger grasp	$9\frac{1}{2}$ months
build with two blocks	$13\frac{1}{2}$ months
turn book pages	$16\frac{1}{2}$ months
name three objects	$21\frac{1}{2}$ months
understand two prepositions	25 months
picture completion	$28\frac{1}{2}$ months
draw a circle successfully once in three attempts with model available	$34\frac{1}{2}$ months
remember one of four pictures	$35\frac{1}{2}$ months

The reader will notice that, once the age-level corresponds to the earlier age-levels tested by the Binet test, the items in the Gesell test begin to resemble those in the Binet test. Looking at the test items as a whole, we observe that they are a combination of performance and verbal items, with the former outnumbering the latter. The early items have a definite relationship to the psychomotor tests for older pupils which we have already discussed.

Eysenck, commenting on such evidence as we have considered above, comes to the following conclusions: that testing the intelligence of children under the age of two has no predictive value for their ultimate adult intelligence; and that there is a slight positive correlation between the intelligence scores of three- and four-year-olds and adult intelligence. However, the important word is 'slight', and Eysenck claims that the weight of evidence strongly suggests that there is so little positive benefit to be derived from testing intelligence before the age of five or six, and so many potential dangers, that such testing should be discouraged. The reference to slight positive correlation serves as a reminder that it is never sufficient merely to have positive correlation; there must be a reasonably high degree of positive correlation. We said, previously, that correlations below ·50 are rarely useful and that, at times, a correlation as high as

·80 or ·90, or even more, is necessary before we can base conclusions on the correlations.*

MEASURING ADULT INTELLIGENCE

There has grown up a belief that it is not feasible to measure intelligence in people whose age exceeds fifteen or sixteen with any degree of accuracy or meaningfulness, and we have already suggested one possible explanation for this. If the belief is well founded, it means that there is little point in expecting meaningful findings when we measure adult intelligence.

One researcher in the United States undertook a long-term investigation. He measured the intelligence of a group of students in early adolescence, and followed their subsequent educational progress, finding that they divided into two groups after the age of sixteen. The groups consisted of those pupils who went on to receive further formal education, and those who did not. The intelligence of the two groups was retested when they were in their early thirties. It was estimated that members of the group which had received higher education had a mental age, on average, two years ahead of those who had not. In their early adolescent years, the mean score for both groups had been very similar. Thus, using tests based on educational achievement, the group, which had received education beyond the age of sixteen, appeared to have gained two mental-age years. But it must be remembered that, if a test which was not basically of the skills acquired and developed within formal education had been administered, the picture might have been different.

After the age when formal schooling ends, we ought to be concerned not with measuring the general intelligence or general ability of adults, but rather with measuring their special aptitudes. Whether one adult is more intelligent than another is often less important than whether he is more suitable than another for a particular vocation.

However, it is useful to consider what measures of general intelligence in adults are available. One of the best-known is the Wechsler Adult Intelligence Scale (WAIS) (9). This must be carefully distinguished from the Wechsler Intelligence Scale for Children (WISC). Wechsler, like Binet, believed that there was a general mental ability. He also found that some types of reasoning and performance in patients suffering from mental breakdown were more seriously impaired than others. Consequently, in the WAIS, there is a combination of items, a verbal scale and a performance scale. On page 99, we give correlations for the verbal scale plus the performance scale with the Binet test, and for each scale separately with the Binet test.

* The reader is referred to the correlation of parts of the test battery with teachers' assessments in the notes and references to Chapter 3, Section 5.

It is important to note two points about the Wechsler test for adults; first, although the term 'I.Q.' is used, as in the Stanford-Binet test, the I.Q. scores obtained by candidates on the tests are not directly comparable; secondly, in the WAIS, the I.Q. is not derived from a mental-age score in the same way as we derived an I.Q. score for children from the Stanford-Binet test (pp. 64–5). Wechsler established norms for the test: a mean of 100 and a standard deviation of 15. Thus the normal or average range was from an I.Q. of 85 to 115.

Wechsler did not accept that mental ability remains constant during adulthood. Because of this, he developed a technique known as standard score conversions for different age-groups within the adult (post-sixteen) age-range. An illustration of this conversion is given in the following table.

	Standard score conversions from WAIS	
Age	*Raw score for WAIS*	*Converted I.Q.*
16	129	115
20	129	111
40	129	114
60	129	121
80	129	136

Standard score conversions for the verbal and performance items are calculated separately.

It is also interesting, as a further illustration of the meaning and use of correlation, that the following correlations were obtained between scores on the WISC and the Stanford-Binet test:

Full WISC (verbal+performance) with Stanford-Binet	·82
WISC (verbal only) with Stanford-Binet	·74
WISC (performance only) with Stanford-Binet	·64.

Another very rough guide to adult I.Q. is provided by the S.R.A. Test of Primary Mental Abilities, prepared by L. L. and T. G. Thurstone. Form AH of the test, to be used with candidates in the 11–17 age-range, consists of a battery of five tests:

> Verbal meaning
> Non-verbal reasoning
> Spatial ability
> Word fluency
> Numerical ability.

From the first two on the list, it is possible to calculate an I.Q. derived from the raw scores, as we shall see in a moment. However, if the tester wishes to obtain a complete ability profile of all candidates, he is at liberty to do so by making use of all five sub-tests in the battery.

H

The two sub-tests, from which the rough I.Q. is calculated, are the verbal meaning test and the non-verbal reasoning test. In the verbal meaning sub-test, the candidate is required to discover in four minutes synonyms for fifty words. The test is a recognition test, since the synonym must be a word in one of the four columns which follow the original word. The candidate is required to indicate the column which contains the synonym, by deleting one of the capital letters A, B, C, D on the extreme right-hand side of the page (10). Here is an illustrative example, not actually taken from the test:

CUNNING   A. strong; B. rough; C. wily; D. persistent. ABCD

The non-verbal reasoning test consists of thirty letter series, or sequences, which the candidate must complete in six minutes, by adding the next logically determined letter. In a number series, 2.4.6.8.10, the next number is 12, determined by the pattern of numbers used. In exactly the same way, if we have the letter series a.c.e.g.i, the next letter in the sequence must be k. Again, the test is a recognition test, since the next letter is always one of six on the right-hand side of the page. Here is an example, not taken from the test, to show the lay-out of the test:

abtcduefvghwij   a g h k m x.

Each of the five sub-tests in the battery has a short warm-up test, to ensure that every candidate knows exactly what he is required to do, when given the instruction to begin. Candidates are also told that it is not expected that they will complete the sub-tests in the main battery, although the present writer finds that a good many applicants for entry to colleges of education, do in fact, complete the verbal meaning sub-test. Far fewer complete the non-verbal reasoning sub-test.

After the expiry of the time limit (four minutes for verbal meaning; six minutes for non-verbal reasoning), each candidate has two raw scores, one point being awarded for each correct answer. These raw scores are out of 50 and 30 respectively. A final adjusted score is obtained by applying the formula $2V+R$, i.e. by doubling the raw score for the verbal meaning test and adding it to the unaltered score for the non-verbal reasoning test. An example is given below:

Raw score on verbal meaning (maximum score possible, 50)   41
Raw score on non-verbal reasoning test (maximum score possible, 30)   18
$2V+R = 2(41)+18 = 82+18 = 100$
Total raw score $= 100$.

The I.Q. is derived from this total raw score simply by looking at a vernier conversion scale, as shown in Fig. 26.

It will be seen that the raw scores, 2V+R, are on one side of the vertical line, and the I.Q. on the other side. Our hypothetical raw score of 100 gives an I.Q. of 109. It is not claimed that this I.Q. is accurate. It does, however, spread candidates over a considerable I.Q. range. All candidates, e.g. for admission to colleges of education, could be assigned a rank-order position on the evidence of their performance on the two tests.

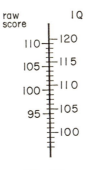

Fig. 26

In the later stages of the 'eleven plus' examination, it became common to increase the test battery by adding teachers' reports (subjective assessment) to the tests of English, arithmetic, and intelligence. Thus a correlation between any item and all the other items in the battery could be calculated.

When we test adults (e.g. students seeking posts in higher education institutions) we have a battery of tests, and similar correlations can be calculated. For example, we may use a 2V+R score; a score on the Maudsley Personality Inventory (see next chapter); the head teacher's reference (or confidential report); together with a measure of scholastic achievement (e.g. results in the 'O' and 'A' levels of the G.C.E.). A candidate who has an I.Q. of 130 may have three 'A' level subjects with a high grade of pass (an 'A' or a 'B'). We can also discover if he had, for example, eight or nine high-grade passes at 'O' level, and we shall know how highly his headmaster rates his intelligence. If the candidate has these high-grade passes, a high intelligence rating from his headmaster, and a high I.Q., the picture is consistent. There is a high correlation between the test result and the other selection criteria.

Alternatively, if a candidate obtains a low score on the verbal meaning, and non-verbal reasoning tests, resulting in a low I.Q., we would expect him, to be consistent, to have a poor intelligence rating from his head-master, low-grade passes in a small number of 'O'-level subjects, and possibly, no passes at all at 'A' level.

Such consistency is not always obtained. There are times when a head teacher's rating of the candidate's ability is at variance with his I.Q.

score on the test. At other times, a candidate obtains a high I.Q., and shows a poor scholastic achievement record. Conversely, some candidates who do not obtain a high I.Q. show an admirable record of scholastic achievement.

These things emphasize the point that we have made before, namely, the older the candidate is, the more difficult it is to be sure that the score obtained for intelligence or general ability is really meaningful. By using a test battery, we have a mixture of criteria. If we add an interview, we use two subjective ratings (reference and interview) and three objective ratings (intelligence test, personality test, and scholastic achievement record). It must, however, be stressed that many subjects at 'O' and 'A' level are not marked objectively, in the strictest sense of the term.

We have spent a great deal of time discussing the problem of testing intelligence, and, in the course of our investigation, we have found that the process is by no means as simple as it sometimes appears on the surface. Consequently, there is no need to offer apologies for the length of time devoted to this important area of measurement. It is all too easy for a teacher to know too little about testing intelligence; it is impossible for him to know too much about it. Ignorance of all the factors involved usually makes for one of two extreme reactions: total acceptance of intelligence testing as though it is some magical form of measurement, or total rejection as though it were some form of witchcraft. It is essential for every teacher to develop a balanced knowledge, not only of the strengths of the different types of intelligence, ability, and aptitude tests, but also of their shortcomings and the ways in which they should be used in conjunction with other methods of assessing and measuring.

NOTES AND REFERENCES FOR CHAPTER 5

1 Until 1951, the Registrar-General used only three categories for classifying data from census returns:

1. Management
2. Operative
3. Working on own account.

As a greater variety of occupations emerged, five categories replaced the three defined above:

1. Management
2. Intermediate
3. Skilled
4. Semi-skilled
5. Unskilled.

Sociologists, in their researches, use a scale divided into seven classes or socio-economic groups. This scale is known as the General Classification

Scale. Readers who are interested in further information about social class and socio-economic status should consult: Cole, G. D. H., *Studies in Class Structure* (Routledge & Kegan Paul, 1955); Glass, D. V. (ed.), *Social Mobility in Britain* (Routledge & Kegan Paul, 1954). See also Burt, C., 'Intelligence, Family Size and Social Class', *Population Studies* (1947), Vol. I, pp. 177–86; and Burt, C., 'The Trend of National Intelligence', *British Medical Journal* (1949), No. 4634, pp. 969 ff.

2 Full details of the Frostig programme and other psychological tests can be obtained from: The National Foundation for Educational Research (NFER), The Mere, Upton Park, Slough, Bucks. NFER also produces very useful occasional publications, which keep teachers informed of current research in important areas such as reading.

3 Remmers, H. H., Gage, N. L. and Rummell, J. F., *A Practical Introduction to Measurement and Evaluation* (Harper International Student Reprint, 1965). (London, Harper & Row, 1966.) Although more technical and statistical than this book this is much simpler than many major works on psychological testing. Readers may well find that it is a useful follow-up to the present book.

4 See also Burt, C., *Age, Ability and Aptitude* (Evans Bros, 1954); and 'General Ability and Special Aptitudes', *Educational Research* (1959), Vol. 1, pp. 3–16.

5 For examples of the actual tests used to measure the seven primary mental abilities, see Chapter 2 of Eysenck, H. J., *Uses and Abuses of Psychology* (Pelican, 1953).

6 *Children and Their Primary Schools* (H.M.S.O., 1967).

7 Two works of this noted American psychologist are relevant to our present purpose: Cronbach, Lee J. and Glesser, G. C., *Psychological Tests and Personnel Decisions* (University of Illinois Press, 1957; Cronbach, Lee J., *The Essentials of Psychological Testing* (Harper International, 1961).

8 It should be noted that the earliest sounds uttered by the infant are no more significant than his earliest motor movements. Just as he exercises his arms and legs, by moving them, so he exercises his mouth and speech mechanisms by uttering sounds. These follow a standard pattern in all normal infants. The commonest sounds are mere repetitions of single sounds – ma-ma; da-da; ba-ba – which parents interpret as indicating that he can now represent 'mammy', 'daddy' and 'baby' in speech. This is not true at this stage, and shows how easy it is to read adult ideas into the actions of children. Similarly, it is dangerous to read Freudian interpretations into the harmless activities of infants.

9 The Wechsler Adult Intelligence Scale developed out of the Bellevue scales, so called because they were developed in the Bellevue Hospital, New York. The hospital contained feeble-minded, psychotics, and illiterates, and the Bellevue Scale, form 1, was developed in 1939 to provide an estimate of the intellectual level of each patient, as a first step to analysing his disposition. The scale (form 1) was greatly used in military hospitals during the Second World War. A second form, published in 1946, was never adequately standardized. The WISC (for children aged 5–15) was published in 1949, and the WAIS, which superseded the Bellevue Scales, appeared in 1955. The WAIS was better constructed and better standardized.

10 We have seen that the term 'standardized' means that both the procedure of administering a test and the procedure of marking the test are standard.

In Chapter 3, we discussed objective marking and objective tests, and said that with such tests, a marking-key was often used. We shall have occasion to mention marking-keys in connection with the Maudsley Personality Inventory in the next chapter. The commonest form of marking-key is simply a card with holes, so placed that the right answer appears in them on each occasion. Marking-keys can be simply constructed for both the verbal meaning test and the non-verbal reasoning test in the S.R.A. battery. If one cuts off the last column of both tests, the letters ABCD for the verbal and the six letters on the right-hand side of the non-verbal test, and pastes these on a strip of cardboard, holes can be punched through the appropriate letter in each instance (Fig. 27).

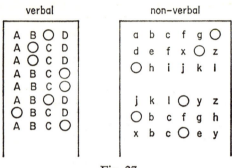

Fig. 27

Every time the candidate gives the correct answer the appropriate letter with a line through it appears in the hole. So, in the first example on the verbal test the letter Ⓒ would appear and on the non-verbal test first question the letter Ⓚ would appear.

GENERAL NOTE

Any reader interested in the development of our ideas about intelligence and the evolution of research in this field should consult: *List of Sir Cyril Burt's Publications*, University of London Press. This covers his writings in book and article form from 1909-65.

Chapter 6

Measuring Personality I

DEFINING PERSONALITY

G. W. Allport (1) describes personality as 'the natural subject matter' of psychology and goes on to say that 'one of the outstanding events in psychology of the present century has been the discovery of personality'.

However, in the same work, Allport finds that the task of defining (2) personality is a difficult one. He finds one idea in the derivation of the word 'personality' from the Latin word *persona* (the mask originally worn by Greek actors, to indicate the role they were playing). In the present century, the importance of role-playing in personality, and the importance of interpreting role-playing as basic to an understanding of personality has been stressed by J. L. Moreno (3).

Allport takes as his starting-point four meanings which the Roman Cicero (4) attributes to the word *persona*:

1. The character or role that a person plays in life (note a similar idea in Shakespeare's 'All the world's a stage' speech).
2. The façade or external appearance which a person displays to other people, marking his true self, which is internal.
3. The collection of peculiarly individual qualities that enables one to live adequately.
4. The distinction and dignity with which one acts out one's role in life.

If we bear in mind the expressions in the four statements above, we shall see that the same ideas occur in Allport's own psychological or scientific definition of personality:

'Personality is the dynamic organization within the individual of those psycho-physical systems that determine his unique adjustment to his environment.'

'BODY-BUILD' AND PERSONALITY

The word 'psychophysical' is a most interesting one. When we talk of psychosomatic illnesses, we mean illnesses which have physical symptoms, but are mental in origin. The Greek word *psyche* means 'soul', or 'mind', and the Greek word *soma* means 'body'. Thus the word 'psycho-physical' implies that personality has a mental as well as a physical component.

The ancient Greeks believed that man, like the earth itself, was made up of four physical elements. When one of the four elements (earth, air, fire, and water) predominated, a certain type of individual resulted. These they defined as: Melancholic, Phlegmatic, Sanguine, and Choleric. We could describe these as respectively gloomy and moody, dour and unshakeable, optimistic and lively, and peppery and hasty-tempered. But examination of physical makeup did not end with the Greeks. In the present century, Sheldon (5), following the lines of Kretschmer (6), has examined the correlation between certain 'body-builds' and different personality characteristics or personality types. The normal or average type is called CHORDOBLASTIQUE. The main characteristic of this type is balanced 'body-build'. The other three types are:

Mesoblastique or Mesomorphic: muscular and athletic, and generally assertive.

Endoblastique or Endomorphic: short and fat (called also Pyknic), and generally easy-going.

Ectoblastique or Ectomorphic: tall and thin (like Conan Doyle's Sherlock Holmes). Such people are also called Leptosomatic.

In Fig. 28, body-build and personality characteristics are combined diagrammatically (based on an idea by Eysenck).

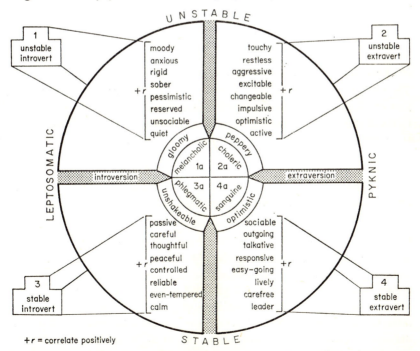

Fig. 28

We can see that the individual characteristics within each quadrant give us more detailed information about an individual's personality than do the terms 'melancholic', etc., just as they give us more detailed information than the terms 'introversion', 'extraversion' (see below).

Figure 28 gives further evidence of the meaning and importance of the term 'correlation'. When personality tests have been used, and the raw data processed by a statistical technique known as FACTOR ANALYSIS, a factor emerges when responses correlate with one another but not with other responses. Thus, a group of responses under the heading 'anxious' would correlate, and another group under the heading 'optimistic' would also correlate. But the 'anxious' responses would not correlate with the 'optimistic' responses. Again, the group of responses shown as 'anxious' correlate with the group of responses shown as 'pessimism', but neither group correlates with 'excitability' or 'aggression'. Thus, all the characteristics in 3 intercorrelate, as do all the characteristics in 4. But there is no positive correlation between the characteristics from 3 and with those from 4 (see also pp. 109–110).

Finally, the details within 1, 2, 3, and 4 are not surprising in view of the terms used in 1a, 2a, 3a, and 4a. If a person is melancholic (overall description) we are not surprised to find that a detailed description of that person includes such terms as 'moody' and 'unsociable', or that it does not include such terms as 'talkative' and 'outgoing.

INTROVERSION: EXTRAVERSION

The reader will notice two key terms, used in Fig. 28: INTROVERSION and EXTRAVERSION. A lot of technical detail is not necessary to make these terms meaningful. A person who is introverted is inward-looking; we sometimes use the word 'introspective' to describe him. The extravert, by contrast, is outgoing. The introvert tends 'to keep himself to himself', and to have rather solitary interests. He is interested in things rather than in people. The extravert likes and seeks people and company. He is gregarious, favouring group activities rather than solitary pursuits.

PERSONALITY CHARACTERISTICS AND JOB SUITABILITY

Bearing in mind what we have already written, and looking at Cattell's statement (7) that 'Personality may be defined as that which will tell what a man will do, when placed in a given situation', we realize how useful it will be if we can measure personality. Let us take a simple example. If we analyse the occupation of a bank clerk, we realize that certain qualities are needed to make a good bank clerk. He must be scrupulously honest, attentive to detail, calm, and a good listener (since the clients of the bank may bring their monetary problems to him to seek his advice).

By contrast, a good salesman would require different qualities. He must be hail-fellow-well-met, persuasive, and persistent. He must be optimistic and possess an unshakeable belief in himself. We can well imagine that, if the bank clerk and the salesman changed places, they might both become utterly frustrated.

We can see now that personality tests, as well as aptitude tests, could well be useful in career guidance. Our power-station operative may have the necessary manual skill to succeed on the test for power-station operatives but has he also the necessary personality characteristics to submit to a somewhat tedious routine day in and day out for some forty years? It is even more clear now why the advice, 'You must obtain passes in such-and-such subjects at "O" level', is meaningless in many cases when pupils seek career guidance. The application of aptitude tests and personality tests are attempts to substitute a scientific system for a system of trial-and-error. If a pupil tries a job, to see if he likes it, without any real guidance, much time and money is wasted. The pupil frequently changes his job, and the employer is forced to put himself to the trouble and expense of training someone else from scratch.

We are not, of course, saying that every individual within a certain personality type is exactly like every other individual within the same type. If the reader turns back to Fig. 28, he will see that there are a number of predictable characteristic reactions to situations within each type. Not only will the unstable introvert act differently in a given situation from the unstable extravert, he will also act differently from the stable introvert. By subdividing both extraversion and introversion into stable and unstable, and both into characteristic reactions in specific circumstances, we are treating personality very much as we treated intelligence in Chapters 4 and 5. We are all the time seeking more and more precise information. To do this, we require more and more sophisticated tests. We can now see that, while 'body-build' may be a general indication of personality, it is only a *very* general one – little more than a starting-point for further investigation. In much the same way verbal precocity, before the age of six, may be a very general indication of high intelligence, but even if it is there is a good deal more that we need to know.

THE PERSONALITY HIERARCHY

We are now in a position to produce a hierarchical diagram of personality (Fig. 29) exactly as we did for intelligence (p. 71).

It will be seen that *g* (general emotionality) corresponds to *g* (general intelligence or general ability), and that introversion and extraversion are the group factors – stable and unstable being subdivisions of both introversion and extraversion, as V and N were subdivisions of the V:Ed (or

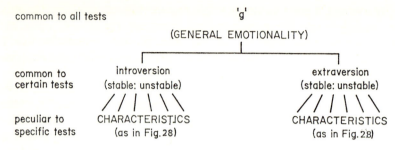

Fig. 29

academic) side, and K and M subdivisions of the K:M (or practical) side, of intelligence. The individual and smaller abilities contained within these larger abilities are equivalent to the individual characteristics (see Fig. 28) within the larger personality groups (Fig. 29). The group factors, introversion and extraversion are also referred to by the technical term.

PERSONALITY DIMENSIONS

Habitual responses and personality
Earlier in this chapter, we said that an individual develops a personality, which enables him to live his life adequately. The personality, therefore, develops as a result of the adjustments made by individuals to the demands of life-situations.

If, however, we had to make a separate adjustment, totally divorced from previous adjustments and from what we had learned from such adjustments, every time we were faced with a problem situation life would be very difficult. In exactly the same way, very little learning would ever take place in the intellectual field, if we had to learn everything as a separate piece of information or as a skill totally divorced from all the other pieces of information and skills we acquire.

To prevent this acquisition of information and skills in isolation, each individual develops learning habits. When set a certain task, some characteristics of it remind him of previous learning experiences and he uses the same technique to assimilate the new knowledge. He makes an habitual intellectual reaction to the problem.

In precisely the same way, we develop habitual emotional reactions to situations, and our behaviour displays some sort of consistency. Because of these habitual reactions, other people are able to predict how we will react in any given situation.

We have now arrived at the point with personality tests (as we did with intelligence tests) where we use personality tests to prognosticate or predict how an individual will behave emotionally, just as intelligence tests enabled us to predict how the individual would behave intellectually. The way in which these 'characteristic reactions' develop is illustrated in Fig. 30. Two key terms appear in Fig. 30: TRAIT and SELF. Allport defines a trait as:

'A generalized and focalized neuro/psychic system with the capacity to make many stimuli functionally equivalent and to initiate and guide consistent forms of adaptive and expressive behaviour.'

This may be difficult to understand, but it can be simply illustrated. A boy is taught by his parents to raise his hat to a lady, to give up his seat on

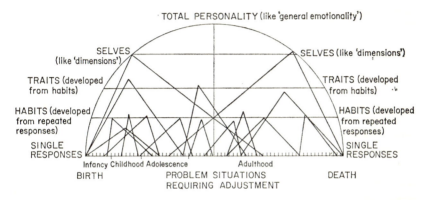

Fig. 30

public transport to a lady, to allow a lady to pass through doors ahead of him, and to open doors for a lady. All these are forms of adaptive and expressive behaviour. The boy adapts to the situation by doing as he is instructed. He also expresses his attitude to ladies by doing such things. A lady, in any of the situations noted, will be the stimulus for the appropriate form of behaviour, and all these forms of behaviour can be summed up by the single word 'gentlemanliness'. Hat-raising, door-opening, and seat-surrender are all habits within the trait of 'gentlemanliness'. Because any lady (the stimulus) is the same as any other lady in these situations, one lady is functionally equivalent to any other lady and evokes the same (habitual) response.

The 'selves', in the diagram, are rather like the dimensions of intro-version/extraversion mentioned on page 108. Thus, we can see that a certain act of adaptive behaviour, when repeated, becomes a habit. Habits of similar nature combine within traits, and traits combine within selves.

It must, however, be realized that we cannot be absolutely sure how any individual will behave in any given situation. We can only predict the direction of his behaviour. We cannot be absolutely sure, for instance, that a person described as being very honest will never perform a dishonest act. What we can say is that there is more likelihood of his being honest, when given the choice between honesty and dishonesty. As we said in Chapter 1, there is a greater probability of his being honest than dishonest. It was this sort of discovery which Hartshorne and May (8) made in their famous experiment.

If we think about the problem, we shall realize that being honest is not identical in every situation. For example, a child may be brought up to believe that it is wrong to steal. He would never dream of stealing money nor would he think of stealing sweets from a shop. However, in company with his friends, he may climb into an orchard and help himself to apples which belong to somebody else. Technically, he is stealing, and, consequently, he is being dishonest. But, the fact he has stolen apples is no indication that, thereafter, he is any more likely than he was before to steal either money or sweets.

MECHANISMS AND PERSONALITY

Sometimes, however, the child may steal in a desperate attempt to protect his self-respect. Many of our everyday actions are what the psychologists call MECHANISMS, or, to give them their full title, EGO-DEFENCE MECHANISMS, since they are forms of behaviour calculated to defend the 'ego', or self. One such mechanism is PROJECTION (see Chapter 7). When we use this mechanism, we criticize faults in other people rather than recognize the same in ourselves.

But, to return to our generally honest child, we can envisage a situation where he moves with his family into a strange district where he has no friends. Moreover, he is unable to make friends, because the group rejects him (a situation we shall consider more fully in Chapter 8). For this reason, the child is willing to do anything which will enable him to gain acceptance. One day, the group dare him to steal, an action which he knows may gain him acceptance, but is out of keeping with his generally honest behaviour. The dishonesty is likely to be repeated only if the original situation arises again.

Another common ego-defence mechanism is RATIONALIZATION. A simple and familiar example of this is the man who applies for a post. After interview, he is told that he has not been successful. Like the boy in the example above, he feels rejected, and to protect his pride he tells his mates that 'he did not want the job anyhow, that he feels sorry for the man who got it, and knows that he himself is lucky not to have obtained it'.

We can see now the importance of the point made on the first page of this chapter, namely that personality is a façade, which masks the real self. We have also said that we develop habitual reactions to specific situations. Now it may be that the man 'who didn't want the job, anyway' was manifesting a characteristic reaction to failure. He might also have used the mechanism of projection and, instead of admitting that he had neither the qualifications nor the qualities required for the job in question, he would see shortcomings in the interviewers. 'They were too stupid to see my real worth,' is a typical reaction. If this man adopts this mechanism every time he is disappointed, he will build up an habitual façade, an attempt to mask one of the real characteristics of his personality, namely, extreme sensitivity. Thus, when we assess personality, we often obtain the information we seek indirectly rather than directly. When a candidate is presented with a problem situation, in the form of a test question, he may give a false answer when he is asked how he would react. Later in the same test, we may ask the same question in a different form. If we now obtain a different answer, this is more likely to be the correct reaction to this situation. Earlier in the test, the candidate was on his guard, and was giving the answers which he thought were expected of him. Later, he forgets the untrue responses he has made, and begins to give responses which reveal his true personality (see also pp. 118–19).

MEASURING PERSONALITY (9)

The evidence of this chapter so far points to similarities between intelligence and personality. Both are concepts or ideas, not tangible objects. Both, as a result, require special methods for measuring them. The term 'personality' is an umbrella, or general term just as 'intelligence' is. Both can be broken down into more specific elements. Eysenck (10), in answer to the question, 'Can personality be measured?', gives a very guarded answer at first, stressing that 'It all depends on what you mean by the terms "personality" and "measurement" ' (11).

However, for the remainder of this chapter, we shall be less concerned with going to the lengths of analysis which Eysenck undertook than with giving some brief idea of the types of personality tests available, together with the strengths and weaknesses of each.

RATING

Rating, in personality measurement or assessment, may be of two kinds: the rating of a person by another, and a person's self-rating. If we wish to know if A is a 'sporty type', we can ask people who know him for their opinion, or we can ask A himself. We may ask half a dozen people who know A, in addition to asking A himself. By doing this, we would hope to obtain a more reliable and consistent assessment (12). However, the situation is not quite so simple as it appears. The heart of the problem is: 'What do we mean by a sporty type?' If we ask six people to describe a Rolls-Royce, we might obtain the following answers:

  i. The most famous car in the world.
 ii. The most reliable car in the world.
iii. The car which the Royal Family nearly always uses.
 iv. One of the most famous status symbols in the world.
  v. A large, smooth-running, and very expensive limousine.
 vi. The car which most people would love to own if they could afford it.

The answers not only tell us something about a Rolls-Royce; they also tell us something about the persons giving them. All six people, asked for a description, interpret the request in terms of their own personality. For example, people who had plenty of money and were, consequently, far from careful in their spending of money, would probably not give answers iv and vi. A republican would not be likely to give answer number iii, unless he wanted to be scathing. Similarly, each of the six people asked, and indeed A himself, might have very definite ideas about what is meant by the term 'sporty type'. Some might think it a complimentary term; others might think it derogatory. Their regard for A would determine the answer which they gave. If, for instance, they respected A, and felt that 'sporty type' was an undesirable classification, they might well give a negative answer.

PROFILES AND THE CONTINUUM

Isolated assessments or assessments on isolated characteristics, such as sportiness or a sense of humour, are seldom meaningful. If we are to build up some sort of coherent picture, we must break down our assessment into specific parts. For example, we may wish to determine how one of our pupils, who is maladjusted, is treated at home. It is little use asking either the child or those who know him: 'Is Tim Jackson treated well at home?' Whatever the answer, we must ask for further information, since 'well' may signify different sorts of treatment to different people. It would be much more meaningful to have a profile of the home, as in the diagram below (Fig. 31).

There could be as many assessment criteria as the person making the assessment thought necessary. Point 4 is the mid-point, and a tick at this point on any of the right-hand criteria would suggest that neither the left-hand nor the right-hand descriptions applied. A tick over the sixth scale-point on the first criterion would mean that, in the opinion of the rater, Tim

Jackson' home was very democratic. A tick after the first scale point on the first criterion would indicate that the rater considered the home to be very dictatorial.

Seven-point scale rating of Tim Jackson's treatment at home.

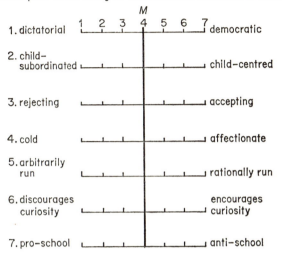

1. dictatorial	democratic
2. child-subordinated	child-centred
3. rejecting	accepting
4. cold	affectionate
5. arbitrarily run	rationally run
6. discourages curiosity	encourages curiosity
7. pro-school	anti-school

Fig. 31

CONTINUUM AND RATING SCALE

It can be argued that the answer of the rater depends on his interpretation of the terms which are at the opposite poles of the CONTINUUM. A continuum is a line between two extremes or poles. However, this use of two opposites and a seven-point continuum is a much better rating system than asking, 'Is Tim Jackson's home dictatorial?'

If we wished to increase the value of this assessment, we could give the profile to a number of assessors, and see if there was a consistent pattern for their ticks. We would see whether these appear in roughly the same half, i.e. to the left or to the right of the mean, on each continuum. If they did, we would be entitled to say that there was evidence of a certain type of home, or of a similar interpretation by all our assessors of the home in relation to the terms which constitute the poles of the continuum.

We could not give this profile to Tim Jackson. If we wished him to rate his home on the same criteria, it would be necessary to reword the terms. Instead of asking him if his home was dictatorial or democratic we would (still using a seven-point scale) ask him: 'When there is a choice to be made in your house, is it made by your parents: always; nearly always; often; sometimes; rarely; hardly ever; never?' Similarly, we could reword criterion v. by asking: 'When your parents make a decision or tell to you do something, do they explain why: always, nearly always; often; sometimes; rarely; hardly ever; never?'

But even here, the terms used cause some difficulty. One research in the United States (13) attempted to find out what percentage of all possible occasions each of the following terms meant. The range of their answers and the commonest answer are given in the second and third columns:

Term	Range of percentage	Commonest answer
usually	70–90	85
often	65–86	78
frequently	50–80	73
sometimes	13–35	20
occasionally	10–33	20
seldom	6–18	10
rarely	3–10	5

Thus, there is almost complete overlap in the ranges and commonest percentage score given for the terms 'sometimes' and 'occasionally'. If we think back to what we said in Chapter 1 about points on a scale, we can see that, for this sample at any rate, the scale was virtually reduced from seven to six points by this overlap. There is also a good deal of similarity between the assessment of percentage of times meant by the highest points on the scale – 'usually' and 'often'.

Another way of presenting a five-point rating-scale is shown below. The trait to be assessed is submissiveness to authority. Instead of asking: 'Is he submissive to authority: always; nearly always; often; sometimes; rarely; hardly ever; never?', five ideas are placed at intervals along the scale and the rater is asked to tick the appropriate one:

1. entirely resigned: accepts all authority
2. respectful: complies by habit
3. ordinarily obedient
4. critical of authority
5. defiant

Comparisons can be made among different groups of people on specific criteria, as we suggested on pages 108–9, when we discussed the qualities which would make a good bank clerk or a good salesman. We could, by this method, produce the type of profile which follows:

		Active in groups	Working with ideas	Avoiding conflict
H I G H	85 75–84 65–74	salesman	salesman	bank clerk
L O W	35–44 25–34	bank clerk	bank clerk	salesman

On page 74 we saw how the abilities profile for individuals compared with that for the total population when measured for the same abilities. We can do the same for the bank clerk and the salesman. In the diagram below (Fig. 30), we take a single criterion – the 'LOW CONFIDENCE——HIGH CONFIDENCE' continuum. We then assign to a point on the continuum seven applicants for the post of bank clerk and seven applicants for the post of salesman.

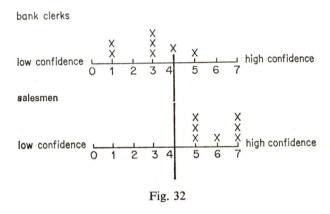

Fig. 32

THE MAUDSLEY PERSONALITY INVENTORY

A well-known 'self-rating test' is the Maudsley Personality Inventory – produced by H. J. Eysenck. The person for testing is presented with forty-eight questions relating to himself. After each question appear three alternative answers – 'Yes', '?', and 'No'. The question mark takes the place of the more usual 'Don't know'; it is simpler, and since the meaning of it is explained in the instructions at the head of the test-sheet, its meaning is perfectly clear to the candidate.

The test is untimed, but the candidates are told that they should not spend a long time pondering over the answers to any of the questions. They are to give their first reaction to each question, by putting a circle round one of the alternatives. An N score (neuroticism or introversion) and an E (extraversion) score are obtained by placing a plastic marking-key over the questions, so that the numbers down the left-hand side cover the numbers of the questions. On the right-hand side of the paper, the numbers 1 or 2 appear over some of the answers in each column, suggesting that the 'Don't know' answers, as well as the 'Yes' and 'No' answers, give some indication of the candidate's personality.

What the test does, in effect, is to ask the candidate to place himself in a number of hypothetical situations and to say, through self-assessment, how he would behave in such situations. In some situations he feels that he would make what turns out to be an introverted response, while in others the response would be characteristic of an extraverted person. As a result of these responses (or adaptive behaviour), a direction of response can be seen showing that some candidates make responses which are predominantly introverted, others make responses which are predominantly extraverted, and the rest make an almost equal number of introverted and extraverted responses. Below are shown four sets of scores, purely for purposes of illustration. In all four cases the '?' responses have been omitted, for simplicity.

Candidate	N	E
Brown	10	36
Smith	36	12
Robinson	36	40
Johnson	15	18

At a glance, we can see that Brown's replies were predominantly extraverted. Smith, on the other hand, gave replies which were predominantly introverted. In both cases, the replies were in a clearly discernible direction.

Robinson and Johnson were in a different category from Brown and Smith. Both of them gave a similar number of introverted and extraverted replies, but, while Robinson scored high on both neuroticism (introversion) and extraversion, Johnson scored low on both counts. There was no clearly discernible direction of responses, as in the case of the first two candidates. From the results, we can say that Robinson is likely to be volatile, and somewhat erratic in his behaviour. Johnson, will be less volatile. His behaviour may be characterized by dullness, dourness, and quiet determination, which might at times, border on 'being difficult'.

A good way to learn precisely what certain combinations of N and E scores mean is to give the test to a group of people well known to the tester. He will have formed some opinion of their characteristics, and can correlate this with the test scores. It is interesting to watch the reactions of some students when we tell them what the tests reveal about their personality. In fact, it is they themselves, if they give honest answers, who reveal their own personality through the medium of the test since it is essentially a self-rating device.

Obviously, the person tested is free to give either honest or dishonest answers. Some candidates may attempt to give the answers which they believe are the ones the tester is looking for. For example, if we use the test as part of a battery for selecting students for colleges of education, some candidates may think that affirmative answers to some questions, will show them in a bad light, reasoning that such answers would disclose a characteristic undesirable in a teacher. To prevent this affecting the results unduly, a 'lie-detector' device is built into the test, by asking certain questions which are related to others. If the candidate answers 'Yes' to one of these, he ought, to be consistent, to answer 'Yes' to the other. The early questions are more likely to produce false replies, since at the start, the candidate is on his guard. Later he may forget what answers he has given to certain questions and, thus, through inconsistency, give the true answer. Again, if he is being very careful in his answers, he may fall behind other candidates. Noticing this, he may accelerate and tend to forget the false answers he gave earlier questions and give true responses to similar questions later in the test.

In the same way, the Edwards (14) Personality Inventory, in the United States, uses 210 pairs of items (considerably more than the Maudsley inventory). Each of the pairs requires a choice to be made by the candidate. In order to check the internal consistency of the answers of any candidate, fifteen pairs are presented a second time at random throughout the test. At this point, the reader might reread Chapter 1, and then ask himself what is the real meaning and importance of the term 'at random'. It is important that the repeated questions do not form a detectable pattern when they occur, the importance of which we stressed when we considered multiple-choice tests.

The Kuder Interest Inventory (15)

This has a special VERIFICATION SCORE, obtained by counting the subject's responses (replies) to certain rarely-chosen items. Subjects making a significant number of these rare responses are deemed to have answered without proper concentration. Readers will recall that the 'number-right formula' was used to eliminate the effect of answering the questions in a multiple-choice test without due attention to the questions or by guessing.

The provision of marking-keys (such as the transparent plastic sheet with the Maudsley Personality Inventory) together with the various lie-detector and correction devices, are all attempts to produce greater objectivity and to increase the validity and reliability of the tests by eliminating distortion. However, Cronbach (16) claims that, in spite of all the efforts which various test constructors have made to reduce or eliminate distortion from data, the ultimate deciding factor in what picture is presented is the ability and willingness of the candidate to provide the person administering the tests with honest responses.

THE 16 P.F. TEST

The 16 P.F. Test is a well-known personality test produced by the Illinois Institute for Personality and Ability Testing. In the introductory remarks to the instructions for Form A of the test, the candidate is told that he is to be asked some questions to see what attitudes and interests he has. He is further told that there are no right and wrong answers, because everyone is entitled to his own views. But, the instructions go on to say that, in order to obtain the best advice from the results (raw scores), the candidate will want to answer the questions exactly and truly.

The wording of these preliminary remarks is especially important. In the introduction to this book, we suggested that many people would be apprehensive, to say the least, if they were told that their intelligence was to be tested. Such people would be even more apprehensive, if told that their personality was to be tested. Intelligence tests make this impression because the candidate fears that he will be made to look foolish. But with personality tests, there is always the fear in the mind of the layman that he will be shown to be mentally unbalanced. There is still confusion in many lay minds between psychology, the study of behaviour, and psychiatry, the study of *abnormal* mental behaviour.

The instructions, therefore, begin by setting the candidate's mind at ease. They suggest that the questions are perfectly harmless, since few people object to discussing their attitudes and interests. Moreover, the fact that the word 'advice' is used, suggests that the candidate, rather than the person administering the test, is most likely to benefit from the test. Readers who in the future will want to devise tests of their own, of whatever sort, should bear these important facts in mind. The wording of any instructions too must be clear, so that the candidate knows exactly what is required of him. He must know whether he has to write words, cross out words, circle numbers, put ticks in boxes, or whatever.

On the back of the 16 P.F. booklet is a sheet for the answer. The total number of questions to be answered is 187, and the candidate can answer by giving one of three alternatives. He indicates his answer by placing a tick in the appropriate box. The boxes are arranged on the answer sheet as shown in Fig. 33.

In the 187 test items there is a small number of reasoning items. In Chapter 5, we noted that Wechsler tested the intelligence of his social derelicts, as part of an attempt to determine their disposition. The inclusion of intelligence items in the 16 P.F. Test provides a further suggestion that there is a

	a	b	c		a	b	c		a	b	c
1	□	□	□	26	□	□	□	51	□	□	□
2	□	□	□	27	□	□	□	52	□	□	□
3	□	□	□	28	□	□	□	53	□	□	□
4	□	□	□	29	□	□	□	54	□	□	□
5	□	□	□	30	□	□	□	55	□	□	□

Fig. 33

connection between personality and intelligence, and we shall examine this more closely in a later section of the present chapter.

In the 16 P.F. Test, as in the Maudsley Personality Inventory, the candidate is asked not to ponder too long over his answers to the items and not to give too many answers in the 'don't know' category. There is more variation in the wording of the alternatives in the 16 P.F. Test than there is in Maudsley, but in the majority of cases the choice is one from three alternatives, occasionally one from four.

BI-POLAR FACTORS

Before we examine the sort of information, which the 16 P.F. Test provides, and the method of presenting this diagrammatically, it is necessary to remind ourselves of the idea of a continuum, and to use this to illustrate the meaning of Cattell's term BI-POLAR FACTOR, revealed by Factor Analysis (17). The two poles of each BI-POLAR FACTOR are, in fact, the ends of a continuum, an idea which we met when we attempted to assess the way Tim Jackson was treated at home (page 115). A number of Cattell's factors are shown in Fig. 34.

```
        A+                                              A—
CYCLOTHYMIA——————————————————————————————SCHIZOTHYMIA
'easy-going'                                       'obstructive'

                          B
                     INTELLIGENCE

        C+                                              C—
EGO STRENGTH—————————————————————————————NEUROTICISM
        H+                                              H—
PARMIA———————————————————————————————————THRECTIA
'adventurous'                                          'shy'
        M+                                              M—
AUTIA————————————————————————————————————PRAXERNIA
'eccentric'                                      'conventional'
        O+                                              O—
GUILT PRONENESS——————————————————————————CONFIDENCE
```

Fig. 34

The results of the 16 P.F. Test can be presented in the form of a personality profile. We have already seen two examples of continua. To remind the reader of the sort of thing we mean, Fig. 35 shows a hypothetical profile, consisting of ten personality traits. For simplicity we have used only a single trait (optimistic) combined with a seven-point rating-scale. OPTIMISTIC——PESSIMISTIC and a ten-point scale, with points 5 and 6 equivalent to our single point 4 (mid-point of scale).

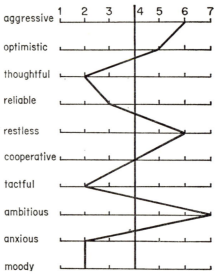

Note that since the fourth scale point is the mid-point of the continuum, it can be thought of as representing *average* aggression, etc., with the points above and below the mid-point representing greater and less than average.

Fig. 35

We could dispense with the points scale combined with a single factor or trait, and use a continuum for each bi-polar factor. By retaining a mid-point on the continuum, we can represent an average on the continuum, or an indication that the individual tested is neither predominantly aggressive nor predominantly submissive, neither predominantly optimistic, nor predominantly pessimistic. In this case, the profile represented in Fig. 35 would appear as in Fig. 36.

If we compare the information, conveyed by Fig. 35 with that conveyed by Fig. 28 (p. 107), we can see a consistent pattern emerging. In the quadrants marked 1, 2, 3, 4 (in Fig. 28) are traits of personality which correlate with other traits within that quadrant but not with traits in the other quadrants. If traits correlate positively with one another, they point in the same direction.

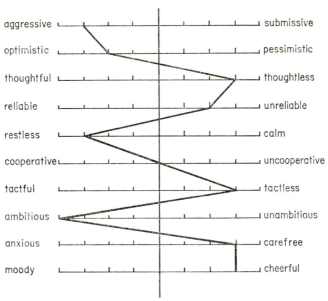

The nearer to one of the 'poles' the individual is placed, on the continuum, the more strongly the trait at the pole characterizes his behaviour.

Fig. 36

If we look at Fig. 35, we see a similar picture emerging. The candidate is rated high on aggression, optimism, restlessness, and ambition, and low on thoughtfulness, reliability, tactfulness, anxiety, and moodiness. We would expect these two groupings of traits in view of what we have learned in this chapter about the nature of personality. The person in question is extraverted. For an introvert, the picture would be reversed; he would score high on such traits as anxiety and thoughtfulness, and low on such traits as aggression and optimism.

The usefulness of a profile rather than a list of statements by a rater about the personality of the individual, is that the one seeking the information can see at a glance what sort of person he is dealing with. He can later compare this profile with his own knowledge of the candidate (if he is known) or with his subsequent behaviour if he is not.

PERSONALITY AND INTELLIGENCE

The other important point which has come to light as this chapter has progressed is the apparent connection between personality and intelligence, the first hint of which came in Chapter 5 on intelligence. Two new indications of a connection between the two have come with the inclusion of a number of reasoning items in the 16 P.F. Test, and the inclusion of intelligence as factor B by Cattell in his list of bi-polar factors of personality. The suggestion is that we cannot measure intelligence satisfactorily without also measuring personality, and that any battery of personality tests should contain some way of measuring intelligence. Eysenck states that speed and accuracy in mental and manual operations differ among groups of hysterics and obsessional neurotics.

THE X FACTOR: SPEED AND POWER TESTS

One of the most important findings in the area that we are considering is the X (or PERSISTENCE) FACTOR. It is, essentially, a personality factor, but one which plays an important role in intelligent behaviour. If a person possesses what we might call 'high X' (or great persistence), he will stick at a task. Thus, if we set a power test of intelligence, we can compare the scores of a given candidate on this type of test with his score on a speed test of intelligence. In the speed test, the candidate is required to answer a number of questions in a given time. Every question is similar in difficulty. We could graph this level of difficulty as shown in Fig. 37.

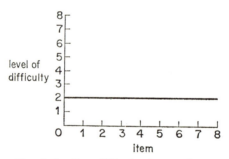

Graph for item difficulty in speed test

Fig. 37

In the power test, the candidate is required to answer a certain number of questions in his own time, but now the items in the test increase gradually in difficulty. The graph for such a test would be like Fig. 38.

It is not difficult now to see the thinking behind the popular accusation that the 'eleven plus' test of intelligence favoured the 'smart Alec', i.e. the boy who can answer the items in the intelligence test quickly. There is a connection between level of intelligence and speed of response to the items in an intelligence test. A pupil with a high level of intelligence naturally sees things quickly. He certainly sees the solution to a problem more quickly than the pupil of lower intelligence. The person with a high ability in mathematics sees the quick method of solving a mathematical problem, while those of lesser ability plod unimaginatively through all the steps, taking a long time, and often obtaining the wrong answer, in spite of all their painstaking work.

To return to our 'smart Alec': it is easy to spot a boy of high intelligence but low persistence, merely by setting a speed test and a power test and

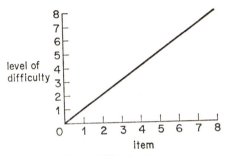

Graph of item difficulty in power test

Fig. 38

comparing his scores on the respective tests. If he scores, for example, 93 out of 100 on the speed test and 68 on the power test, there is little to worry about. It would appear that he continues to bend his best efforts to solving problems whether these are of the same difficulty throughout, or whether they increase in difficulty as the test proceeds. If, however, his scores are 93 on the speed test and 27 on the power test, one may well wish to have further information about his degree of persistence, and administer a personality test which measures persistence (see next chapter).

It has also been suggested (18) that, because of the importance of the X factor, any battery of tests for secondary school selection, ought to contain a report from a teacher who knows each candidate well. If this report contains an assessment of persistence, it can be most useful to the selecting body. Three criteria could then be used to assess suitability for grammar school selection (see table below).

	Score on speed test	Score on power test	Teacher's rating for persistence
A	72	39	good
B	81	27	average
C	90	56	average
D	61	43	good
E	81	61	very good

To make the information even more reliable, we could add the score from a personality test of persistence.

Knowledge of the X factor helps us to understand another type of pupil in the secondary school. He is usually described as a steady plodder, or as not very bright but very hard-working. This type of pupil is usually highly regarded by his teachers, while the so-called 'smart Alec', who is likely to quit when the going becomes difficult, is not. The steady plodder may be a child with a not very high I.Q., perhaps even a border-line case, when the secondary selection test was held. For the sake of illustration, let us suppose that his I.Q. is 110, but that his persistence is very high. Such a child is often described in yet another way as making the best of what ability he possesses. The more one analyses the problem, the more one realizes just what a complex business assessment and testing is. We have repeatedly seen that one raw score is of no real value, and that assessment or rating on a single characteristic, such as sense of humour, is almost equally useless. It now appears that the results of a single test, or even a number of tests of one area (e.g. intelligence or personality) are a much less reliable guide than a battery of tests including tests of intelligence and personality.

PROBLEMS POSED BY RATINGS

We have already seen that one of the serious problems of any self-rating test of personality is that the people tested may or may not give true answers. Although there are devices which attempt to remove distortion, there is no guarantee that they are entirely or even largely successful.

In an appraisal of rating, we find problems similar to those which we met, when we considered the teacher's mark in Chapter 1. To end this chapter it will be useful to bring together some of the weaknesses of the rating system.

Just as teachers, in awarding marks, rarely use the whole scale which they claim to use, so raters rarely make use of all the points on the scale or continuum. The tendency in many instances is towards generosity, if the request is for a rating of a desirable quality. The top end of a continuum for example UNCOOPERATIVE $\overline{\quad 1 \quad 2 \quad 3 \quad 4 \quad 5 \quad 6 \quad 7 \quad}$ COOPERATIVE is used much more than the lower end. Only the totally uncooperative tend to be rated below the mid-point of the scale. This is particularly noticeable when the person rated is applying for the same sort of job as the rater. Thus, if headmasters are asked to rate applicants for entry to colleges of education on a five-point scale of suitability for teaching, they tend to concentrate too much on grades 'A' and 'B'. Similarly Cronbach (19) tells of company commanders who rated their own junior officers in only the top two categories out of five on efficiency reports.

The problem of not using the whole of the scale or continuum leads to the second weakness – failure to discriminate sufficiently. We have already seen that a three-point scale, by its very nature, discriminates less well than a five-point scale, and that both discriminate less well than a seven-point scale. But most scales are reduced by the rater's failing to use all the points to produce fine discrimination. The complementary error to using the top end of the scale too often, is bunching ratings round the mid-point, an error which appeared in our examples of teachers' marking.

Thirdly, there is the weakness of ambiguity resulting from personal interpretation of the trait or quality which is being assessed. This is even more likely to happen when the quality for assessment is an omnibus one. We often talk about rating teachers or about producing ways of measuring the good teacher. We can see at once that A may think that a teacher is good if his class is absolutely quiet and well-behaved, when he enters the room to carry out his rating. B, on the other hand may give this teacher a very poor rating, since he is looking for a teacher who allows the class plenty of freedom and has the children moving about and doing rather than sitting about and listening. In such circumstances the rating is more a self-assessment of the rater projected into the person rated, than a rating of the other person.

This projection of one's own personality into a rating or assessment situation is a most important point. It suggests that the person who requires the rating to be made ought to know the rater well. Eysenck describes people as being tough-minded or tender-minded. The former would be likely, for example, to favour the return of capital punishment, while the latter would be horrified by the very thought. The former would be much more likely to rate an average to weak performer as utterly disastrous, while the latter would rate him as 'not up to the high standard of some others I saw, but by no means a failure'. Such terms as 'average' and 'excellent' are meaningless, because they are open to such wide ranges of rater interpretation, but, when we give the raters a chance to put their rating of an individual into their own words, similar discrepancies of interpretation are likely to occur.

Fourthly, there is the problem of rater-error. We saw, when we examined the problem of marker-error, in essay marking, that the error factor could be calculated for each marker, and that when the error factor has been calculated, a particular marker's marks can be adjusted or corrected to allow for his inconsistency. We have seen, however, that personality measurement lends itself in general to less accurate standards of measurement, and that rating is wide open to error. The tough- or tender-mindedness of the rater is only one source of error, which makes it a technique requiring most careful handling.

Such evidence as we have presented so far suggests that ratings of personality may be both invalid and unreliable. They are invalid, because they do not in all cases measure what they claim to measure. For example, in the hypothetical situations above, keeping a class quiet or allowing a class freedom of activity cannot be synonymous with being a good teacher. Yet either situation may so affect the overall impression made on the rater, that he rates the teacher good or bad on the strength of them.

We have also suggested that while traits of personality give some consistency to human behaviour, and hence help others to make accurate predictions, they do not ensure that a given individual will behave in exactly the same way in every situation, since no two situations are identical. Rater variability and behaviour variation are unlikely to produce reliability in rating. Cronbach reports that the best inventories of personality show reliability of ·80 and above, but that many have much lower reliability.

There is evidence that rating/rerating over a short period of time has much greater reliability than over a longer period. This is not in the least surprising, for the longer the time lapse between the initial and the final ratings of an interest or attitude, the greater the opportunity for change. Similarly, with memory tests the shorter the period of time between test and retest, the larger the amount of material retained, or the smaller the amount of material forgotten. The table below shows figures obtained by Kelly, working in the United States (20).

Area tested	*Correlation test/retest 1 week*	*Correlation test/retest 20 years*
Interests		
Architect	·95	·60
Office manager	·95	·65
Minister	·89	·63
Values		
Economic	·70	·50
Political	·75	·49
Personality		
Self confidence	·85	·61
Sociability	·79	·46

The figures are interesting. We should expect the short-term interests of an architect, an office manager, and a minister to be very consistent, since they would almost certainly largely centre round their occupations. Such interests would change very little in the course of a week. Over a twenty-year period, each might tend to develop more interests outside the sphere of his own occupation.

On the other hand, economic and political values are much more likely to fluctuate over the short term. We are all aware how rapidly the trends of political opinion polls can change. Moreover, one's political and economic values depend much more than one's regular interests on the mood of the moment. If, between the test and retest, the 'big end' on one's car has 'gone', involving great expense, one's reply would no doubt be coloured by this recollection. Similarly, political events can greatly influence a reply even a week after the original test.

Sociability is also something which is very much at the mercy of prevailing moods. There are times when even the most sociable people want to be alone. The answers given, when this happens, are likely to be very different from those given after the end of a successful party.

NOTES AND REFERENCES FOR CHAPTER 6

1 Allport, G. W., *Personality; a Psychological Interpretation* (Holt, Rinehart & Winston, 1937).
2 See also Burt, C., 'The Description and Measurement of Personality', *British Journal of Psychology* (1948), Vol. 1, pp. 134–6.
3 Chapter 10, 'Moreno' in Bischof, L. J., *Interpreting Personality Theories* (Harper & Row, 1964). Moreno is also responsible for the development of sociometry, which will be the subject of discussion in Chapter 8 of this book.
4 Publius Cornelius Cicero (106–65 B.C.), a leading defence counsel in Ancient Rome, was a prolific writer. His works covered philosophy and current affairs of his day. He was expert in a large number of areas and had tremendous influence on later thinkers in moral philosophy, political philosophy, literature and jurisprudence. He was also something of a poet and prided himself particularly on this accomplishment. He would undoubtedly have made a most interesting subject for modern personality testing.
5 See Chapter 4 of *Interpreting Personality Theories* (see 3 above). In a graphic presentation of his 'body-types', he shows that the Endomorph (short and fat) loves company, bakery and beer. The Ectomorph (tall and lean) likes Bach and books. There is a correlation of −·32 between the interests of the two types showing that they are very different. A correlation of +·32 would give slight overlap, while −·32 shows that there is a gap between the two, as shown:

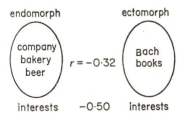

In the same presentation Sheldon shows that the Mesomorph (muscular type) is interested in sport. The interests of the Mesomorph and the

Endomorph have a correlation of −·29. The interests of the Mesomorph and the Ectomorph have a correlation of −·58. This is not unexpected, since we would expect a greater degree of similarity between the interests of an extravert and an athlete, than between those of an introvert and an athlete. As further visual evidence of the meaning of negative correlations and the significance of degrees of negative correlation, the three sets of interests are illustrated diagrammatically below:

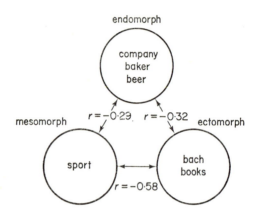

6 Kretschmer, like Jung, took his personality types from the field of psychiatry. He is therefore concerned with types, and the mental breakdown to which each is prone. Eysenck relates 'body-build' and mental breakdown when he shows that the pyknic (extravert) is liable to the manic-depressive form of breakdown, while the leptosomatic (introvert) is liable to hysteria, when he breaks down.

7 Cattell, Raymond B., *The Scientific Analysis of Personality* (Pelican Original, 1965). Although this is a Pelican, and excellent reading for those with some experience, it is not a book to be treated lightly by the inexperienced.

8 Hartshorne, H. and May, M. A., *A Study in Deceit* (New York, Macmillan, 1928).

9 See also, Burt, C., 'The Assessment of Personality' (26th Maudsley Lecture), *Journal of Medical Science*, pp. 1–28.

10 Eysenck, H. J., *Sense and Nonsense in Psychology* (Pelican, 1957). The most useful part of the book for our purposes is Part 2: 'Personality and Social Life'.

11 These questions, and ones like them, play a most important role in modern (analytical) philosophy. For their importance in this area, see: *The Philosophy of Education*, Schofield, op. cit.

12 Remember what we said in Chapter 1 about the size of samples.

13 The research referred to is that of R. H. Simpson, reported as 'The Specific Meanings of Certain Terms Indicating Different Degrees of Frequency', in the *Quarterly Journal of Speech* (1944), No. 30, pp. 328–30.

14 See Edwards, A. L., *The Social Desirability Variable in Personality Research* (New York, Dryden, 1957). (London, Holt, Rinehart & Winston, 1957.) The reader who thinks that he would be interested in studying some

research findings is reminded of the list of articles given towards the end of the present book, to be found in the *British Journal of Educational Psychology*.

15 An example of the area in which Kuder carried out his researches can be found in Kuder, G. F., *Research Handbook for the Kuder Occupationa. Preference Record* (Chicago, Science Research Associates, 1957), pp. 27–38.

16 The reference is to Cronbach, Lee J., *Essentials of Psychological Testing* which has been mentioned several times already.

17 'Factor Analysis' is a complex statistical technique. It was through applying factor analysis that the seven primary mental abilities and the minor abilities grouped under the seven emerged. It was through use of factor analysis that the personality traits emerged. If a number of test items correlate positively with one another and negatively with other items, a factor emerges. This is yet another instance of the supreme importance of correlation in all forms of psychological measurement. Factor analysis is carried out by computer, after the data from the experiment has been programmed for factor analysis.

18 Vernon, P. E., *The Structure of Human Abilities* (Methuen, 1950; 2nd ed., 1965).

19 See 16 above.

20 Kelly, E. Lowell, 'Consistency of Adult Personality' in *American Psychologist* (1955), Vol. 10, pp. 659–81.

K

Chapter 7

Measuring Personality II

PERFORMANCE TESTS

Performance tests of personality, like performance tests of intelligence and aptitudes, are non-verbal. They require the person tested to do something, and are designed to test specific reactions by individuals in structured situations. Other non-verbal tests involve the use of diagrams and shapes.

Cronbach makes two important points about performance tests of personality (1): first, that unsatisfactory as rating and self-rating techniques are in many ways, performance tests of personality have reached 'a much less mature stage of development'; secondly, because there are 'no performance tests of salient importance', there are few clear principles determining their precise usage and usefulness. The first of these statements reminds us that, when we considered psychomotor (or performance) tests of aptitude (see Chapter 5), we found that such tests had reached a stage of development comparable only with that of tests of the seven primary mental abilities twenty years previously.

Performance tests do not provide accurate measures of personality; they merely provide the tester with raw data, from which standardized scores have not been derived. Consequently, what the tester obtains from these raw scores is best described as an impressionistic assessment. In view of what we know already about raw scores and about single scores or a single set of scores in isolation, there is a suggestion that performance tests of personality ought to be only one of a battery of personality measures.

We have seen that methods of rating an individual for a particular quality are not always completely satisfactory. An alternative method of assessing is observation. This, however, may be a long process requiring much time and patience, and, even then the information required may not always be obtained. The writer recalls visiting a child guidance clinic, where an autistic child (2) had been observed with great care daily for nine weeks before her behaviour or play gave a clue to the real cause of her trouble. Eventually, after refusing to play with any of the toys provided by the clinic, she chose a small celluloid doll, which she proceeded to bury daily in the sand-pit, showing signs of extreme agitation as she performed the action. The root cause of the trouble was the birth of a brother, when she herself was nine years old, and the subsequent withdrawal of her parents' attention from her. However, there are many times when we need to have a measure of a particular trait much more quickly than this, especially in the case of normal subjects. In the child guidance clinic, the process was slow because it was diagnostic. The child guidance workers had to wait for the child to show them what was disturbing her. When we know what we are looking for, we can structure a situation and accelerate the process of finding the answer.

A common structured situation is the stress interview. Here, the interviewer is looking for the degree of self-control in the candidate, and bases his assessment of this trait on the success he has in provoking the candidate. It must not be thought that this is the standard interview procedure, which will be described in Chapter 9. In the stress interview, the use of deliberately provocative tactics may provide the answer about the candidate's level of self-control much more quickly and effectively than long periods of observation in everyday situations. In everyday life he may, because there is nothing unduly provoking or frustrating, remain perfectly calm, controlled, and equable, which might lead us to suppose that he is ideally suited to a very frustrating job. A stress interview may cause us to alter our opinion.

This type of situation was structured by WOSB (3), during the Second World War. As part of the selection process for officers, various performance situations were utilized to enable the testers to determine, against pre-determined criteria of officer-suitability, who were the right men for the job. The most famous of the WOSB stress situations was that known as 'Kippy and Buster', in which two men were planted with instructions to make life difficult, if not impossible, for the candidate. One of the *agents provocateurs* was to be openly hostile, the other quietly uncooperative, and the assessors observed what reaction their behaviour prompted in the potential officer. Some candidates became angry and almost succumbed to the temptation to deal physically with Kippy and Buster. Some became so discouraged by their behaviour that they abandoned all attempts to obtain their cooperation. Others became moody.

Another carefully structured situation is that for selecting personnel for Special Branch work. Here an interrogation session is structured. The candidate is subjected to extremely tough interrogation often carried out while he is suffering considerable discomfort, e.g. after he has been deprived of sleep for a considerable period. Naturally, it is not possible to inflict all the unpleasant treatment on the candidate that a desperate enemy may well inflict. However, it does reveal that different people quit at different stages in the situation – that they have different breaking-points. At this point, it is important to emphasize that, to obtain the best measure of the quality being tested, the structured situation should resemble the real thing as closely as possible. Thus, in combat-training, the soldiers will be much more likely to take cover and stay there if live ammunition is used rather than blanks. In the latter case the individual will know, possibly even unconsciously, that he can take risks and become careless without penalty, neither of which courses is desirable in the heat of real combat.

We can now draw up a list of points about performance tests which will serve as some guide to their suitability and as some indication of what those who structure them seek to achieve:

1. An attempt is made to structure the situation so that it is uniform for all. This is really an attempt to produce validity, to make sure that, for every candidate, it measures the same thing and measures what the tester wishes to measure. This is comparable to the attempt to eliminate distortion from rating and self-rating.
2. It is impossible, and, in most cases, undesirable to attempt to eliminate variations in behaviour from one individual to another. Indeed, in the 'Kippy and Buster' and the interrogation situations, the tester wanted very much to separate those who could cope with the situation from those who could not. However, the tester knows what particular trait he is looking for. In the two situations mentioned, all observers are looking for resistance to frustration, endurance, and powers of persuasion; they are not looking for sense of humour, pleasantness of manner, etc., although these may be contributory factors.
3. The person tested is not told what is being looked for. Indeed, on many occasions, he is deliberately misled by the persons carrying out the test, by being told that they are looking for something entirely different. Readers will recall that in the 16.P.F Test (see p. 120) the written instructions told the candidate that they were interested in his interests and attitudes, as the basis for giving the best advice.
4. The tester makes detailed notes of the exact reactions of every individual tested. One candidate, in the interrogation session, may openly exhibit fear in his features, while another may apparently show total indifference to the pressures brought to bear. We said, when talking about rating scales, that raters did not usually discriminate finely among the candidates rated for a particular quality. If the tester in the performance tests merely gives the breaking-point of each individual interrogated, in terms of minutes, there is one criterion for discrimination. By noting the specific characteristics of the candidate's behaviour throughout the test, he builds up a number of detailed, individual pictures.

OBJECTIVITY AND PERSONALITY MEASUREMENT

Some personality traits are more easily measured objectively than others. In Chapter 6, we mentioned the X factor of persistence, and found that it was an important link between personality and intelligence. There are a number of objective measures of persistence, but we shall describe only two.

The first is the dynamometer. One form of dynamometer is the 'try-your-strength' machine in a funfair. To test your strength, you put a coin in the slot, grasp the handle, and pull. Your pulling-power is registered in pounds on the dial above the handle.

It will be seen at once that, if we are merely attempting to measure an individual's strength, the test is an objective one. Each candidate is measured on a scale which is the same for all candidates. Each pull is recorded in terms of the same units, and there is no room for a subjective interpretation that A is stronger than B, although he gained a lower score on the machine.

But it is also possible to use the dynamometer as a test of persistence. Since the machine is the same for all those tested, we are attempting to standardize the procedure of a performance test. (Remember that tests are standardized for procedure as well as for scoring.) What the tester is looking for now is the same as what was being sought in the interrogation and the 'Kippy and Buster' situations – the reaction of each candidate when he nears his breaking-point. Some people, subjected to the dynamometer test, step back from the machine when they have moved the needle a little way round the dial and make no further effort. Others spend much more time forcing the needle as far round the dial as they can. Yet others continue to heave and strain for a considerable time, even when it has become apparent to all that they are not going to move the needle any further. (The reader will notice here a parallel between the speed and power tests of intelligence shown in Chapter 6.)

This is another important point. We can be sure that our dynamometer test is a valid measure of pulling-power. It is more difficult to be sure that it is also a valid test or measure of persistence. To obtain further information in this direction, we could correlate whatever measure of persistence we use in the dynamometer test with the candidate's score on the power and speed tests of intelligence. If the speed test of intelligence measures only intelligence, and the power test intelligence and persistence, while the dynamometer test measures strength and persistence, one would expect a higher correlation between the dynamometer test score and the power test score than between the former and the speed test of intelligence. One would expect a higher correlation still between the dynamometer score and a rating for persistence since both claim to be measuring the same trait.

The tests which we have mentioned, particularly the dynamometer and the interrogation test, raise another important point, indeed, one of the most important points in teaching, namely that of MOTIVATION. We have already said in this chapter, that two apparently identical situations are rarely identical in performance tests. A simple example will illustrate this point. If a young man is with his girl friend and sees the dynamometer, his motive for taking the test is to impress her. He wants to take the test and undergoes it voluntarily. He can see some point in doing it, because he can see some point in impressing his girl friend with his masculinity.

When the same youth is to be tested for persistence and is required to take the dynamometer test, the situation is apparently the same as in the previous example. The same individual and the same piece of machinery are involved. But it is unlikely that the youth will be as concerned to impress the tester as he was to impress his girl friend. We have thus introduced into the situation what psychologists call a VARIABLE. A variable is the opposite of a constant. It is something which changes from one situation to another, while a constant remains the same. In these situations, the machine is the only constant. The youth has changed because his motivation is not the same; because his motivation is different, his performance is not the same.

Let us look at our interrogation again. Real interrogations are carried out in solitude. The person interrogated is removed from his friends, so that the only other people with him are those attempting to break him. Many sportsmen play better in front of an audience, and better in front of large crowds than before a handful of people. Similarly, the victim of an interrogation would probably hold out longer, if he knew that people whom he respected were watching. He would want to impress and would feel ashamed to be beaten. By removing the audience, the interrogator removes a powerful motivating element and has already gone some way to achieving his purpose.

It will be readily seen that this has important implications for children learning. We have all had to deal with the child who is quite unable to remember the simplest thing that we tell him in school. Yet he can reel off the names of the teams that have won the F.A. Cup for years back and he can also tell us the names of all First Division sides without hesitation. In this case interest is the motivating factor. Nor does this apply only to children. Recently, a friend of mine bought a particular make of car. Until that time I could not recall seeing a single car of that make in my home town. Now, every time I go out into the town, I see at least a dozen cars of the same make, many of them of the same colour. I am now interested in that sort of car, and am motivated to notice them so that, if my friend is out in his, I do not fail to wave to him. If the teacher can find what will motivate each child to perform well in school, the battle is more than half won.

Another objective test of persistence is a jigsaw puzzle with certain key pieces missing, or with certain pieces of the wrong shape but bearing the right picture. Again the measure of persistence is the point at which the examinee quits. Those who quit early can next be given a puzzle in which all the pieces are present and of the correct shape. They will often quit at exactly the same point of time as on the first attempt.

If, however, we feel that both the dynamometer and the jigsaw puzzles validly measure persistence, we can obtain scores on both for all our candidates, and work out the degree of correlation. If we obtain a high positive correlation, the suggestion is that they are both measuring the same thing. If we obtain the same high positive correlation between the two performance test scores and an external criterion which is known to be a valid measure of persistence, we are entitled to claim that both our performance tests are also valid measures of persistence.

Hartshorne and May, to whose work we have already referred, attempted to measure personality traits in children objectively. They structured objective tests of honesty, consisting of situations in which there was the opportunity for children to cheat. In every case, the children believed that they would not be detected, but the investigators had ensured that detection was possible. One test consisted of getting the children to answer a number of questions and then to allow them to mark their own scripts, the object being to discover how many children altered wrong answers to right ones.

Another test in the battery consisted of a number of plain wooden boxes in which amounts of money were placed. In every case, the investigators were able to tell which child had had which box and how much money had been in each box originally, although the children were misled into thinking that detection was impossible, because their names were not on the boxes and the tester had said that the amount of money in each was unknown to him.

As we have said earlier (p. 112), we have here two different situations. Some of the children would probably not cheat in either situation; others would not hesitate to cheat in both. Yet others would alter wrong answers to correct ones, because this was 'only cheating' (a minor delinquency) but would stop short of stealing the money. Moreover, children would react differently from adults in these situations. Indeed, if we gave a child these tests and retested him in adulthood, there might well be a low correlation between test and retest.

The question of motivation could enter in here also. Although the children had been led to believe that there was no chance of their being detected if they cheated, a particularly anxious child could still remain unconvinced that 'teacher would not find out'. If this child refrained from cheating or stealing because he was anxious to please the teacher and wanted her to believe that he would not cheat or steal, he would be positively motivated. His motivation would be to win his teacher's approval.

On the other hand, if the child knew that the teacher would be displeased if she caught him cheating or stealing, and refrained on this account, he would be negatively motivated, because he wished to avoid the teacher's displeasure.

We can see, now, that any of our tests can be adapted to particular needs by controlling the motivation variable. We could obtain a score on the dynamometer test by allowing the candidate an attempt in the presence of his girl friend and in her absence. She could also be present and absent at the jigsaw test and at the interrogation, to see how her presence or absence affected the candidate's performance. When we use the observation method of assessing personality traits, however, we do not know what the motivating factors are.

The two situations above are comparable to the situations in classical and operant conditioning (4). In classical conditioning, the stimulus is directly under the control of the experimenter. It is a known constant in the experimental situation. In operant conditioning, the stimulus is not under the control of the investigator; it is an unknown variable quantity. The experimenter may feel that he knows what the stimulus is, or what prompts the subject to perform certain actions, but he cannot claim to know what the stimulus is.

It must, also, be stressed that the two tests of persistence, which we have described, contain what might be called an ability or aptitude factor. In the case of the dynamometer, one of the candidates may be a weight-lifter, another a very unfit person. The former has developed much greater ability in and aptitude for feats requiring strength. He may, therefore, be more strongly motivated to continue and more interested in the performance test anyway. Again, we can see that the jigsaw puzzle involves something akin to perceptual ability. The question, if it does contain an ability factor, is whether this prevents it from measuring persistence? The answer must again be that correlation with the score on a known measure of persistence and correlation with the score of a known measure of the ability or aptitude involved in the test is the best way of answering this question.

RELIABILITY OF PERFORMANCE TESTS OF PERSONALITY

What we have said previously about validity and reliability has suggested that the two are not unconnected. If a test is invalid, as a measure of persistence, we know that it is measuring something other than persistence, and we would not expect it to be reliable as a measure of persistence.

Cronbach made some cautious statements about the level of maturity of performance tests of personality. Later he stated that some were more reliable than others. The reason for this is the lack of standardization in these tests compared with tests in other areas, e.g. reading-age. Even when there is some agreed form or standard for marking the tests, individual testers may well adapt the tests, however slightly, to meet particular requirements. We cannot, therefore, compare the persistence of one person with that of the total population, as we can compare mental age or the reading age of that person with that of all others of the same physical age.

An example of the reliability of some of the Hartshorne and May tests of honesty is shown by the correlation between test and retest scores. When children were retested six months after the initial testing, there was a correlation of ·75 between test and retest scores. But, when the group was tested in early adolescence and again in early adulthood, the test/retest correlation fell to ·37. By contrast, a different sort of test – the Witkin Rod and Frame Test (5) – showed a test/retest correlation of ·86 over a period of one year.

The correlations from the Hartshorne and May tests of honesty suggest that the test is unreliable, because the correlation between test and retest for the two groups differs so greatly. Nor is the correlation of ·75 between test and retest scores for the first group exceptionally high. By contrast, the Witkin Rod and Frame Test seems much more reliable.

However, there is another explanation. We have already said that some traits are more easily measured by objective and performance tests than others. The Witkin test is not measuring honesty and cannot, therefore, be compared with the Hartshorne and May tests. The drop in correlation (test/retest) for the children and the adolescent/adult groups, could, equally well, indicate that honesty in children is not the same as honesty in adolescents and adults. It is feasible that certain changes take place in a trait, such as honesty as the individual becomes older and more experienced, develops different motives for doing things, and has to find for himself a personal code of values, standards, and morals. We may claim to be measuring honesty in both cases, but we may not be measuring exactly the same thing.

PROJECTIVE TESTS

PROJECTIVE TESTS are diagnostic. They are designed to discover areas of emotional disturbance, in the same way as diagnostic intelligence tests were designed to discover areas of intellectual weakness manifesting themselves in poor school performance. Emotional disturbance manifests itself in poor adjustment to problem situations, and in failure to come to terms with life.

Cattell (6) states that it is a natural step from getting people to state their preferences in art and music to getting them to tell their fantasies as they look at pictures or listen to music. Thus a diagnostic projective test provides a person with the opportunity to read into a situation (often represented pictorially) things that are not there in fact. The things which the person reads into the situation are the things which are causing him to be emotionally disturbed.

Wenig, an assistant of Cattell, defined two sorts of projection which he called TRUE PROJECTION and NAÏVE PROJECTION. True projection is of unconscious, or barely conscious, anti-social motives and is really the province of the psychoanalyst (7). In naïve projection, the individual, like a child, interprets the behaviour of other people in terms of himself. By seeing his faults in others, he attempts to rid himself of the shame and guilt which these faults cause him. When given the opportunity to perceive a pattern or picture, he misperceives it, or perceives it in a way convenient to his feelings at the time. He sees things in a picture that are not there, or makes up a dramatic story about the activities of people in a picture who are actually not shown as doing anything in particular. A man crossing a road is misperceived as going to attack the man who lives in the red house on the other side, although the picture does not show any man at all on the other side of the street.

THE BENDER TEST

The Bender Test (8) is a test of perception. Lines, waves, dots (in various arrangements), and geometrical figures are shown, and these symbols (eight in all) have to be copied. The test cannot be said to measure any single trait, and examinees can interpret the test in hundreds of different ways. The responses are interpreted by the tester, and immediately we realize that subjectivity enters into the test.

Eysenck discovered that there were differences between the answers given by neurotics and normal people to the items in the Maudsley Personality Inventory. Similarly, Gobetz (1953) (9) found that neurotics and normal people differed on four criteria when given the Bender Test. The neurotics (i) drew a line of dots sloping upwards instead of level, as shown on the perception test sheet; (ii) drew an incorrect number of wave crests; (iii) counted aloud the number of dots and other items while they were reproducing them; and (iv) crowded the figures, which occupied the whole sheet in the test presentation, into half a sheet when they reproduced them. The differences between the performance of the neurotic and normal groups were 'statistically significant'.

THE RORSCHACH TEST

This is sometimes known as the Rorschach Ink-blot Test, since it developed out of the interpretations, which emotionally disturbed subjects made, of ink-blots on pieces of paper. The modern Rorschach consists of ten cards bearing symmetrical, coloured shapes. In the Bender Test, the examinee is given a specific objective task, namely to reproduce certain symbols. In the Rorschach, he is merely invited to say what he sees, or to say what the shapes remind him of. The Bender Test tests mental efficiency, the Rorschach Test invites emotional response. Some subjects become very agitated while making their responses, and read into the cards animals, dragons, giants, and even sexual organs.

An attempt has been made to produce objective rules for scoring the test, but these have been severely criticized in some quarters. The scoring takes into account whether the subject uses the whole blot or figure in making his projection, whether he uses the part of the blot used by most subjects, or whether he perceives (or misperceives) unusual details. The effects which the colour of the blot has on the subject's interpretation are taken into account, as is the extent to which the subject sees movement in the shape. It will be seen that it is very difficult to produce norms for such a test to which thousands of different responses are possible. It is much easier to standardize the procedure of giving the test than it is to standardize the scoring. Eysenck says that the test is so prone to errors of interpretation that, as a measure of personality, it is virtually useless. Benton (10), on the other hand, claims that he found that the interpretations of responses made by subjects had a validity greater than chance. He adds, however, that the correlation (r), between such interpretations and definite personality traits is low ($+ \cdot 35$).

THEMATIC TESTS

A THEMATIC TEST is used by the tester to obtain information about the content of the subject's thoughts and fantasies. Such a test seeks information about cognitive ability, emotions, and attitudes, and is designed to give a profile of the whole person to a much greater extent than the Bender Test and the Rorschach Test.

THEMATIC APPERCEPTION TEST (TAT)

The Thematic Apperception Test (11) (abbreviated to TAT) was the work of Murray (1938). It requires the subject to look at a picture and to interpret it by telling a story. He is invited to say what led up to the scene in the picture, why such events occurred, and what the consequence will be. He is, therefore, given only the middle of the story and has to invent a beginning and an ending. The manner of his invention gives an indication of his state of mind or emotional condition. The subject really identifies himself with the character in the pictorial situation shown to him and reads his own disturbances into him.

The TAT consists of twenty pictures, and men and women subjects are shown different pictures. To administer the full test takes two one-hour sessions, although some investigators use a shortened version. We have previously stressed that, in personality tests, the purpose of the testing is often deliberately hidden from the person tested. Subjects taking the TAT, are told that their imagination is being tested. Most people feel flattered by this, rather than apprehensive.

Certain response-types are looked for by the tester. These include the defeatist attitude, the anti-authority attitude, and pre-occupation with sexual matters. As with the Rorschach, the tester observes whether the whole test picture is used, how obsessed the subject is with details, and how systematic he is.

When one picture is finished, the candidate goes on to the next. At the end of the test, the tester checks the stories for consistency of reaction. For instance, if the person tested shows aggression to an overbearing authority-figure in one picture, does he show this consistently throughout the test? Are ego-defence mechanisms, shown in one situation, repeated consistently in all? Although all the pictorial situations are from real life, some subjects resort to fantasy and magical interventions in their interpretations. The tester looks for common core elements among such individual details, in an attempt to bring some degree of standardization into his interpretation. It is possible, for example, to calculate the number of stories invented by the people tested, which have a sad ending or end with someone or something being destroyed, or with the female character depicted as wicked or dominant. In one research (12) seven boys, who were rated high on aggression and low on fear of punishment as a result of their TAT performances, showed high aggression in everyday life. But, of nine rated high for aggression and high for fear of punishment, only two were actually aggressive in their everyday behaviour. The suggestion here is that high aggression, indicated by test responses, is much more likely to appear as real life aggression if the person has a low fear-of-punishment rating. Again, we are reminded that a single rating, like a single raw score, may be a comparatively meaningless piece of data.

THE CHILDREN'S APPERCEPTION TEST (CAT)

The CAT is a version of the TAT modified for use with children between the ages of three and ten by Bellak (13). Many of the pictures contain animals, since it is common, as we shall see later, for children to project their own hopes and fears into animals. Children are often willing to tell things to Teddy and to attribute to Teddy things which are a source of conflict in themselves. They believe that, if they tell Teddy these things (i.e. if they project them into Teddy), grown-ups will not learn their secrets.

Thus, children who are emotionally disturbed will frequently refuse to answer a direct question such as, 'What is the matter?' They will, however, frequently reveal their troubles through one or other of the projective techniques. As with TAT (the adult form), the tester looks for certain conflict areas such as the jealousy of brothers or sisters (technically referred to as 'siblings'), or feeling rejected by one or both parents. As with the adults, the details of the children's stories may also be highly individualistic, but the themes cluster round predictable areas of disturbance.

OTHER WELL-KNOWN PROJECTIVE TESTS

Since we have dealt with the essential features of diagram-based and picture-based projective techniques in the above section, we will mention the remaining tests only briefly before considering what might be called verbal types of projective tests.

1. *Blacky Pictures*
This test consists of cartoon situations involving a small dog. Cartoons are very popular with children and it will be noted that an animal is used once more. Few children are suspicious of a cartoon; its attraction diverts the child's mind away from the idea of a test. The test is psychoanalytical, in that it looks for sexual responses indicating areas of disturbance. Cronbach asserts that the validation is inadequate.

2. *The Four-picture Test*
This is a variation of the TAT. The four pictures contain two of solitary figures and two of social situations.

3. *The House, Tree, Person Test*
This requires the child to draw. Houses, trees, and people are common elements in the drawings of young children, and there is little doubt that drawings reveal personality characteristics and problems. A child known to the present writer left school during the lunch-hour, set fire to a building, and then returned to school in the afternoon and produced a most dramatic drawing of his delinquent action. There is, however, considerable doubt about the way drawings should be interpreted. We have mentioned elsewhere that it is very easy to read adult interpretations into children's actions, and this is equally true of their drawings. As a result different testers tend to stress different elements in the drawings.

4. *'Make-a-picture-story' Test* (abbreviated to MAPS)
This is closely related to the TAT and CAT. The subject, instead of being asked to tell a story about a pictorial situation, is required to make his

own story situation out of cardboard cut-out figures. It is less structured than the TAT and CAT, since only the figures, and not the figures in a specific situation, are provided.

5. *Rosenweig Picture Frustration Test*
The basis is again a set of cartoon situations, where one of the characters is the underdog. The subject has to identify with this character and describe his feelings and reactions to being the underdog. There is an objective scoring system for the test but no clear principles for interpreting individual scores in relation to norms for the total population, showing once more the difference between tests in the fields of personality and ability.

However, it is again important to note the interrelationship of personality and intelligence. The Bender Test was a test of perception, and it was shown that certain types of disturbed people performed less well than did normal people. Their perception appeared to be distorted by their mental disturbance.

In 1934, Thurstone examining the results of Moore's experiments, made discoveries related to the points which we have been making. Thurstone listed five 'family of behaviour' headings and subdivided these into individual behaviour characteristics. The combination of intelligence and personality elements in these families, is shown below:

MANIC: destructive, excited, irritable, prone to tantrums.
DEPRESSIVE: anxious, tearful, retarded movements.
COGNITIVE: prone to logical fallacies, perceptual defects, memory defect, reasoning disorientation (confusion).
HALLUCINATORY: prone to strange delusions both visual and auditory, prone to hallucinations and to 'hearing voices'.
CATATONIC: mute, negative, 'shut-in' personality, stereotyped actions.
It will be seen that there is a definite connection between many of the characteristics under the various headings in this list, and the reactions to the projective tests which we have analysed in this chapter. Such terms as 'logical fallacies', 'perceptual defect', and 'reasoning disorientation', show why emotionally disturbed individuals are likely to read things into pictures. 'Memory defect' and 'perceptual defect' show why a certain type of disturbed person reproduces the symbols of the Bender Test so inaccurately. A 'shut-in personality', for example, would be likely to cramp the reproduced symbols into half a page. The external evidence of the test is a guide to his inner feelings, which are also taut and cramped.

EGO-DEFENCE MECHANISMS

It may be helpful at this stage to list and describe briefly, the main EGO-DEFENCE MECHANISMS, to which we have already made a number of references. This information will help the reader to see the sort of things which subjects are likely to read into the pictures of projective (diagnostic) tests. As we have already said, information about personality, especially about a disturbed personality, is often obtained indirectly. It is not obtained from the response made by the person tested, but by deductions made by a skilled psychologist from those responses. By these deductions, the psychologist is able to penetrate the façade which the subject has built up as a protection.

1. *Rationalization*

The subject gives some plausible and socially acceptable excuse rather than the real reason for his actions. 'I didn't accept the post, because my wife did not wish to live so far away from her mother.' In fact, it was probably the man's mother who did not wish him to move so far away from her, but it would have hurt his pride to make such a confession.

2. *Projection*

This we have already examined: see p. 112.

3. *Repression*

This is a Freudian term. Things which are unpleasant to the conscious mind are buried in the unconscious, whence they continue to affect behaviour without the individual being aware of it. It may be many years before the effects come to light. For example, a man in his thirties is under particularly heavy stress, and his behaviour suddenly becomes inexplicable. Examination shows that the bizarre behaviour is the result of the reactivation of some particularly unpleasant childhood memory. One classic example is that of the man who suddenly found himself unable to enter a bus or train. Examination showed that he had been accidentally shut in an entry as a small boy. During his period of stress in adulthood, his mind was no longer capable of keeping the painful memory deep down in his unconscious. The thought of being shut in a train connected with the unpleasant experience from his childhood. If the reader wishes for a simple explanation, he should imagine himself pressing a very strong spring down with his foot. Sooner or later, the foot becomes tired, and he has to remove it and allow the spring to leap into the air, which it has been attempting to do all the time.

4. *Compensation*

Here the subject hides a defect by exaggerating another area in which he can succeed. The unattractive girl devotes all her energies to making a career for herself. The child who is unsuccessful at school work concentrates all his energies on football. (This leads to the fallacy that those who are poor intellectually are good at games.) The Greek orator, Demosthenes, to hide a speech impediment, practised for years with pebbles placed under his tongue, and eventually became the greatest public speaker of his day. From these examples we can see that there is a connection between mechanisms and motivation.

5. *Fantasy*

This is a withdrawal mechanism. The subject, unable to cope adequately with reality, withdraws into a fantasy world, where he can imagine himself as a hero and a great success. James Thurber's book, *The Secret Life of Walter Mitty*, centred upon such a character. The schizophrenic lives partly in the world of reality and partly in the fantasy world without realizing the difference between them, and his conversation may switch from fact to fantasy in the same sentence. This is most disconcerting for the listener, but the schizophrenic does not realize that anything is wrong.

6. *Regression*

This is expressed in such terms as 'childishness' and 'infantilism'. The subject, unable to perform successfully in present circumstances, regresses to an earlier form of successful behaviour. It is an 'attention-seeking mechanism'. One of the commonest forms is enuresis (bed-wetting) in older children and adolescents, because, in infancy, bed-wetting brought parental attention. It is the unconscious mind which prompts the action – the adolescent does not make a conscious effort to wet the bed.

7. *Sublimation*

This is sometimes called 'sublimation of the instincts', since it is the substitution of socially acceptable behaviour for unacceptable behaviour in which the subject would like to indulge. Some argue that some people are in the teaching profession because they wish to dominate other people's minds, and that others join the army because it legalizes aggression and killing.

All these mechanisms make it clear that it is tremendously important to 'run the goose down' in problems of emotional as well as intellectual deviant behaviour (i.e. behaviour which differs from the normal). For this reason, many school punishments, such as automatically given caning for certain offences, provide no solution to the underlying problem. Three boys may be caned for playing truant, but their reasons for playing truant may be vastly different. One may play truant because he is poor at Mathematics, and he wants to avoid a day which begins with a double period of Maths. Another may be late for the first time in his school career, and know that the master who takes the first lesson punishes lateness with detention. The boy has never had a detention and is proud of his record, so he plays truant to preserve his record. A third boy may have played truant because his friends (or those he wishes to have as friends) dare him to play truant as his passport to group acceptance.

'MAKE-UP-A-STORY' AND 'SENTENCE-COMPLETION' TECHNIQUES

All children love stories. They are a natural part of childhood. Most children like to 'make up a story'. For this reason, there is a ready-made diagnostic test for use with small children. If a child is disturbed at school, there are certain causes which the teacher can guess at, such as an unsatisfactory home atmosphere, jealousy of brothers and sisters, or unhappiness at school. Direct questioning is hardly ever successful in eliciting the vital information, for the child, like the adult, is capable of building up protective façade. But he will readily project, and he does not realize that adults can easily tell when he is projecting his own troubles on to other children, or even animals. In making up a story, therefore, they are really confessing what is the root of their trouble by projection.

The teacher must bring into the story all the elements which she suspects could be contributing to the emotional disturbance. She begins the story and allows the child to fill in the blanks at the appropriate places. The story might run as follows:

'Once there was a little boy (or girl). What shall we call him? [the child supplies the name]. Now, this little boy lived in a house; what do you think the house was like outside? ... And inside? ... This little boy had a ... Did he have a daddy, and a mummy and brothers and sisters ...?' and so on.

Gradually, the teacher obtains a picture of the child's home and of its atmosphere. It is not suggested that an instant diagnosis can be made, but the 'make-up-a-story' technique helps us to gain the child's confidence without revealing the reason for our inquiries. The 'complete-a-sentence' technique is similar in many ways. It will be apparent, at once, that the making-up-a-story is effective with very young children who are either unable to write or to think and write sufficiently well to supply the information required. Moreover, children of this age are always listening to stories, and write much less frequently. They would have to concentrate so hard on the act of writing that the object of the exercise would never be achieved. The 'complete-a-sentence' technique is thus for use with older children who have got beyond the 'being-read-to' stage.

In the 'sentence-completion' test, the teacher must again decide exactly what possible areas of disturbance there are, and ensure that there is at least one sentence relating to each. It may be necessary to place at various points sentences which ask for the same information in slightly different words, to check for consistency. If a child continues to give an answer indicating a particular cause of disturbance, the answer becomes 'too frequent for chance, and becomes significant. The reader should note that we are employing here the same technique as in the Maudsley Personality Inventory and other tests of normal personality. A specimen set of sentences is shown below:

My class teacher ....
My father and mother ....
My brothers and sisters ....
The boys in my class at school ....
The girls in my class at school ....
The worst boy in the class ....
The people I like best ....
The people I hate most ....
The things we learn at school ....
In school, I like ....
In school, I hate ....
The things I like at home ....
The things I hate at home ....

The wording of the sentences is most important, and the age of the child must be taken into account. He must be able to understand the wording. For example, it is much better to put 'hate most' than 'like least'. 'Hate most' provides a better balance for 'like most'. The point of the wording, however, is not the impression it makes on an adult, but whether it asks clearly for the information we require in terms which the child can understand.

Each teacher must decide how much cueing will be given. For example, we could considerably restrict the answer to the second sentence by adding 'are' (My father and mother are ...). But we might then miss valuable information as to what the parents do. By adding the word 'are', we make it impossible for the child to write 'hate me'. We can also see why this test is not suitable for very young children. With them, a great deal of cueing would be necessary, and the freedom which is provided by the 'make-up-a-story' technique would be lost. Moreover, we would be liable to get such unhelpful answers as: 'My class teacher is ... a lady', or 'My class teacher is ... Mrs Jones'. Such naïve answers would not necessarily indicate emotional stability; they would merely reflect the limited verbal experience of the child when he is required to write instead of talk.

We do not suggest that all cases of emotional disturbance can be diagnosed by either of these methods. The child at the child guidance clinic (mentioned in Chapter 6) would not have been helped by this method, since she refused either to speak or to write. Many disturbed children become so withdrawn that they refuse to communicate in any way. For this reason diagnosis has to be made through some significant performance in play. Even then, we may have to wait for a long time for results, and perhaps refer the child to guidance experts. However, many lesser problems of disturbance may yield to the two techniques we have described.

TESTS OF SUGGESTIBILITY

The reader will recognize that suggestibility is a very important trait in the field of personality and in everyday life. The degree to which we are open to suggestion is a problem which many people must solve to obtain a livelihood. Television advertising assumes that many thousands of people are open to suggestion, provided that the suggestion is presented in an appropriate way, so that we must link with suggestibility the less pleasant word 'conditioning'. If we are conditioned to perform a certain act, we do not do it because we are so motivated. Indeed, we may to some extent be motivated not to do it, or motivated to do the opposite (these are further examples of negative and positive motivation). Moreover, if we are conditioned to perform some act, we have no rational choice in the matter. The consequences of such conditioning are brilliantly depicted in Aldous Huxley's *Brave New World*, where children are conditioned to hate flowers and all beautiful things, by making them suffer unpleasant experiences whenever they come into contact with them.

Psychologists over the years have been concerned to develop tests which measure suggestibility. Six of these tests are particularly important and are described below:

1. The 'Body-sway' Test
Some readers may be familiar with this test, for it has long been used as a party game. The subject is blindfolded and told to stand to attention and to remain quite relaxed. A 'hypnotic voice' then tells him: 'You are falling forward'. To make the test more objective for research purposes, a record is made of the voice so that every subject heard exactly the same voice, although it might sound different (more hypnotic or more convincing) to highly suggestible subjects. The amount of sway of each subject is measured by a device called a KYMOGRAPH.

2. *Arm-levitation Test*

The subject is told to stand to attention in a relaxed manner and to raise his arms shoulder-high. He is then told repeatedly (by record, in scientific experiments) that his arms are becoming lighter and that they are rising. As in the body-sway test, the amount of 'arm-levitation' can be measured accurately. On both tests, there will be different amounts of body-sway or arm-levitation according to the suggestibility of the subject.

3. *The Chevreul Pendulum Test*

This test differs slightly from the other two in that the suggestion is stated once at the outset, whereas in the other two the suggestion is repeated for the duration of the test.

A line is drawn on a flat surface with a piece of chalk, and the subject is told that a metal pendulum will swing along the chalk line, since it repre-sents one of the earth's magnetic lines. Many subjects accept this scientific evidence, since it is in accordance with what they themselves know about magnetism.

As the tester hands the pendulum to the subject, he may gently set it in motion to 'prove' his point. Observers state that many highly suggestible subjects, without realizing what they are doing, actually move their arm to keep the pendulum swinging.

The three 'performance scores' on these tests correlate highly with one another. This means that they are tests of the same thing. In a similar way, we saw in Chapter 4 that an intelligence factor emerges when scores on a number of tests correlate highly with one another and do not correlate with other scores from other tests. In a moment, we shall see that the scores obtained on these three tests, while correlating highly with one another, do not correlate with the scores from three other tests of suggestibility. Since the scores from these other three tests correlate highly with one another, we know that the two test batteries measure different types of suggestibility. We shall deal with this in more detail when we have described the second battery of three tests.

1. *The Odour Suggestion Test*

The subject is told that he is to undergo a test to determine how sensitive he is to smells. Subjects are motivated to succeed on this test, since they feel that to have a highly developed sense of smell is desirable, and allows them to be seen in a good light. The subject is, then, seated in a corner of the room and blindfolded. The tester sits in the opposite corner of the room and uncorks a bottle of scent. He approaches the subject, who must say, 'NOW' the moment he detects the smell. After each 'NOW', the subject has his blindfold removed so that he can see how near the perfume was brought before he detected its odour. After several trials with real perfume, a bottle of distilled water is used. Subjects with a high degree of suggestibility 'detect' the 'odour' very quickly. It must be realized, too, that they have become conditioned to hearing or sensing movement by the tester, and also to saying, 'Now'. There is, of course, no guarantee that they only say, 'Now' in the trials with the real perfume, when they actually detect the odour.

2. *Increasing Weights Test*
The subject is seated at a table on which there are fifteen identical boxes, numbered on the outside 1–15. The first four boxes contain weights of 20, 40, 60, and 80 grammes respectively. Each of the other boxes contains 100 grammes. The subject is required to lift boxes 1 and 2 and to declare which is heavier. He then lifts 2 and 3 and declares which of those is heavier, and so on, with each pair of boxes. Many subjects, noting that the weight in the first five boxes does, in fact, increase, continue to say, 'Heavier', even when they are balancing boxes containing equal weights.

3. *Memory Suggestion Test*
There is a similarity of principle between this test and the pictorial projection tests which we mentioned earlier. In the 'memory suggestion' test, a picture containing a large number of details is used. The subject is asked to memorize the details, as in the well-known 'Kim's game'. After fifteen seconds, the picture is removed and the tester asks the subject a number of questions about the picture. Suddenly, the questioner asks: 'Was the dog, in the bottom right-hand corner, sitting on the floor or on the armchair?' Many subjects will say, 'On the floor', or 'On the armchair', although there was no dog in the picture at all.

The last three tests correlate highly with one another but do not correlate with the first three. The first three are tests of PRIMARY SUGGESTIBILITY, the second three of SECONDARY SUGGESTIBILITY. Primary suggestibility does not correlate with intelligence. Highly intelligent people as well as dull ones may become 'victims' of the suggestions made in the first three tests.

Secondary suggestibility, however, does correlate with intelligence. This is a most important fact, since highly intelligent people are less easily conditioned by suggestion than dull ones. The educational implications of this are far-reaching. The need to give reasons for what we teach is often stressed by educators. In view of what we have said about secondary suggestibility, it seems that this applies even more with dull children than it does with bright children. Moreover, when we talk about teaching critical thinking (and O'Connor (14) has this as one of his five aims of education) it seems that dull children are in greater need of this than very bright ones. The dull children are the more likely to become the victims of mass advertising and other forms of suggestion.

A third type of suggestibility (TERTIARY SUGGESTIBILITY) also has implications for teaching (15). The subjects are presented with an inventory of questions related to burning social issues. They record their 'honest' replies to these questions, which are collected and recorded. The subjects are then presented with a second set of questions, which is much larger than the first, but contains all the original questions. The subjects are told how some person of authority and status, such as the Prime Minister or the Archbishop of Canterbury, has answered these questions. They then answer the questions, and the tester is able to see to what extent the subjects alter their original answers to the first set of questions to make them correspond with the answers of the 'authority figure'. Some will do this to a greater extent than others, because their level of tertiary suggestibility is higher.

The implication for teaching is simply this – the teacher is an 'authority figure' in the eyes of children. Some children have what almost amounts to 'hero-worship' for the teacher. Teachers not only teach facts, they also convey attitudes and beliefs, and the child of high tertiary suggestibility is likely to accept everything that the teacher says as 'gospel truth'. He is even likely to take seriously remarks made by the teacher in jest. All too often we are unaware, as teachers, just how much impact our remarks can make on certain children. We talk about individual differences, and we are careful to say that, although the most obvious differences are in height and weight, followed perhaps by intelligence, we must not forget such differences as motivation, social class, parental encouragement, personality, temperament, and ambition. Rarely, however, does one hear mention of individual differences in suggestibility.

SUMMARY

In the last two chapters, we have covered a good many aspects of personality measurement. We have seen the difficulties posed by such measurement as well as the necessity of measuring personality and the advantages of having the results of such measurement.

It has also been suggested that some methods of measurement may be more effective than others. They may also be more effective in certain directions. To take one example, we can see that, if we are asked to rate someone for suggestibility, our rating may be entirely contradicted by the results of suggestibility tests. The reason is simply that, if we are asked to rate someone for suggestibility, we assume that we are rating a unitary trait, that is, one characteristic. In fact, we find that there are three types of suggestibility.

In the introduction to this book, we stressed that we were not conducting a crusade to convert people to accepting tests unthinkingly. It is stressed again that, whenever tests are used, the user must be aware of their weaknesses as well as their strengths. Exposing the weaknesses does not eliminate the strengths, as some people appear to imagine, it merely emphasizes that the tests are not infallible. This one ought to know anyhow, because we have discovered that there is no such thing as perfect correlation. Tests always correlate less than $+1$ with other criteria.

With tests of personality, special care must be taken. For example, even the experts differ considerably in their interpretation of projective tests. Some believe that tests like TAT measure stable traits, which can be seen in the behaviour of individuals and give consistency to that behaviour. Others believe that what is revealed by a test such as TAT is motivational strength or motivational direction, and that the strength and direction may change with changed circumstances. There is, also, the possibility that the test itself, if improved, would produce more reliable results. One experimenter, Soskin (1954 and 1959), showed that, when two sets of judges were asked to rate individuals, and one group knew only the social background of the subjects, while the other had the results of TAT and Rorschach tests, the latter tended to be too severe, and tended to expect the worst in the subject. This is, perhaps, both natural and an indictment of projective tests of this type. Such tests are looking for maladjustment. Many of them show that abnormal subjects, such as neurotics, give significantly different replies from those given by normal subjects. Consequently, people using these tests are constantly receiving maladjusted responses, and may tend to look for such responses in people whom they rate. They may also tend to magnify out of all proportion the odd maladjusted response, when they use a different sort of approach.

We can say, as our own last word on the subject, that, although there are many problems in personality testing, and although psychologists realize that there is still a long way to go before they are satisfied with the standards of measurement available, we cannot afford to avoid attempting to assess and measure personality. More and more, the importance of measurement in this field is appreciated. What the teacher must realize is that there are many ways of measuring personality, that not all of them measure the same thing, and that there are many weaknesses in the techniques as well as considerable strengths. The teacher must be well aware of these and, also, absolutely sure what he is attempting to measure. Without this latter knowledge, he cannot even choose the most appropriate test from the available ones.

NOTES AND REFERENCES FOR CHAPTER 7

1 Cronbach, Lee J., *Essentials of Psychological Testing*, op. cit.
2 The autistic child is the non-communicating child. Some severe emotional problem has resulted in the child shutting itself off completely not only from the source of the emotional problem, but also from everyone and everything in the outside world. Because the child will not communicate, it becomes extremely difficult to apply any sort of technique for getting to the heart of the matter. The autistic child is, as a result, handed over to experts, who use all the skill and expertise at their disposal to solve the problem.
3 WOSB – the initial letters of War Office Selection Board, a body of people who selected officers during the Second World War. The selection process developed was subsequently modified and used in other spheres. The 'Country House' selection system used by the Civil Service, lasting for a whole weekend, was a similar selection process.
4 Perhaps the most famous operant conditioning situation is the Skinner Box. A white rat, which has been starved, is placed in a box, which is empty save for a food-hopper and bar at the far end (see diagram below).

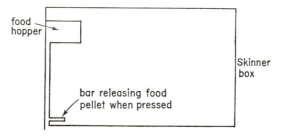

It is natural for the hungry rat to sniff about and to perform a number of random actions, which we call 'trial-and-error' behaviour, since there is no reason, pattern or sequence for such actions. Eventually the rat, apparently by accident (or chance), presses the bar of the food-hopper and the pellet of food is released.

The problem for the psychologists is: 'What precisely is the stimulus which evokes the response of pressing the bar?' Is the sight of the bar the stimulus, or does the rat merely press it by chance as part of his random or trial-and-error behaviour?

In classical conditioning, as we have seen (Chapter 3), Pavlov controlled the stimulus on every occasion. He showed the dog the meat, *and* rang the bell, switched on the metronome or light, or exhibited the black square, or whatever stimulus he was using at the time.
5 The Witkin Rod and Frame Test involves a subject strapped in a chair in a darkened room. The chair can be tilted and the subject has to decide when a rod, several feet in front of him, is in an upright position. The rod itself is luminous. Later, in an attempt to supply diversionary cues to disturb the subject's KINESTHETIC ACUITY, the luminous rod is placed in a luminous square which is tilted. The subject again has to judge when the luminous

rod is in the vertical position. Many subjects choose a position part way between the vertical and the tilt of the square as the vertical position. Readers who have experienced an eyesight test will recall sitting in a darkened room and being asked if a luminous rod several feet in front of them is to the left or to the right of a luminous dot.

6 Cattell, Raymond B., *The Scientific Analysis of Personality*, op. cit.

7 The term 'psychoanalysis' is linked with such phenomena as the animal magnetism of Mesmer, from whom the word 'mesmerism' was derived, with the hypnotic treatment used by Freud in his early days, and with the depth interview. The process is based on the belief that the human mind consists of a conscious part and an unconscious part. Everything makes an impression on the conscious mind, but we cannot retain everything in the conscious part of the mind. Consequently, much of the material that we have to 'remember', but which we shall not require to use for a long time, is placed in the unconscious mind, much as a shopkeeper uses the back of his premises as a store for stock which he is not immediately using. Later, when we have to remember or, more strictly speaking, to recall the stored material, we have to bring it from the unconscious to the conscious part of the mind.

Psychoanalysts claim that the mind deliberately pushes into the unconscious part things which are unpleasant and which it does not want to remember. For the psychoanalyst, forgetting is a deliberate act. However, any unpleasant impression is a source of energy. Just as we cannot destroy energy in the physical world, so we cannot destroy the emotional energy generated by repressing unpleasant experiences. From time to time, these unpleasant experiences are the cause of emotional disturbance. Because they re-emerge from the unconscious in a form not identical to their original form, the sufferer is unaware of the cause of his disturbance. The psychoanalyst, by hypnotism, drugs, and depth interviews, claims to be able to probe the unconscious mind of his patient, and, by locating the cause of the trouble, to bring the patient face to face with it, thus ending his disturbed state.

8 Bender, Lauretta, 'A Visual Motor Gestalt Test and its Clinical Use', *Research Monograph of the American Orthopsychiatric Association*, No. 3 (1938).

9 Gobetz, Wallace, 'A Quantification, Standardization, and Validation of the Bender-gestalt Test on Normal and Neurotic Adults', *Psychological Monographs*, 67, No. 6 (1953).

10 'Influence of Incentives upon Intelligence Test Scores of School Children', *Journal of Genetic Psychology*, 49 (1936), pp. 494–6; 'The Experimental Validation of the Rorschach Test', *British Journal of Medical Psychology*, 23 (1950), pp. 45–58. Both articles are by Arthur L. Benton. Although the second is the one directly relevant to the reference in this chapter, both are important, since we have already seen the connection between intelligence and personality, and between personality and motivation. A motive is an internal urge to action, an incentive an external inducement to action. Thus, if a child runs an errand for his mother, because he is anxious to please his mother, 'anxiety to please' is his motive. If, however, he has to be bribed to run the errand, the money offered becomes an incentive to run the errand.

11 The term 'apperception' is a most interesting one and is found in the writings of the educational philosopher/psychologist Herbart (1776–1841).

There is a distinct connection between the idea of apperception and what we said (in 7 above) about the parts played by the conscious and unconscious mind in learning and retaining.

Herbart's idea was that material taught entered the conscious mind From there, as we have already seen, it sinks into the unconscious mind. What enters the conscious mind is a perception. Later, when similar material is taught, or, in psychological terms, when an equivalent stimulus confronts the learner, another perception enters the conscious mind. But, the learner, seeing the similarity between the new material and the old, recalls from his unconscious mind the old material. Old and new now combine to form an APPERCEPTION MASS. The process is represented diagrammatically below.

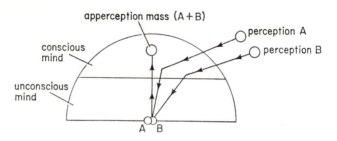

From this we can see that, when the subject is confronted with a projective test, certain features about the test remind him of certain experiences, which he has pushed down into his unconscious mind. On seeing the picture in the test, he brings to the surface these experiences and reads them into the picture, thus showing the tester what he wishes to know.

12 Mussen, Paul H. and Naylor, H. K., 'The Relationship between Overt and Fantasy Aggression', *Journal of Abnormal Psychology*, 49 (1954), pp. 235-40.

13 Bellak, Leopold, *The Thematic Apperception Test and the Children's Apperception Test in Clinical Use* (New York, Grune & Stratton, 1954).

14 O'Connor, D. J., *An Introduction to the Philosophy of Education* (Routledge & Kegan Paul, 1957).

Chapter 8

Sociometric Measurement

SOCIOLOGY AND SOCIOMETRY

SOCIOLOGY is a comparatively new discipline within the field of education, which, for our purposes, can be defined as 'a study of those formal and informal groups within which learning takes place'. SOCIOMETRY is a technique of measurement within sociology useful for determining the natural structure and cohesiveness of groups in school. It is a measure of inter-personal relationships, of social adjustment of individuals to groups. Some discussion of important terms and features within sociology will help us to understand sociometry better.

Sociology cannot be separated from psychology. When we discussed culture bias in Chapter 4, we were referring to a psychological phenomenon determined by sociological factors. The two elements are clearly shown in the titles of two books, Allison Davis's *Social Class Influences upon Learning*, and Stephen Wiseman's *Education and Environment* (1), in which he describes research findings of the effect of the home environment on school attainment, measured intelligence, and so on (2).

FORMAL, SEMI-FORMAL AND INFORMAL GROUPS

We have said that sociometry measures group cohesiveness and the adjustment of individuals to groups. Sociologists recognize two distinct types of groups: primary and secondary. Primary groups are those in which we make intimate face-to-face, spontaneous relationships. Such groups include the family, the peer group, etc. In secondary groups members come into only indirect contact through formal relationships. Inter-personal relationships are functional and fragmentary. Schools and large industrial concerns are secondary groups.

The school has three structures – formal, semi-formal and informal. The formal structure consists of the overall discipline and groups which all must attend. The most obvious of these is the instruction class, which is teacher-dominated, even when non-directive methods (3) are used. The teacher is in authority (4) and has special group status.

Semi-formal groups are those which are available but which do not require compulsory attendance. These are usually referred to as out-of-school or extra-curricular activities (5). In such groups, e.g. the science society, relationships are more relaxed and spontaneous than they are in formal groups. They are teacher-led but not teacher-dominated. In schools in the United States, they are often entirely controlled by the pupils. In Britain, staff and pupils attend these semi-formal groups, because they share a common interest. Semi-formal groups also exert a socializing influence on pupils, but the influence is of a particular type. In semi-formal groups, staff and pupils frequently see one another in a very different light from that of the classroom. The atmosphere of such groups is more relaxed, spontaneous, and natural than in the classroom. Many such groups are educational, but in a less obvious way than the classroom. The group member is less aware that he is receiving education, because the teacher is more inclined to help and guide than to control and instruct. In some cases, semi-formal groups provide the teacher with quite a different impression of some individuals. They reveal different traits of personality, because the situation has changed. A boy who, in class, is little more than a nuisance and a source of distraction for many of his classmates, reveals positive powers of leadership in the cycling club. There, he brooks no nonsense from his group companions, and takes it upon himself to ensure their good behaviour on outings, which he himself plans and organizes down to the last detail. In this situation, he would earn a high rating for responsibility. His classroom behaviour would earn a low rating on the same personality trait.

Within the formal groups, such as the class, there are informal groups, or more correctly, informal sub-groups. Within these sub-groups, different pupils mix for their own reasons. It is often thought, quite erroneously, that children deliberately choose their friends against the criterion of social class. It may be that children of a certain social class do group themselves together, but this is not because they are consciously aware of class. We usually choose friends because of their attractive personality or because their interests coincide with ours. No single class has a monopoly of pleasantness of personality, but interests and social class do tend to correlate positively. Working-class and middle-class children may not mix because of different interests within their classes. In the same way, the interests of a group of lower working-class men correlate highly. Thus we have the equivalent of a 'factor of interests' emerging for upper middle-class and lower working-class men.

Children reflect the interests of their parents. But, a child at school chooses his friends, not because he is consciously aware that Jim belongs to the lower middle class, but because Jim's interests coincide with his. The criterion for selecting friends is common interests, not conscious awareness of the social class to which they belong.

Informal groups may be formed on a number of criteria. The criteria which children use for forming their own groups may be totally different from those which the teacher uses for assigning children to groups or sub-groups. The criteria used by children for forming groups may include travelling on the same school bus, living in the same street, attending the same Church, playing in the same youth club team, and many others. These criteria include activities outside as well as inside the school.

Every group of this kind has its natural leader. This is an individual whom the group is prepared to follow, because he satisfies certain criteria imposed by the group. Again, these criteria may be completely at variance with those which the teacher uses in selecting a group leader. Thus the inexperienced teacher may appoint as form captain a pleasant clever boy, and find, to his astonishment, that the class refuses to accept him. Cleverness and pleasantness are not necessarily criteria against which *they* would make their selection of the group leader. They prefer to follow the natural leader of the group who satisfies *their* selection criteria. In that case, they will regard the form captain as a leader imposed by authority and reject him. If teachers are surprised at the power wielded by some scruffy, not over-bright youth within a classroom, they are showing that they do not appreciate the gulf that exists between adult and child (or adolescent) selection criteria for leadership. For such teachers, sociometry will be a most useful field of study.

There is, also, a connection between the different structures which we have described in this chapter and the role-playing theory of personality which we mentioned in Chapter 6. In fact, Moreno, the author of the role-playing theory, is also one of the pioneers in the field of sociometry. A child must have self-respect. If he is a failure within the formal structure of the school, he will try doubly hard to be a success within the semi-formal and informal structures. This may well lead to a head-on clash with authority. Tom may be almost synonymous with poor academic performance. No matter what the lesson, Tom is always the one who gives the wrong answer, or who does not know the answer, whose ignorance causes amusement. Tom may find self-respect in one of two ways. He may actually capitalize on the laughter, which he gains by his wrong answers. In this case, he will not be motivated to give the right answer, but to gain acceptance as a clown. He is unlikely to be motivated to improve his scholastic performance.

On the other hand, he may channel his energies in a different direction. Unable to succeed within the formal group, he may well seek success in the semi-formal group. He may devote all his energies to playing the clarinet, so that his name becomes synonymous with success in the school orchestra. If the school orchestra is the semi-formal group which carries greatest prestige in that particular school, he again achieves success, acceptance, status, and prestige, without having to concern himself with improving his academic performance. We can see here the ego-defence mechanism, which we referred to as substitution. It is also known sometimes as compensation, since the individual seeks to compensate for failure in one sphere by achieving success in another.

We have stated, both in this chapter and in Chapter 6, that role-playing figures prominently in studies of personality and in sociometry. In Greek and Roman comedies (6), there were stock characters, and there are also stock characters in every formal group. One such role is the funny man. The present writer has seen many students, who have been taught about sociometry and the natural leader of the group, mistaking the funny man for the natural leader, and trying to win him over to their side. But the funny man is frequently playing his role, not because he is the natural leader of the group, but to gain group acceptance. The terms on which the group accepts him is that he makes them laugh. Again, such a character may find success in buffoonery because he fails to win academic success or distinction on the games field. His buffoonery becomes an ego-defence mechanism designed to distract attention from his shortcomings in other directions.

Another stock character is the 'goat', as certain sociologists name him, i.e. the butt for the humour of the rest. The goat is usually some unfortunate individual, who, through physical clumsiness, natural gaucherie, or social naïvety, becomes a byword for stupidity. The jibes of the rest of the group are always directed at him. It is not difficult to see that, in some cases, this could lead to problems of adjustment for the goat. In other cases, he capitalizes on his role and makes this the instrument of his acceptance.

Finally, there is the 'awkward customer'. His role is to be obstructive on every possible occasion. He is often the rallying-point for troublemakers in the group. By identifying with him, they play the submissive role of follower and gain acceptance indirectly, because the troublemaker protects his followers against any action taken by other members of the group.

The important task for the teacher is to isolate these role-players and by tactful investigation, to try to determine exactly why they play their particular role. The cause may be partly home circumstances, partly school situations of which the teacher is unaware. We shall have more to say about this when we consider the usefulness of the TARGET SOCIO-GRAM. For the moment, it must never be forgotten that delinquency rarely begins with premeditated viciousness. Much more frequently it is a case of the individual resorting to socially unacceptable solutions to problems, when socially acceptable methods have failed. Even young children are reluctant to discuss problems, especially when discussing them appears to place them in a bad light. Adolescents are frequently even more reticent. For the reasons given above, the teacher must attempt to detect ego-defence mechanisms and try to find a way behind them to the real problem.

For the infants school teacher, the problem centres on the fact that children have a life of their own, and learning patterns decided by their family, in terms of their social class or socio-economic status, for five years before the formal learning patterns of the school are encountered. The roles which are learned and played out during those five years may be in harmony with the role which the children are required to play in school. In other cases, there may be 'role conflict'. The learning patterns, and code of behaviour in the home may set up a conflict in the young child, who finds that the values of the school are at variance with the values which he has been taught to recognize at home. In another direction, many middle-class children are placed under tremendous emotional stress because their parents demand success which they are incapable of achieving. In yet other cases, certain children have never had satisfactory child-mother relationships (7) and consequently find it almost impossible to fit in with informal groups, much less with formal groups.

Teachers are, therefore, concerned with the social and emotional adjustment of the children or adolescents whom they teach. They are concerned with these areas, not only because they are important in themselves, since the child must, ultimately, learn to fit into society, but because the degree of emotional and social adjustment achieved affects the academic performance of the child in school. Poor social or emotional adjustment may well be a factor which results in limited measured intelligence (Hebb's intelligence B).

In Chapters 2 and 6, we discussed rating, and saw instances of teachers being required to rate children for a particular personality trait, such as reliability or loyalty. The evidence on which many teachers base such ratings is the behaviour of the individual in formal groups. They either do not know, or do not take into account, in their ratings, the behaviour of the individual in informal groups. We have stressed that traits are guides to behaviour, but that, since no two situations are identical, no two reactions to situations by any individual are identical. A child may appear to be particularly disloyal to his teacher, because he is shielding a friend. Conversely, he may appear to be loyal to the teacher, but only at the cost of being disloyal to his friend. In neither case can a satisfactory rating of loyalty in that individual be made by a teacher who is not aware of all the facts of the situation.

It is all too easy to allow a rating to limit the help which one can give to a child in one's role as a teacher. We can say that Bob Smith is unsociable, but sociometric investigation may reveal that Bob Smith is totally rejected by his classmates (his peer group(8)). Thus he is deprived of a context in which he can learn to be sociable. If a child is rejected, the compensatory ego-defence mechanism does not permit him to 'crawl' to the group for acceptance. Rather he adopts a 'don't care' attitude, which makes him appear to be defiant. In actual fact, he is protecting his pride and trying to avoid being emotionally hurt by his rejection. The situation is rendered more difficult by the fact that he often does not know why he is rejected by the group. In other cases, he may know the reason but not be able to alter the situation. He may, for example, have been brought up very strictly in a sheltered home. His school groups may require a more permissive form of behaviour. The child is then faced with the choice between betraying the ideals which his parents have taught him (this will result in feelings of guilt which will hinder emotional adjustment), and trying to preserve the ideals of his parents at the price of rejection by the school group.

THREE IMPORTANT AREAS OF KNOWLEDGE ESSENTIAL FOR TEACHERS

To sum up what we have so far said, we can say that there are three areas of knowledge of tremendous importance to the teacher:

1. The criteria which children themselves use to assess success or to determine the degree of acceptability of their group, as distinct from the criteria which adults, especially teachers, use in assessing these same areas.
2. The internal structure of the class (formal group) in terms of the informal sub-groups which develop as a result of the application by the children of these criteria.
3. The best methods available for obtaining this necessary information, and the best method of solving the problems which arise from this informal grouping, and which manifest themselves through socio-metric methods of investigation. The method used will depend on a number of factors. Among the most important are the age of the children involved, their social background and previous learning habits, and the skill of the teacher in handling the various methods available. A badly used technique will yield little, if any, valuable information, and may well worsen instead of improving the situation.

ANECDOTAL RECORDS : SYSTEMATIC RECORDING

Two common techniques of measurement, in the field of sociometry, designed to reveal inter-personal relationships, are the SYSTEMATIC RECORD and the ANECDOTAL RECORD. The former is close to the personality rating-scale which we have already studied. The rater attempts to isolate units of behaviour, which indicate how well or poorly developed are the relationships between one individual and others.

For example, we may wish to find which workers in a factory are disrupting influences, and which workers, by their behaviour, produce group cohesion. We may also wish to know which workers are easily distracted from the task in hand, and what is the source of such distractions. In our systematic record, we write down these units of behaviour on a separate record sheet for each worker. Over a period of time, we can compare any given worker with his own behavioural tendencies to see how consistent these are and to what extent he deviates from them, what are his reasons for such deviation, and so on. We can also compare any given worker with all the other workers on any of the criteria selected, i.e. on any unit of behaviour. We are reminded here of the two methods of marking described in Chapter 2: the first, where we attempt to use the marks for pupil X to see if he is up to, above, or below his own standard (evaluation); the second, where we attempt to compare his progress with that of all the others in the group (rank-order placing).

Naturally, it is difficult to record all the details of such units of behaviour. While we are observing A, we may miss some significant form of behaviour from B. Moreover, even the actual behaviour observed may be too varied for direct tabulation, unless we have certain behavioural categories in mind. One method of facilitating recording is the method devised by Bales in 1951 (9). He listed twelve categories (or families) of behaviour. These would be listed on each person's sheet, and a tick placed against any form of behaviour, which corresponded to the details within any of the categories. Examples of the categories and of smaller units of behaviour within the category or family are given below:

DISPLAYS SOLIDARITY
i. raises the status and morale of others
ii. gives help where needed
iii. praises and gives reward where suitable.

SHOWS TENSION RELEASE
i. makes jokes for the benefit of the group
ii. makes jokes for the release of his own tension
iii. shows satisfaction with: { his own performance / other people's performance.

ASKS FOR ORIENTATION
i. seeks information
ii. requires repeated confirmation of this information
iii. requires repetition of information and of circumstances to produce security.

SHOWS ANTI-SOCIAL TENDENCY
i. displays passive rejection of ideas

M

    ii. refuses to give help to those who need it
    iii. is formal and not easily or lightly approached by others.

There is a similarity between the systematic recording of what might be called social traits and the rating of personality traits as discussed in Chapters 6 and 7. The recorder decides, in advance, the areas of social behaviour which he will study, and either ticks, or refrains from ticking, the smaller units of behaviour within the categories. It is possible, from the information obtained to build up a profile of social behaviour for each individual. This would require a bi-polar presentation of the units of behaviour as in Figure 39.

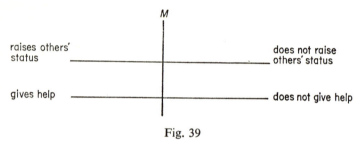

Fig. 39

In this way, a profile similar to that for specific personality traits (pp. 121–23) can be produced.

    Three points can be made at once about anecdotal records:

1. They require a great deal more time to compile than systematic records.
2. They provide much less structured information.
3. The recorder notes *all* aspects of behaviour in every case, and, when the report is finished, looks for trends and significant behavioural acts. He does not, at the outset, have in mind specific criteria, as does the compiler of systematic records.

Cronbach stresses that systematic records are useful in research. We ourselves have given an example from the factory floor. He also says that they have limited use in personal guidance. We can see that this is because everyone is assessed against the same criteria determined in advance by the recorder. He decides that people with specific behavioural tendencies are useful to him, like the factory owner for example. People lacking these behavioural tendencies are less useful to him. He would not, for instance, wish to appoint a disrupting influence as foreman.

    When we compile an anecdotal account of, for example, the behaviour of a class of seven-year-old children, we are hoping that certain areas of activity will reveal the specific needs of each individual. In the light of the evidence which the children give to the observer in spontaneous activity, he will be able to decide what kind of treatment is best for each individual.

In addition to the information which the children themselves supply, the recorder will have access to information about the child's home background. It is most important to see his behaviour in class against his home background, since the home is the first socializing agent. The degree of socialization in class may be explicable only in terms of the success or failure of the home as a socializing agent. We give below a purely fictitious specimen anecdotal report.

Thursday, September 12, 1969. Anecdotal report on James Middlewhite; aged six years and nine months (6;9).

'James comes from a poor home in the Blackfield district of Scarpond. His father (a labourer at the docks, when employed at all) is frequently out of work, and, for long periods, stays away from home entirely, leaving the mother to look after four boys and two girls. The ages of the boys are 12;3, 11,0; 8;6, while the girls' ages are 3;0 and 0;6.

'The mother is Italian and speaks very poor English. She is painstaking and has been to the school on several occasions to ask about James. She seems eager to obtain advice, but almost totally incapable of acting on it. She is always clean, but often untidily dressed in clothes which are ill-fitting and shabby. James is always clean bodily, but always comes to school in clothes which have obviously belonged to someone else, either one of his elder brothers or a stranger.

'James seems completely unable to adjust to the company of the other children. He makes no advances to them, and retreats from their advances to him. Two girls in particular try to mother him, but he seems suspicious of their approaches. If boys attempt to play with him, he runs into a corner and frequently bursts into tears. He does, however, show great affection for the rabbit which is kept in the classroom. His most frequent act is to squat cross-legged on the floor in front of the hutch, curled up and sucking his finger, while he rocks slowly backwards and forwards. From time to time, he timidly touches the wire netting of the cage.

'James's vocabulary is very limited. He knows hardly any of the children in the class by name and does not respond to remarks they make to him. He makes remarks frequently about the rabbit, but these are cryptic, taking the form: "Rabbit hungry", or "My rabbit sad". On approximately three-quarters of the number of occasions on which he speaks of the rabbit he refers to it as "my rabbit".

'When he first came into this class a year ago, he showed no interest at all in the books, which we keep in the corner for the children to read whenever they wish. Towards the end of the year, he occasionally picked up a book from the rack, but immediately threw it to the ground. He never made any comment, nor was there any change in his "dead" expression.

'On one or two occasions he has shown enthusiasm for drawing. What he produces is barely recognizable, and there is a good deal of scribble surrounding objects such as houses. He does, however, react emotionally when drawing. On one occasion, he moaned throughout the entire process, which lasted some fifteen minutes. On another occasion, he appeared to be drawing a man and repeatedly shouted out during his drawing, without uttering specific words.

'James appears to be happiest at mealtime and has a good appetite. However, he never displays enthusiasm over his food. If he wishes to have more, he never asks. The servers have been instructed to ask him each day if he would like second helpings. When asked, he pushes his plate towards the server. If he does not want more, which is a rare event, he covers his plate with his arms and body and stares defiantly, not at the server, but at the teacher sitting at the head of the table. He appears to think that he is withholding something from her by his actions.'

The frequency of the anecdotal accounts has to be decided by individual teachers. In the case of disturbed children, such as James in our example, it may be advisable to make them frequently, in the hope that some significant act of behaviour will emerge which will enable the teacher to find the key to the child's problem. It is not difficult to understand that the problem stems from a poor home atmosphere. But every child is an individual, and each poor home poses a specific problem. In the case of James, the starting-point of any investigation may well be his attachment to the rabbit.

A good deal of interpretative skill is needed to make the best use of anecdotes. The teacher must record frequent as well as rare actions, and be able to interpret the latter in terms of the former. She must also know areas of particular significance such as the type of speech used, the breadth or narrowness of vocabulary, physical aggression or withdrawal, the consistency of aggression and against whom it is most often directed, what incidents produce definite withdrawal as distinct from apathy, and so on.

A series of anecdotes is possibly better than a continuous single serialization. Threads and patterns of behaviour are more readily seen in shorter accounts and comparisons are made more easily. If, for example, the teacher adds weekly to a single anecdote, the details may obscure the themes which emerge. If the reports are made at monthly intervals, the mind of the interpreter has rested from this particular situation and may see things more clearly. Parents rarely notice how rapidly their child is growing physically because they see him every day. Grandparents who see the child less frequently notice the increase in size much more. They also make such remarks as, 'Ah, he's counting much more confidently now than he was last time we saw him.' Parental reaction to this is often: 'Oh, is he? We hadn't really noticed.'

'PEER-RATING' TECHNIQUES

Systematic and anecdotal records both involve the teacher as sole judge and jury. The teacher determines the assessment criteria in the systematic records, and, in the anecdotal records, he collects and interprets the data. As a member of the formal structure of the school it is his task to discover why certain individuals' efficiency of performance in formal areas of study is impaired. We have seen that such decreased efficiency is often the result of emotional disturbance, which only the teacher can diagnose successfully.

There are, however, certain occasions when the teacher is not in the best position to obtain the information he requires by conducting the investigation himself. In these situations, the pupils can *tell* him more than he can discover for himself, using his own techniques. These circumstances enable the teacher to use PEER-RATING TECHNIQUES.

The term PEER GROUP is commonly used in sociology. It simply means a group of one's contemporaries. The peer group has its own characteristic structure, its own criteria for admitting individuals to membership, its own code of behaviour, its own interpretation of normal and deviant behaviour. These do not always correspond to the equivalent in adult society. At times there is, for example, a distinct clash of values between adult and adolescent interpretations of normal behaviour. Infants and junior school children tend to be dependent on the teacher and to accept the adult code. But, as these children approach adolescence (10), they come, simultaneously, nearer adulthood and begin to become independent, to develop minds of their own.

A child is not automatically accepted into the peer group. He has to adjust to such groups, just as he had to adjust to the formal groups of home and school. Those whose behaviour deviates from the code are rejected by their peers. Peer-rejection is a much more serious matter for the adolescent than is rejection by adults. In some cases, the rejection by adults may almost be equivalent to a mark of distinction, in the eyes of his peers.

THE 'GUESS WHO' TEST

In view of what we have said above about adolescents, it will come as no surprise when we say that it is much easier to use sociometric measurement, whether adult-based or peer-based, with younger children than with adolescents. This will become even clearer as we examine some of the methods available in peer-rating.

In the 'GUESS WHO' TEST, the children are given a paper on which a number of sentences have been written. They are told that this is a very exciting game and that they are really playing 'detectives'. They have to put down the name of the boy or girl (or boys or girls, if the sentence describes more than one), who in their opinion is being described.

It will be seen at once that the 'Guess who' test, like the sentence-completion test (p. 148), can be used only with children who are able to understand fully the meaning of the sentences. At a certain age, too, pupils would suspect that they were being required to tell tales, since the sentences describe both pleasant and unpleasant characters. Although the group may not like certain children, they may prefer to deal with them in their own way rather than tell the teacher who they are. Sentences suitable for inclusion in a 'Guess who' test might be:

   i. This boy is the best runner in the class. He is also very good at football and drawing.

  ii. This boy is always annoying the girls.

 iii. This girl is always criticizing the boys even when they try to ignore her.

 iv. This pupil is a great favourite with both boys and girls, is always happy and joins in with everything.

It is impossible to devise a standardized score for tests of this kind. However, the subjectivity, which is present in the rating of pupils by the teacher is eliminated since the responses are made by the pupils. The simplest method of scoring is to give one plus mark ($+1$) for each time a pupil's name appears after a sentence describing a good quality, and -1 after each sentence where a bad quality produces that pupil's name. In the final analysis, a plus score and a minus score can be obtained for each child. This can be adjusted, as in the 'number-right' formula, by subtracting the number of adverse appearances (negative scores) from the number of appearances in complimentary situations (positive scores).

Some teachers expect certain names to appear after certain sentences and not after others. Frequently, their expectations are not fulfilled and they are surprised. This is further evidence that children's criteria are not the same as the criteria used by adults. If they were, there would be little or no point in such techniques as 'Guess who'. In this test, the teacher is looking at individual children through the eyes of their peers.

NECESSARY FEATURES TO MAKE A 'GUESS WHO' TEST EFFECTIVE

Since teachers will make up 'Guess who' tests for themselves, they must be acquainted with certain essential features. These can be summarized as follows:

i. Each pen portrait should contain a number of characteristics. For simplicity, in our examples, we presented only one or two such characteristics. Older children deal with numerous characteristics better than younger children do.

ii. The characteristics included should fall into the 'good' or 'bad' categories. If they are clearly definable in this way, the marking of the test is simplified.

iii. The wording of the pen portraits must be such that it is easily understood by the children. Young children will require very simple wording and obvious characteristics. Older children may be able to cope readily with subtleties of wording and characteristics.

iv. The teacher should ensure, especially with very young children, that every child in the class has an opportunity to be mentioned. This is not as easy as it appears at first glance, since, as we have said, children's assessment of their peers does not always correspond with adult assessment. Thus, the teacher may think that a particular question is certain to result in the naming of a specific child, only to find that quite another name is given. By adding more characteristics, the teacher may make distinctions between pupils clearer. For example, A may be good at running and very tall, but he does not show kindness to girls. The three characteristics in combination make it more likely that B will be named.

SOCIOMETRIC SUMMARY SHEETS : TARGET SOCIOGRAMS

Two more complex and time-consuming ways of obtaining and recording a picture of the group structure of a class from peer-ratings are the SOCIOMETRIC SUMMARY SHEET and the TARGET SOCIOGRAM (see Fig. 40 and 41). The symbols on the target sociogram (see pp. 173–4) are standard sociometric symbols, but their position on each target is unique and derived from data on the sociometric summary sheet.

Separate sheets and targets must be constructed for each rating situation. If the children are asked to form a number of committees, different names will appear on different committees with, possibly, a small nucleus of very popular individuals common to all the committees. For example, different selection criteria will be used by the group for choosing members of a sports committee than for choosing a work-programme committee.

It will be appreciated that, if the teacher is prepared to collect this type of material and produce sociograms, he will have a detailed picture of his class structure, which can be seen at a glance. He will know the degree of cohesiveness of the class as a whole (main group) as well as the members of the constituent sub-groups. He may be able to give specific help to individuals who find it difficult to fit in. Once he knows where they fail to fit in, he has taken the first step to determining why. Some sub-groups will be regular, others will be occasional. Very popular children will figure in all or most regular groups. Less popular children may be assigned to occasional groups, e.g. the charity committee for collecting money at Christmas and Easter. They would not, however, be on the more prestige-giving committees, e.g. the games committee, which meets every week.

In compiling data sheets and constructing sociograms, two types of choice occur, a 'within-sex' choice and a 'between-sexes' choice. In the former, a boy chooses a boy or a girl chooses a girl; in the latter a boy chooses a girl or vice versa. The technical terms WITHIN-GROUP DIFFERENCES (or variance) and BETWEEN-GROUPS DIFFERENCES (or variance) are important research terms. Explanation of them will reveal a parallel with the within-group and between-groups choices.

Let us suppose that, in a certain area of the country, we wish to compare the level of attainment in mathematics of fifth-form pupils in the A and D streams. We take, as our sample, the A and D stream fifth-formers from thirty comprehensive schools. There are, thus, thirty groups, each with its own within-group variance, i.e. the difference in mathematical attainment of the A and D stream fifth-formers.

In addition to expecting the A stream fifth-formers in any given school, to have a higher level of mathematical attainment than that of the D stream, we would expect both the A and D stream groups in some schools to have a higher level of mathematical attainment than their counterparts in some other schools. The degree of superiority of a group in one school over its counterpart in another is the between-groups variance.

Sociometric choices can be one-way or mutual. In one-way choices, A chooses B. In mutual choices, A and B choose each other. Mutual choices can be within-sex or between-sexes. It will be appreciated that, if we combine both types of choice, we obtain the following combinations:

i. One way (within sex) choices
ii. One way (between sexes) choices
iii. Mutual (within sex) choices
iv. Mutual (between sexes) choices.

The degree to which the sexes integrate and segregate differs at different age-levels. The types of choices made indicates whether, at the age-level tested, socialization is within-sex or between-sexes.

An example of the sociometric summary sheet is given in Fig. 40.

		BOYS				CHOSEN		GIRLS				
	Charles	David	Henry	Leonard	Thomas	William	Audrey	Betty	Carol	Lucy	Mary	Olive
Charles		ab–	abc									
David	a––				––c		a–c			a––		
Henry	ab–					a–c						
Leonard	abc											
Thomas		a–c										
William			–b–	a––								
Audrey												abc
Betty									a–b	–bc		
Carol							a–b			ab–		
Lucy							––c	–bc				
Mary							––c			–bc		a–c
Olive							abc	a–b		ab–		

(Side label: CHOOSER — BOYS / GIRLS)

–indicates no choice on this criterion. Thus a–c means choice on criteria a. and c: no choice b.

Fig. 40

The number of names on the sheet may vary from one situation to another, but the following points are common to all sheets:

i. The same number of names, in the same order, must appear along the top and the side of the sheet.

ii. There must be vertical and horizontal divisions to indicate the two sexes. In this way within-sex and between-sexes' choices can be recorded.

iii. There must be a symbol for each criterion on which the pupils are asked to make their choices. In the example below there are three criteria, designated *a*, *b*, and *c*.

iv. Questions must always be asked consistently, i.e. the three questions below ask, 'With whom would you LIKE to . . .? It is also possible to ask three questions beginning, 'With whom would you NOT LIKE TO . . .? The first type will produce acceptance answers, the second type will produce rejection answers. It matters little which type is chosen, but all questions must be worded in the same way. It would be interesting to compile data from acceptance questions, in some situations, and from rejection questions, in others. We shall see later that there is a difference between children who are neglected, i.e. not chosen on the 'like to' questions, and those rejected, i.e. those named on the 'not like to' questions.

From the data above, the teacher can determine:

i. Single (within sex) choices
ii. Single (between sexes) choices
iii. Mutual (within sex) choices
iv. Mutual (between sexes) choices.

The between-sexes choices are easily disposed of. There are no mutual between-sexes choices. Nor is there any one-way between-sexes choice by a girl. There are only two instances of one-way between-sexes choices by a boy. David chooses both Audrey and Lucy on criterion *a*, in addition to choosing Audrey again on criterion *c*. None of the remaining five boys chooses any girl on any of the three criteria. This sex segregation could mean that the age of the pupils is one where little interest is shown in the opposite sex, or that the activity concerned lends itself to single-sex committees, e.g. organizing sports, where boys and girls compete separately.

Charles and Henry exercise within-sex mutual choices on criteria *a* and *b*. In addition, Charles makes a one-way within-sex choice of Henry on criterion *c*. Audrey and Olive provide an even better example of a complete mutual within-sex choice, since they choose each other on all three criteria. Carol and Lucy make a mutual within-sex choice on criterion *b* only. Carol makes a one-way within-sex choice of Lucy on criterion *a*, balanced by a one-way within-sex choice of Carol by Lucy on criterion *c*. Readers may wish to complete the analysis of the summary sheet, noting any other one-way or mutual choices and determining their direction.

SYMBOLS USED IN TARGET SOCIOGRAMS

The basic symbols representing boys and girls are:

On each sociogram, the name of the boy or girl must be combined with this symbol, thus:

A one-way within-sex choice is represented for boys by:

and for girls by:

A mutual within-sex choice is shown for boys thus:

and for girls thus:

A one-way between-sexes choice is shown thus:

A mutual between-sexes choice is shown thus:

A within-sex sub-group, formed as the result of both one-way and mutual choices, would be shown for girls thus:

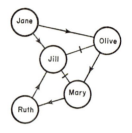

and for boys thus:

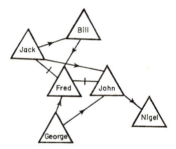

A between-sexes sub-group, based on one-way and mutual choices, would be shown thus:

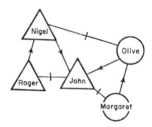

A complete target sociogram is shown in Fig. 41: selection is on a single criterion, namely 'like to work with' for one activity only (unlike the three criteria of the data sheet on p. 171). The single criterion was adopted for simplicity of presentation.

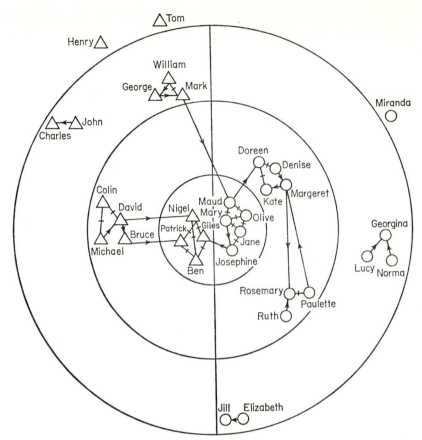

Those in the centre circle are 'stars'. Those outside the target (Henry: Tom: Miranda) are 'isolates', because they choose no one. They may be 'neglectees' if no one has chosen them or 'rejectees' if everyone has refused to choose them on the criterion 'not like'.

Fig. 41

There are a number of technical terms given to people as a result of their placing on the sociogram:

Stars: these are children (boys or girls) who appear near the centre of the target. The more choices an individual obtains, the closer to the centre he is placed.

Isolates: this term refers to those who appear near the perimeter of the target, or even outside the perimeter. An isolate is one who does not not choose anyone when given the opportunity. He does not wish to select group members to work with him.

Neglectee: a neglectee will also appear near or outside the perimeter: of the target. He is the child who is chosen by no one, or perhaps by one individual, when the question is worded, 'I would like to work with . . .'

Rejectee: he (or she) also appears at or beyond the perimeter of the target. He (or she) is the one who receives the most mentions, when the question is worded, 'The person I would least like to work with is . . .'

Thus a neglectee is a child who makes no impression on his peers, while a rejectee makes a strong impression. It is, however, a strong unfavourable impression. By contrast, the star makes a strong favourable impression on his peers.

The rank-order of choices may also be indicated on a sociogram. For example, if asked to nominate three people with whom he would like to work, and place them in order of preference, a child might write:

1. George
2. Bill
3. Henry.

This would be represented symbolically (Charles is the child making the choice) as:

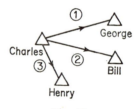

Fig. 42

Many teachers would be concerned to discover why some children make isolates of themselves and why others becomes neglectees and rejectees. By comparing their position on the target sociogram with information from other sources, e.g. systematic records, anecdotal records, and 'Guess who' tests, this information may be obtained. There are always two reasons for applying sociometric techniques:

1. To help the teacher, by obtaining an accurate picture of the internal structure, and degree and direction of internal cohesiveness in the class.
2. To help the children by finding where they lie within the group structure, and, as a result of finding the reason for the position of

the unfortunate ones, supply the best help and advice to improve their socialization.

NOTES AND REFERENCES FOR CHAPTER 8

1 Wiseman, Stephen, *Education and Environment* (Manchester University Press, 1964).
2 The 'measured intelligence' would be 'intelligence B' (see Chapter 4, pp. 75–77).
3 Non-directive methods are informal methods of teaching, which allow a good deal of child-directed activity. The non-direction is a term describing the teacher's role in this situation.
4 See Peters, R. S., *Ethics and Education* (George Allen & Unwin, 1966), Chapter 9, for discussion of the teacher's authority.
5 There is a school of thought, in the United States, which defines 'curriculum' as 'all the activities in which the child participates in school'. In this case there is no division into curricular and extra-curricular activities.
6 The comedies referred to are those by the Greek, Menander (342–292 BC), and the Roman, Plautus (254–184 BC). The plays of Menander are called the 'New comedy' to distinguish them from the 'Old comedy' of Aristophanes (448–380 BC). The stock characters were part of the tradition of these plays, and the audience looked forward to their entry. In the Roman plays, two such stock characters were the 'gullible master' and the 'cunning slave' who always got the better of his master. At some point in the play, the slave would come close to being flogged, but would, by use of his cunning, avoid the punishment. These characters reappear in the Restoration comedies.
7 A most readable book in this important area of psychology is Bowlby, J., *Child Care and the Growth of Love* (Pelican, 1953).
8 Membership of the peer-group is part of the socializing process, which begins in infancy and ends with adulthood. The peer-group figures prominently in adolescent culture. The 'gang' is a particularly good example of a peer-group.
9 Bales, R. F., *Interaction Process Analysis* (Addison-Wesley, 1951).
10 Adolescence is that period in human development between childhood and adulthood. It is divided into the period of puberty (roughly between the ages of 11 and 15), and the post-pubertal period. This is adolescence proper. It is impossible to set precise limits, in terms of age, to adolescence. Many writers put the lower limit as 11 years and the upper limit as 20. It is, thus, the period which the lay term 'teenager' covers. During adolescence, the sexual development of the individual is completed by the appearance of the sexual characteristics of manhood and womanhood. The period is the last chance for the individual to come to terms with life, before he enters adult society and takes his place as an individual responsible for his own actions. It can be (but is not necessarily) a period of conflict. The adolescent begins to show his independence of parental restrictions and adult domination. One thing which is almost guaranteed to cause resentment is treating the adolescent like a child. It is for this reason that we suggested, in this chapter, that the teacher should use sociometric techniques with great care when applying them to adolescents.

Chapter 9

Interview and Questionnaire

It is appropriate to consider the INTERVIEW and the QUESTIONNAIRE within the same chapter because they have certain fundamental features in common. Points which make for a good interview are also essential in the compilation of a good questionnaire. Both interview and questionnaire seek information by asking questions. The interview is a personal, face-to-face situation; the questionnaire (sometimes referred to as the MASS INTERVIEW) is an impersonal situation.

THE INTERVIEW

Many people, quite erroneously, believe that they are good interviewers, and that the interview is an excellent selection technique. Moreover, many people, when seeking a post, would much prefer to be selected, or rejected, by interview than as the result of their performance on certain tests of ability and personality.

INTERVIEW VALIDITY AND RELIABILITY

It is easy to rid our minds of the results of an unsuccessful interview by projection. We feel sorry for the interviewer, because he was unable to pick out our good qualities. Thus, while we pride ourselves on being good interviewers, we attribute our failure to obtain a specific post to interviewer incompetence. The whole process is much less sinister than being rejected by a battery of objective tests. Ironically, our opinion of the interviewer may be entirely justified, as we shall see later in this chapter. If we said that the interview was subjective, and that its validity was doubtful, as also was its reliability, we should be less enchanted with interviews than we are.

We have said earlier that, if a test is both valid and reliable, it should assign people to roughly the same rank-order position each time it is used. If it does not, it is unreliable. Moreover, different tests of intelligence, each with its own norms, should assign individuals to the same rank-order positions. If we look at an experiment involving interviewers, we shall see why we claim that the interview is neither valid nor reliable.

Eysenck records a situation where interviewers, whose daily routine included interviewing candidates for posts, were asked to place fifty-seven candidates in rank-order, on a given criterion. In an interview, such a criterion is usually suitability for a certain job, whether it be that of a professor, a commercial traveller, or a bus driver.

When the data from these interviewers was collected, it was found that one candidate was placed first in the rank-order by one interviewer and fifty-seventh by another. There have been similar examples when teachers have been asked to mark 'borderline' essays, i.e. essays to which a mark of, say, 50 per cent has already been given by one marker. In the re-marking, the same essay has been awarded marks as widely different as 20 per cent and 80 per cent.

To return to our interview experiment, it must be noted that the candidate, who appeared first and fifty-seventh on two rank-orders, was the same candidate, just as, in our essay-marking example, the essay, which received marks of 20, 50, and 80, was the same essay. The candidate and the essay are constants, so the variable (or error factor) must be the interviewer or the marker. And this happens even though experienced teachers are thought to be good at marking and experienced interviewers good at interviewing.

If we seek reasons for this inconsistency in interviewers, we can say, at once, that, in many interview situations, there are no valid criteria for selection. The interviewer knows that he is looking for a salesman or an assistant teacher, but he has no clear idea in his mind of the qualities he is seeking. He allows the candidate to impress him as a person. Now, it is quite possible for a man to be most charming, but a poor salesman. He lacks the tough-mindedness required for the hard sell. He may impress everyone with his personal charm, but that alone is not sufficient for the job under consideration. Interviewers often see candidates who are about to replace someone, and they are not always sure whether they wish the new man to be like the previous one or different from him. In addition to this, we tend to look favourably in interviews on people who are like ourselves. This may be all right if we are selecting someone for a similar job to our own, but not otherwise.

However, the fault does not lie entirely with the interviewer. Suppose that we are interviewing candidates for the post of sewing-machine operative. What qualities are we looking for? Even if we know the skills which a sewing-machine operative must have, can a face-to-face interview determine whether the applicant has these skills? It is easy to see, as with our power-station operatives. that a test of the necessary skills, produced as a result of job analysis, would reveal beyond doubt the answer to our question. But are verbal questions the best way to provide evidence of manual (performance) skills? Frequently we find the interviewer asking such futile questions as: 'Do you think you will like the job?' or 'Do you think you will be able to do the job?' The fact that the candidate is present

N

for interview strongly suggests that the answer to both questions will be 'Yes'.

Every interviewer builds up a picture of each candidate. This picture suggests suitability or unsuitability. But scarcely ever is an attempt made to check this picture against an external criterion. One obvious external criterion would be whether or not the applicant subsequently proves to be good at the job. Such validation of the interview would require the interviewer to list the qualities which caused him to draw a favourable picture of a successful applicant. Then, on the next occasion, he would have a list of qualities for which he would look. Scarcely any interviewers do this, each interview being treated in isolation.

Moreover, instead of obtaining precise and relevant criteria for validating the interview, we tend to choose irrelevant criteria. Jones stayed with the firm for thirty years; we therefore chose the right candidate at interview. But, in the course of those thirty years, no fewer than forty employees left the firm because they found it impossible to work with Jones. Again looking back, we find that Thomas, whom we appointed to a junior teaching post years ago when other members of the committee wanted Isaacs, is now a headmaster. On this evidence, we argue that we picked the right man. But did we? Was our task not to pick the best man for a junior teaching post, not the potential headmaster of fifteen years later? In any case, the two are not necessarily synonymous. The skills required to be a good teacher are not necessarily the same as those required to be a good headmaster.

From time to time, researchers do follow up interview selections, just as we saw that they follow up the predictions of the 'eleven plus' examination, to decide how valid the prediction is. We have already seen that some qualities are difficult to assess in an interview. Both these points are made by Iliffe in the following passage (1):

'It is common experience in British Universities that both headteachers' reports and interview assessments are poor predictors of academic success. Overall performance in school-leaving examinations generally shows a higher statistical relationship to results in final examinations, though not enough to justify the rigid cut-off level applied by some selectors.'

This quotation supports the point which we have previously made that a test of academic attainment (final leaving examination) is a better, or more valid, predictor of subsequent academic success than is the interview or headmasters' references or confidential reports. This is in line with our argument that we would be more likely to make a valid prediction of success in machine-operating by setting a machine-operating test, than by interviewing our prospective machine-operator.

However, we also saw that Jones, who was good at his job (i.e. he was able to perform the necessary manual operations), had certain defects of temperament which made it impossible for others to work with him. Such defects would not be revealed by a performance test, but they might suggest themselves at an interview.

In the first part of this book, we talked about a test battery. One such battery consisted of an intelligence test, tests of attainment in school subjects, and subjective teacher ratings. What we are now suggesting is that an interview may be much more satisfactory as part of a test battery than as the sole instrument of selection. While it often fails to tell us things which could be found by other means, it does tell us some things which it would otherwise be most difficult to discover, as we shall see when we consider the advantages of the interview (pp. 183–4).

We can illustrate the usefulness of items in a test battery quite simply. If we apply the Maudsley Personality Inventory to a candidate and obtain his N and E scores, we can give this information to the interviewer. If the candidate is strongly introverted, shy, or anxious, the interviewer can plan his interview strategy so as to get the best out of the candidate. If he takes a tough line, the candidate may become too nervous to do himself justice. On the other hand, to take a gentle line with a candidate who is highly extraverted and tough-minded might result in the interviewee taking over the dominant role in the interview and interviewing the interviewer. Conversely, the interviewer might think that he detected, in the interview, certain personality traits. By consulting the test scores, after the interview has been completed, he could obtain objective evidence which would either confirm or deny his impressions.

Much of the success or failure of the interview depends on the opening few minutes. If interviewer and interviewee establish rapport (good two-way communication) there is a good chance that the interview will be a pleasant experience for both. However, in some interview situations, both interviewer and interviewee impress each other so unfavourably at the outset that there is tension throughout the interview.

NECESSARY FUNCTIONS OF THE INTERVIEWER

Madge (2), talking about the use of interviews in social science investigations, states that the interviewer must discharge a number of duties, if valid interview results are to be obtained. These include:

1. Listening to the candidate in a friendly, patient, but intelligently critical manner.
2. Refraining from showing an authoritarian attitude and suggesting that his status as interviewer makes him superior and sets him at an advantage over the candidate.

3. Refraining from giving advice or moral instruction.
4. Avoiding asking questions in such a way that the candidate is compelled to give the reply which the interviewer wishes (3).
5. Avoiding prompting the candidate towards certain answers, when it is much more valuable to allow the candidate to give the information which he thinks fit. This may be much more revealing in the end.
6. Avoiding entering into argument with the candidate.
7. Using questions or statements in the interview only
   (*a*) to prompt the interviewee to talk freely and coherently. It is important that every interviewee be given this right in full. If he goes off at a tangent, he should be allowed a certain time to realize that he is entering irrelevant areas and given the chance to bring himself back on to the right track. If he fails to do this of his own accord, he should be gently guided back on to the right lines by the interviewer;
   (*b*) to congratulate the candidate on the quality of his answers, the originality of his ideas, and so on;
   (*c*) to clarify points on which there is uncertainty, and to ascertain precisely what the candidate means in places where the interviewer could interpret the candidate's remarks in a way detrimental to him.

WEAKNESSES IN INTERVIEW TECHNIQUE

Iliffe, in the work already mentioned, lists the following weaknesses in interview technique:

1. Lack of definite aim or purpose in the interview (this links with what we said about lack of clear selection criteria in the interviewer's mind).
2. Too many questions which can be answered monosyllabically, instead of allowing the candidate to develop a theme.
3. Asking questions which only elicit information already possessed by the interviewer through application forms, confidential reports, etc. Such questions merely indicate that the interviewer has no clear idea of procedure; for example, 'Ah, you are Mr Smith. I see that you come from Barnsley. Is that so?'
4. Asking the questions in such a way (including certain voice intonations) that the candidate is led to believe that the question must be *answered* in a certain way.
5. Pursuing a single question well beyond the stage where it serves any useful purpose, either as supplying information or establishing an opportunity for the candidate to show himself in a good light.
6. Restricting the time so much that there is no real chance of making maximum use of the interview possibilities.

7. Failing to develop one's own interview technique, which would be most effective in obtaining the essential information, and being unduly influenced by the views and techniques of other interviewers.
8. Failure by interviewers to discuss techniques of interviewing among themselves, and to determine what part each shall play as a member of the interview panel.

It is not denied that some people are, by nature, better interviewers than others. But, however skilful, he can still learn things which will improve his technique.

THE ADVANTAGES OF THE INTERVIEW

So far, most of the points we have made have stressed the imperfections of the interview. This does not mean, however, that it has no strong points, or that, in some cases, it may be not only the best but the only way of achieving a desired aim. The credit side of the interview can be summarized as follows:

1. The interview is a face-to-face situation, in which two people enter into a structured conversation. To this extent the interview is a familiar, real-life situation. It enables each side to have a look at the other. No employer would like to take on an employee without seeing him. Nor would an employee like to join a firm without meeting somebody from the firm.
2. The interview is a method acceptable to both sides, but the acceptability is often for the wrong reasons, sometimes for no better reason than that it is familiar. Nevertheless, an unacceptable selection method, e.g. tests of intelligence, could cause considerable initial tension which might impair performance.
3. The interview, especially the skilfully-handled interview, provides a highly flexible situation. Different approaches can be tried, and, if the candidate is unhappy with one approach, another can be tried. If the candidate is unhappy with a test, no such alterations in approach and content can be made.
4. The interview is relatively quick and economical.

The reliability of the interview has been shown to be no more than ·50 or ·60; the validity is even lower. There is also some evidence that the interview, far from increasing the predictive validity of a selection test battery, may actually decrease it. This means that, in some instances at least, we could place greater confidence in the correctness of the prediction if the interview did not take place at all. This suggests that the interview ought to be used less for predictive purposes than as a means of allowing the two sides to meet and exchange ideas.

THE QUESTIONNAIRE

The QUESTIONNAIRE has been described as a MASS INTERVIEW, or an INTERVIEW IN WRITING. Thus, it may be said that the questionnaire resembles the group test, while the interview has more in common with the individual test. The three most familiar questionnaires are probably the annual income return for the Inland Revenue, the Registrar-General's census form, and the opinion poll.

These questionnaires are all useful illustrations of the two main reasons for using the technique to gather information. The return of income and the census form both seek factual information. The person concerned must declare the amount and sources of his income, and details about himself and the composition of his family and household. In the opinion poll the person completing the questionnaire is asked to state his opinions, beliefs, or preferences. The questions in such a setting are often hypothetical, since the person is not immediately required to put what he says into practice. He may be asked, for instance: 'If there were a General Election tomorrow, would you vote (*a*) Conservative, (*b*) Labour, (*c*) Liberal, (*d*) Communist?'

We can see that, while the reply is indicative of something, in particular of the person's political persuasions, there is no guarantee that he would actually vote in the way he says. People tend to change their minds over a period of time for various reasons which the reader can fill in from his own experience. Asking a single question, then, may prompt a reply reflecting a temporary or a permanent state of mind or belief, just as a personality questionnaire may prompt answers reflecting a stable personality trait or a less stable one.

Even the seemingly 'factual' questions in the opinion poll are not so much questions requiring a factual answer as ones requiring us to make a value judgment. We may, for instance, be asked: 'Do you think that Mr X or Mr Y would make the better Prime Minister?' Recalling what we said earlier (see Chapter 3) about subjectivity and objectivity we realize that our answers to this type of question are subjective.

CONSTRUCTING A QUESTIONNAIRE

It is important to consider the construction of a questionnaire for two main reasons. Firstly, the teacher during his career is much more likely to want to construct a questionnaire for his own use than an objective test of intelligence or personality. Secondly, the construction of a questionnaire seems deceptively simple. In fact, those who attempt it, soon realize that it is by no means as simple as it appears at first sight. The reason for this is that, although we ask questions every day of our lives, we often ask them very badly. Students will no doubt recall that, during their periods of teaching practice, they have been criticized by their tutors for not asking questions effectively. What we are asking is so obvious to us, because we know the answer, that we forget that the answer is far from obvious to the person questioned. Because of this, our questions are not put clearly.

When we study linear programming (4), we learn how to ask questions. A question in such a programme is phrased to ensure that it is virtually impossible for the learner to give the wrong answer (5). The information is given in what is known as a 'frame', consisting of between ten and twenty-five words, and is followed by a 'question', usually in the form of a statement, in which the learner is required to fill in a blank. A very elementary example of 'frame' and 'question' would be:

'In 55 BC, Julius Caesar invaded Britain with a large army.
Julius Caesar invaded Britain in — — — —.

Two points should be noted: first, the wording of the information in the frame and the wording of the question are very similar – a form of cueing; secondly, there is another form of cueing in the layout of the blank, which corresponds exactly with the date to be filled in, full stops and all.

It is a mistake to think that a question in a questionnaire will always produce the right answer. It may produce the answer in the required form in ninety-nine out of a hundred cases. But in the hundredth case, the answer given will show that the question, for one candidate at least, was ambiguous. A simple example will illustrate this point. When confronted by the question: 'Do you vote Labour or Conservative?', most people would answer either, 'Labour' or 'Conservative'. But it is possible to answer, 'Yes' to this question without being either wrong or stupid. For example, there may be a person who, in the last six general elections, has four times voted Conservative and twice Labour. He has voted in only six elections, and the idea of voting Liberal has never occurred to him. Such a person would be perfectly entitled to answer the question with 'Yes'. To remove all possibility of ambiguity, we must reword the question: 'In a General Election do you generally vote (*a*) Conservative (*b*) Labour (*c*) Liberal (*d*) For some other party?'

OPEN AND CLOSED QUESTIONS

It is clear that in a questionnaire there can be two types of question: OPEN-ENDED (sometimes called just OPEN) and CLOSED (or FIXED

ALTERNATIVE). We cannot say that one type is right and the other wrong, but that both types have their merits, depending on the situation in which they are used. If we wish to give the person answering free rein, so that we can afterwards analyse his words for significant details or patterns, we use open questions. If, on the other hand, we wish to limit the directions of the replies, we use the fixed alternative question. Perhaps we have run a course in Modern Mathematics and decide to use a questionnaire to obtain audience reaction to it. When we planned the course we had a number of aims in mind, and, not unnaturally, we wish to know to what extent we were successful in achieving them. To determine this, we would normally ask a number of fixed alternative questions.

However, at the very end of the questionnaire, we may want to include one question which allows free expression of opinion, to obtain an indication of what the audience would like in future courses. So we might ask:

'Kindly make any observations (either favourable or unfavourable) about this course, which are not covered by the other questions.'

and:

'If we were to run another course on Modern Mathematics, what features would you particularly like to see included?'

Note the use of the words 'favourable' and 'unfavourable' in the first question. One may obtain one set of responses to a questionnaire if it is answered anonymously, and another set if the respondent is required to place his name at the top of the paper. This applies especially to adverse comments. It is particularly important to let respondents remain anonymous if delicate topics are being examined. Many people will fabricate favourable comments if their names are disclosed. The same people may well give most enlightening unfavourable comments if they are permitted to remain anonymous.

There are times when it is not possible to let people remain anonymous, because we wish to repeat the questionnaire later, to see if their views have changed. For example, we may give to applicants entering colleges of education a questionnaire relating to attitudes to teaching. It might include such questions as:

'Do you think teachers are born and not made?'
'Do you think that teaching-machines are just expensive gimmicks?'

Subsequently, say, towards the end of the three-year course, we may wish to put these same questions again to see whether, in the light of what they have learned on the course, the students have changed their minds. We may also wish to compare the answers they gave when the questionnaire was included in the entry-test battery (when they were trying to obtain places in college) with the answers they give when they know that they have obtained places. In such a situation, it is necessary to know the names of the respondents.

We can sum up the advantages and disadvantages of open and closed questions as follows: The open question is effective in showing the respondent's attitude to a situation, since the words he uses to answer the question are his own. We have seen that there is the possibility of his not understanding the question or the situation to which it refers, but this will be revealed in his answer. The wording of the answer may also be helpful by revealing something about an individual or a group of individuals. The writer once carried out a research where children were required to translate passages of Latin (6) using three methods and types of aid. At the end of the test period, they were asked:

'Have you found the method helpful? If the answer is "Yes", state in what particular ways it helped you.'

One child wrote: 'I found the method helpful, but I can't say how.' Another wrote: 'I don't get higher marks in class for translation, but I feel more confident.'

The first reply shows that many fifteen-year-olds find it difficult to put their thoughts into words. They have feelings, but cannot always clearly express them. The second reply was most revealing, showing that, although the expected improvement, i.e. in marks obtained, did not occur, the method had been valuable, because it increased the pupil's confidence when translating Latin. There is always the possibility that such increased confidence will lead to higher marks eventually.

Again, the wording of open questions is less stereotyped and nearer to the wording of everyday expressions than is the closed question. This may have its effect on the respondent's answer, e.g. by producing greater spontaneity. More spontaneous reactions are nearer to true reactions than non-spontaneous reactions produced by heavy cueing. In this respect, closed questions can be classified as 'leading' or 'loaded' questions.

Closed questions produce greater uniformity of response. This makes for easier analysis of the replies. The closed question attempts to standardize the method of reply so that a standardized method of answer analysis can be provided. Closed questions ought to reduce the number of 'non-responses', the reactions of those who do not understand the question. They should also reduce the number of irrelevant responses often elicited by open questions from those who miss the point of the question.

It is advisable to present a standard pattern of closed questions, that is, it is not a good idea to have some YES/NO answers, some with four alternative answers, and some with three, plus the odd question with five alternatives. Such a mixture makes marking more difficult, as well as presenting a confused pattern to the respondent. He becomes used, after the first few questions, to the *a*, *b*, *c* format or the always, sometimes, never format.

Whichever type of question is used, the instructions at the beginning must be clear. The questioner must also decide whether he wishes to disclose the real reason for setting the questionnaire or to give an alleged reason, as we saw with the 16 P.F. Test (Chapter 7).

SUMMARY OF POINTS FOR CONSTRUCTING A QUESTIONNAIRE

Evans (7) makes four simple but vital points for those constructing questionnaires. They really amount to a formulation of aims by the constructor:

1. To have perfectly clear in his own mind, and subsequently to convey to the respondent, the purpose of the questionnaire (but see point about 16 P.F. Test above).
2. To decide, in the light of this purpose, precisely what information is required.
3. To analyse this information into its component parts and make sure that the questions within each part are consistent. We saw this principle applied to main areas and sub-areas of knowledge when constructing objective tests (Chapter 3).
4. To ensure that the questions are so worded that they will stimulate the answer required.

The reader should note that this fourth point is really saying that questions must be valid, or that, in order to be valid, questions must actually ask what they are intended to ask. The technical term for this is ITEM VALIDITY. Note also that item-inconsistency is likely to affect both the validity and the reliability of the questionnaire.

Phillips (8) gives the following guidelines for determining the order of questions:

1. On a given topic, general questions should usually precede specific questions. In the FUNNEL TECHNIQUE, the initial questions for each section are open and the remaining (specific) questions are closed. (Note that this combination produces a regular, not a random, pattern.)
2. The sequence of questions should follow the same logical order. It is bad practice to cause the respondent to make abrupt transitions from one thread, or theme, to another. Such transitions will be likely to affect his answers. The time sequence is a simple logical sequence,

i.e. questions are asked about the past, present, and future, in that order. Readers will note that this is closely related to our own point about consistency of format (p. 187). The constructor should always ensure that his questions follow the PARABLE TECHNIQUE, i.e. proceeding from the familiar to the unfamiliar, from the concrete and simple to the abstract and complex.

3. Care should be taken to avoid questions the content of which may antagonize the respondent and colour his answers to subsequent questions, or even cause him to refuse to answer them. Such questions would probably be about religion, income, sex, etc.

Finally, in this section we can make four essential points for those who use the questionnaire as a fact-finding technique:

1. Seek the minimum of information which is meaningful in the circumstances.
2. Ask questions which you are reasonably sure all respondents can answer.
3. Provide questions which can be answered by writing 'yes' or 'no', or by deleting one or the other, or by underlining or ticking one of a number of alternatives.
4. Omit any question which allows a biased answer.

THE QUINTAMENSIONAL PLAN

In order to produce a questionnaire as free as possible from the defects mentioned so far in this chapter, a technique known as the QUINTAMEN-SIONAL PLAN (because it has five parts or elements) has been devised. It relates to question-design, and the stages are as follows:

1. Begin with the information stage (to be used as a screening or filter process). This may require the construction of a short pre-test before the main test. The preliminary questionnaire will indicate whether the people answering it have considered the issues involved. In the preliminary questionnaire, the tester may wish to follow-up 'yes' items with further investigation.
2. In stage two open-ended questions are used, to allow the respondent to answer in his own words.
3. In the third stage, closed questions are asked.
4. In the fourth stage, follow-up items are used. These may be in written or oral form. The aim is to see why the person holds the views expressed. The process is technically termed REASON ANALYSIS (9).
5. This stage may be termed a 'pressure interview', to see whether the

subject (respondent) can be persuaded, under pressure, to alter his views. The technique is thus designed to determine the tenacity with which the person holds his views.

It must be stressed that the average teacher may neither desire, nor have the time available for such a lengthy process as the Quintamensional Plan. It is included here to show just how much work is required if we are to make the questionnaire as reliable a technique as possible. The reader should recall to what lengths Binet, for example, went to ensure item validity in his test.

BIAS IN THE QUESTIONNAIRE

Before we examine the problem of bias in the questionnaire, it is necessary to say a word about alternative methods of administering this type of test. These can be classified as follows:

1. The whole process is carried out by post. Questionnaires are sent out to the sample by post, and a covering letter and a stamped and addressed envelope are included. In many cases, a preliminary letter, designed to discover whether the people concerned are willing to cooperate, is advisable. The sample may have been a random sample, taken from, say, a list of members of a science teachers' organization.
2. The whole process is carried out in person. The compiler of the questionnaire, either alone, or accompanied by helpers, who have been taught a standardized procedure for the questionnaire, delivers them to the sample, explains how he wishes the questionnaire to be filled in, superintends the filling in (answering any questions which arise), and collects the papers.
3. A combination of methods 1 and 2. In the General Census, the forms are sent to householders. Subsequently, workers who have been carefully instructed in procedure, call to collect the forms and give any assistance which is needed to interpret the form and its questions. (It is quite surprising how even supposedly intelligent people react to a questionnaire.)

It should be noted that, in this third method, the tester may, especially with mature people, distribute the questionnaire in person, allow the respondents to go away and complete it, and later collect it from them. It should be stressed that this method also poses problems. There will always be some who fail to fill in the questionnaire, either because they have forgotten, or because they have not had time, just as there will always be those who will fail to return it by post. If we distribute 100 questionnaires, and receive only sixty back, we cannot ignore the outstanding forty. To ignore them would result in bias, since we shall make the same conclusions from a sample of sixty as we would from a sample of 100.

Consequently, we can say that bias, in a questionnaire, results from ignoring nil responses or from wrong sampling.

In Chapter 1, we considered various methods of sampling. We saw, for example, that different results will be produced by entirely random sampling within groups which proportionately represent the areas of society from which they come. Bias from sampling error, in questionnaire investigations, occurs when the tester does not make certain at the outset that the method used to select his sample is completely suitable for his purposes. If we want to obtain a picture of the views of people in general, our sample must be typical of people in general. If we wish to compare the views and attitudes of working class and middle-class, we must ensure that our samples are typical of working-class and middle-class people.

If it is important in representative sampling, to ensure that the same proportion from each of the classes investigated is included in the sample, it is also important to attempt to estimate what the replies to the questionnaire would be from those people who fail to return it.

In 1946 certain figures relating to the births of children were obtained in the Census. D. V. Glass, examining the data, found that 230,000 forms had not been returned, representing 17 per cent of the total number sent out, or a reduction of 17 per cent in sample size. A reminder was sent to each of the 230,000 people concerned, and this produced another 50,000 returned forms, but there still remained 180,000 unaccounted for, representing a 12 per cent reduction in the size of the original sample. Glass now made a distinction between the 180,000 and the original 230,000, deciding that those who failed to return the form after a reminder were more like those who returned the form after being reminded, than those who needed no reminder.

Since Glass was examining the birth statistics, he was able to check the correctness of his assumption against an external criterion, just as it was possible to check the predictive validity of the 'eleven plus' against the external criterion of the 'O'-level examination. Glass discovered that the figures, which he obtained after adjustment in the light of his assumption, came closer to the true figures than the unadjusted figures did. In other words, his derived score was closer to the correct answer than the raw score. Thus, he obtained proof that to interpret an 83 per cent return as if it were a 100 per cent return is unjustified.

COMPARISON OF INTERVIEW AND QUESTIONNAIRE

The following points of comparison can be made between the interview and the questionnaire:

i. *Cost:* although we have suggested that the interview can tell us important things about a person, it is only feasible to interview small numbers. Group tests of intelligence represent a great saving in time over individual tests; similarly, there is a saving in money as well as time if we send out questionnaires to obtain the views of several thousand people.

ii. *Standardization:* the questionnaire is in a standardized form. It is worded in exactly the same way for each individual. Interviewers do not always use the same words, nor the same intonation in dealing with different candidates. The manner of asking the questions in an interview is determined by the impression which the candidate makes on the interviewer. On this score alone, it is impossible to standardize interview procedure.

iii. *Flexibility:* the interview, provided that it is well handled, is much more flexible than the questionnaire. A person may not understand the question in either situation, but, in the interview, it can be rephrased. Similar help can be given when the questionnaire is used only if the tester is present when the questionnaire is completed.

iv. *Motivation:* we are generally motivated to make a good impression on an interviewer. It is quite possible to be entirely lacking in motivation to complete a questionnaire. This is a similar impersonal situation to that where people are expected to learn from a teaching-machine. People may even put down wrong or facetious answers (especially to open questions) from a sense of frustration.

SUMMING UP

We hope we have shown in this chapter that both the interview and the questionnaire require very careful handling. It is easy to conduct an interview or a questionnaire badly; it is difficult to do either well.

Both the interviewer and the user of the questionnaire ought to be fully conversant with the techniques necessary to produce good results. It is useless to suppose that because a person can talk, he can interview, or that because anyone can ask questions, everybody can construct a good questionnaire.

We have seen that the interview has poor validity and reliability. There is little more guarantee that the questionnaire, even when properly handled, is any more valid and reliable. For this reason, only tentative generalizations should be made from the data of questionnaires. Even when people make every effort to answer the questions properly, many unconsciously produce either dramatized or stereotyped answers.

Consequently, both techniques must be handled with great care. In both cases the real difficulties are in inverse proportion to the apparent simplicity of the technique.

NOTES AND REFERENCES FOR CHAPTER 9

1 Iliffe, A. H., *The Foundation Year in the University of Keele* (Unpublished research report, 1962–4).
2 Madge, J., *The Tools of Social Science* (Longmans, Green & Co., 1953).
3 Further discussion of this point is undertaken in Schofield, H., *The Philosophy of Education*, op. cit.
4 For a comparison between a linear programme and a lesson, see Schofield, H., *A Teachers' Guide to Lesson Preparation* (Normal Press, 1972). In a 'linear programme, the information is given in a single sequence of frames, each of which follows on directly from the previous one. The alternative method of producing a programme is to make a branching programme, in which the learner is sent down side-lines, either to give him further opportunity to understand a point which he has missed, or to follow up a main point with examples. The two types of programme can be represented diagrammatically:

linear

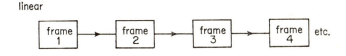

Branching

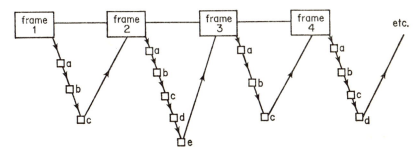

5 B. F. Skinner believes that learning takes place most effectively when the learner is prevented from making mistakes. This is the opposite view to that of the popular philosophy that 'we learn by our mistakes'. Skinner argues that any wrong response is bad because it may be the first step to the

194 | *Assessment and Testing*

establishment of a wrong habit. If we continue to make the wrong response, the response becomes habituated, just as right responses become habituated. Therefore, argues Skinner, we must ensure as far as possible that only right responses are made. So, when we construct a programme, we validate it by trying it out on a sample, chosen on the criteria of age and ability. We retain only those questions which 90 per cent or more of the sample answer correctly. If an item is answered by less than this percentage, the question is considered to be invalid, and must be restructured or replaced. For further information about B. F. Skinner, the reader should consult Morrish, Ivor, *Disciplines of Education* (George Allen & Unwin, 1967).

6 Schofield, H., *Latin by Stave Analysis; a Linguistic Approach to Grammar and Translation* (Educational Explorers, 1969).
7 Evans, K. M., *Planning a Small-scale Research; a Practical Guide for Teachers and Students* (NFER, 1968).
8 Phillips, B. S., *Social Research: Strategy and Tactics* (New York, Macmillan, 1966).
9 The idea of reason-analysis comes from Paul F. Lazarfeld. An appraisal of the idea can be found in Zeisel, H., *Say it with Figures* (Harper & Row, 1957).

Chapter 10

Points to note in choosing tests; examples of tests

We have already stressed that the first decision which must be made before any test is used, is whether a teacher-made or a standardized (commercially produced) test is the more suitable. We have also outlined points for and against the selection of both types of test. Teachers who intend to construct their own tests will find most helpful information about technique and procedure in Green, J. A., *Teacher-Made Tests* (Harper & Row, 1963).

Those who decide to use commercially produced tests should always make sure of the following points:

1. *The precise name of the test*
It is essential, for instance, to distinguish between the Army Alpha Test and the Army Beta Test. Similarly, the Eysenck Personality Inventory, the Eysenck-Withers Personality Inventory, and the Junior Eysenck Personality Inventory all differ in detail and, consequently, in test content, age-range, etc.

2. *The exact content of the test*
For example, the Binet test is largely verbal, while the Pintner-Paterson Performance Scale is a non-verbal test, the content of which includes object-assembly, form boards, Healy pictures, etc.

3. *The exact aim and purpose of the test*
Some tests are of general ability, some of special ability, some of scholastic aptitude. Sometimes the aim of the test is indicated by the title: the Cattell (SRA) Test of Primary Mental Abilities, the Morrisby Tests of General Ability, the California First-Year Mental Scale; but others, for example A.H.4 and A.H.5 (also known as the HEIM tests), and the Lorge-Thorndike Intelligence Tests do not. Tests may also be prognostic or diagnostic, clinical or non-clinical (1).

4. *The precise age range for which the test is intended*
Some tests supply this information in the title. Some tests are for a specific and limited age-range only, e.g. the Cattell Infant Intelligence Scale, and

o

the California First-Year Mental Scale, while others such as the Stanford-Binet test, are applicable to a much wider age-range. Similarly, A.H.4 and A.H.5 give no clue to the age-range. Both are applicable to adults, but A.H.4 is useful for a general cross-section of the population, while A.H.5 is for use with very able adults, e.g. entrants to the professions and universities.

5. *The validity and reliability of the test*
These details should always be shown in the test manual, for example:

'These scores correlate approximately ·45 with grades and, combined with an ability test, yield a predictive validity of about ·60. The test can be faked and is not recommended as an admissions test.'

or

'The short scales have extremely low reliability (·40 to ·45) and the information on norms is unsatisfactory. Not recommended for the assessment of individuals.'

6. *The norms of the test*
We suggested a major area of norms when we talked about the age-range suitability of tests. The age-range norm is the mean score for children of a given age. The ages may be given in whole years 7;0: 8;0, half years 7;6: 8;6, or some other division such as two months – 8;0: 8;2: 8;4: 8;6. In each test we are interested in:

    a. The age of the sample tested (in standardizing the test)
    b. Mean score of the sample tested (in standardizing the test)
    c. Standard deviation from the mean (in standardizing the test)
    d. Number in the sample used to provide the norms
    e. Composition of the sample; local, regional, national, international.

7. *Number of tests available for the purpose in mind*
If there are several tests with *apparently* the same purpose and content, these should be carefully examined, to see whether they are *in reality* the same.

If the teacher decides that one is much the same as another in aim and content, he should check with the test manual to see if one was validated with a larger sample than the other, is credited with greater validity and reliability.

8. *Should more than one test be used for a specific purpose?*
Whether or not to seek a second opinion rests with the teacher and whether he thinks that he can obtain more information from more than one test than from one. Great care must, however, be taken for example not to use two tests of general intelligence with different norms (e.g. the

Stanford-Binet Test and the Wechsler Adult Intelligence Scale) or two tests of general intelligence both using the same measure (e.g. I.Q.) but having different means and standard deviations.

9. *How much skill and time are needed for proper use of the test?*
This is a most important point. We saw that it is very easy to produce and use a bad questionnaire, less easy to produce a good one and handle it correctly. Even if we use a commercially-produced test, we shall not obtain the best results unless we know the best way of administering it and have the time to mark it and analyse the information which the marks give us. In this respect, it may be necessary to retain information from test data over, say, ten years, before a picture which has really important implications begins to emerge.

10. *How much cost is entailed in purchasing tests?*
The cost of a single test may appear to be low. However, some tests are sold in lots of twenty-five, which means that even a test costing 5p involves an outlay of £1·25. In many instances, we require more than one batch; to test forty children in a class would involve the purchase of fifty tests and an outlay of £2·50. Since most pencil and paper tests can be used only once, the expense is a recurring one.

To help illustrate the importance of these points, a selection of tests is given below. The list is not exhaustive, nor must it be assumed that these tests are, automatically, the best in the area indicated by their titles.

1. *Tests of general ability*
Stanford-Binet Test: age-range $2\frac{1}{2}$ to superior adult.
Pintner-Paterson Performance Scale: age-range 4–16; results depend heavily on speed.
Otis Quick-scoring Mental Abilities Test: subdivided into alpha section-grades 1–4; beta section-grades 4–9; gamma section-grades 9–16. Scores are valid predictors of school achievement. The score is an I.Q. The alpha section does not require reading skill.
Gesell Development Schedules: age-range 4 weeks to 6 years; tests: *a.* motor; *b.* adaptive; *c.* language; *d.* personal/social behaviour. Described by Anastasi as a refinement of the qualitative observations routinely made by pediatricians.

2. *Tests of aptitude and ability*
Morrisby Differential Test Battery: for grammar school and university samples, especially those with natural mechanical aptitude, rather than with the principles of mechanics.
A.C.E.R. Speed and Accuracy Tests: tests: number-checking, name-checking, classification skill in subjects; 13 years of age and above.

A.C.E.R. Mechanical Comprehension and Mechanical Reasoning Tests: separate answer sheets are provided so that test booklets may be re-used. If candidates scribble on the booklets, however, the accuracy of the subsequent tests may be affected. Age-range, 13 years and over.
Scholastic Aptitude Test: by R. A. C. Oliver, for University applicants: Verbal and Mathematical Sub-tests.

Vision Tests
Farnsworth Dichotomous Test for Colour Blindness: distinguishes between functional colour blindness and moderately defective colour vision.

Art Aptitude Test
Graves Design Judgment Test and Meier Art Judgment Tests: the former is used for guidance and selection and requires the appraisal of ninety sets of two- and three-dimensional designs, the latter requires the evaluation of 100 pairs of pictures as a test of artistic principles.

3. Miscellaneous aptitude tests
Moss/Hunt Test of Social Intelligence, designed to test:
    a. judgment in social situations
    b. recognition of mental states of speaker
    c. memory for names and faces
    d. presence or lack of sense of humour
Watson/Gleser Critical Thinking Appraisal Test, measures ability:
    a. to draw inferences
    b. to recognize implied assumptions
    c. to apply deductive reasoning
    d. to judge relevance of an argument

4. Attainment tests
Carlton Picture Intelligence Test: for children passing from infants to junior school; scores as I.Q. standardized on 30,000 children.
Moray House Picture Intelligence Test (M.H.T(pic) 1): norms for children between $6\frac{1}{2}$ and 8 years; standardization same as for famous Moray House test for top junior age-range.
Southgate Group Reading Test: word selection and sentence completion tests for 7;0 to 9;6 age-range.
Manchester (Wiseman/Wrigley) Tests: age-range 14–16 years, and standardized for 14,000 children: useful for guidance at 15 plus, and consist of:
    Manchester Mechanical Arithmetic Test (senior)
    Manchester Reading Comprehension Test (senior)
    Manchester General Ability Test (senior)
    Manchester Graded Ability Test (senior)

Northumberland Standardized Tests: work of Sir Cyril Burt to test (in pupils in the 10–14 age-range):

 a. Arithmetical ability
 b. Ability in English
 c. Intelligence

5. *Personality and attitude tests*

The Bristol Guides of Social Adjustment: a clinical (1) test battery.

Eysenck Personality Inventory: provides neuroticism/extraversion scores for adults.

Eysenck/Withers Personality Inventory: produces same dimensional results as the above for the I.Q. range 50–80 (subnormal).

Junior Eysenck Personality Inventory: adapted from Eysenck Personality Inventory for use with 7–15-year-olds; norms given for 10,000 school children and groups in child guidance clinics.

6. *Diagnostic tests*

Standard Reading Tests, Daniels and Diack: text-book published by Chatto and Windus, containing various tests of backwardness in reading in the junior school.

English Picture Vocabulary Test 2: for age-range 7 – 12 years.

Raven's Coloured Progressive Matrices: for age-range 6–11 years.

Frostig Programme of Tests of Perception: details from NFER.

Royal National Institute for the Deaf Picture Card Test: simple means of discovering if hearing acuity is average, or if full otological examination is necessary.

Wepman Auditory Discrimination Test: details from NFER.

NOTES FOR CHAPTER 10

The term 'clinical', applied to a test, means that the test is one administered by experts in a clinic to groups of deviant patients. Eysenck, working at the Maudsley Hospital's psychiatric unit, found that neurotics gave different answers from normal people on personality inventories. Clinical tests are diagnostic. Non-clinical tests are the tests, such as we have mentioned throughout this book, which are used in schools, colleges, universities, industry and commerce for the measurement and selection of normal people.

A very useful book is *Tests for Guidance and Assessment, 1969*, published by NFER and obtainable from: Ginn & Co. (Test Services) Ltd, 18 Bedford Row, London, W.C.1. NFER tests may be ordered by members of the teaching profession on the production of a written authority from their Head Teacher. Students requiring tests for research should obtain the written authority of their supervisor.

Chapter 11

Glossary of the main technical terms used in this book

Ability test: a test designed to show the individual's present level of efficiency in a specific area, e.g. comprehension of words.

Achievement test: a test designed to show to what extent the person tested has achieved the objectives of a particular course. 'Backwardness' can be defined as 'underachievement', usually in the area of one or more basic skill, e.g. reading.

Age norms: the average (mean) score produced on any test by samples selected according to age.

Aptitude: the potentiality to succeed in a particular area of activity; aptitude tests are designed to show which individuals are likely to benefit from training in a given occupational area, or area of schoolwork.

Battery (test battery): a group of tests with scores standardized on the same population, used as a totality on subsequent populations. A test battery might consist of a test of general ability, an objective test of English, an essay-type test, a test of arithmetical ability. The purpose of the battery, as distinct from a single test, is to increase the predictive validity (see also 'validity').

Correlation: the degree of sameness in two people, items, situations, etc. Perfect correlation (never found) is identity, and is represented symbolically by +1. Perfect negative correlation (complete oppositeness) is represented by −1. Correlation (represented symbolically by *r*) is always shown in the form: $r = \cdot895$ or $r = -\cdot325$.

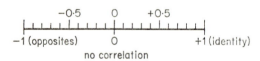

Continuum: a line, or scale, between two extremes or poles. +1 and −1 are the poles of a correlation continuum and ·895 and −·325 are points on the continuum. Another well-known continuum is that of Cattell's bi-polar factors of personality, where the poles might be surgency and desurgency. Life is a continuum between birth and death, and one's age represents a point on this continuum.

Criterion: a standard against which performance is evaluated, or a judgment or selection made. An external criterion is some standard outside a test (such as the 'O'-level examination) against which the predictive validity of the test is measured. In this case, the test would be the 'eleven plus'.

Culture-bias: the effect which living in a particular environment has on an individual's test score. The culture-bias of verbal tests of intelligence is that they tend to favour middle-class children. Tests designed for western children would be culture-biased against, say, Pakistani children.

Diagnostic test: a test used to diagnose weakness in specific areas of achievement or personality.

General ability: often referred to simply as intelligence. It is the ability to deal successfully with a wide variety and range of problem situations.

Group test: a test administered by a single tester to a number of candidates simultaneously.

Halo effect: the tendency to rate an individual as good or bad on all criteria because he appears good or bad on one; failure to be sufficiently analytical in one's judgment.

Histogram: a graphic representation of mark or score distribution in column form instead of curve form.

Mental age: a method of measuring the people taking the Binet Test. It represents the age for which the candidate's score is typical or average. Mental age can be the same as, greater than, or less than the candidate's physical age.

Multiple-choice test: a test in which there are a number of alternative answers to each question.

Non-verbal test: a test whose items consist of symbols, diagrams, pictures. Such tests are useful, for example, with children before they can read, deaf children, and immigrants.

Normal curve of distribution: a curve of probability which is symmetrical about its mean (which is also the mid-point of the scale or continuum). Approximately two-thirds of the population lie between one standard deviation above the mean ($+1$ SD) and one standard deviation below the mean (-1 SD).

Objective test: a test which will give the same score for any individual, regardless of who marks it, since the marks awarded are predetermined and cannot be influenced by the preferences or prejudices of the marker.

Performance test: a test requiring motor or manual responses, as distinct from verbal or paper-and-pencil responses.

Prognostic test: a test which prognosticates future performance in the light of present evidence.

Projective test: a test of personality where the subject is presented with a verbal or visual stimulus or pictorial situation and is allowed to read into the situation what he wishes. What he reads in gives a clue to the cause of maladjustment.

Random sample: a sample chosen from the population so that each person has an equal chance of being selected; a sample not selected according to specific criteria.

Rating-scale: a continuum of *n* points (usually 3, 5, or 7) on which a person can be rated or assessed.

Raw score: the actual score obtained by an individual on a test, not adjusted by use of statistical techniques.

Recall: the production of an answer by an act of memory.

Recognition: producing the right answer from a number of given alternatives by recognizing its rightness.

Reliability: the extent to which a test is self-consistent, and will give comparable results when applied to the same person on a number of occasions.

Skew: the amount of deviation of a distribution curve from a symmetrical distribution. Skew may be positive (mean score below the mid-point of the scale) or negative (mean score above the mid-point).

Sociogram: a diagrammatic representation, using certain conventional symbols, of social relationships between individuals. It reveals such phenomena as social adjustment and maladjustment or internal group cohesion, and is used in sociometry.

Sociometry: the measurement of interpersonal associations and degree of social adjustment.

Special ability: an ability in a specific area, as distinct from overall or general ability.

Speed test: a test where the individual is required to answer a certain number of questions in a given time.

Standard deviation (SD): measure of distribution of scores about the mean.

Subjective marking (also called impression marking): a system of marking which can be altered according to the prevailing attitude or opinion of the marker.

Validity: the extent to which a test measures what it claims to measure. Predictive validity is the degree of success in predicting what the test claims to predict.

Verbal test: a test which asks questions in words and is designed to test the individual's comprehension of words and of problem situations expressed verbally.

Z-score (*also called standard score*): a score derived from a raw score on a given test. By deriving the standard score from the raw score on *n* tests, a comparison can be made between the individual's performance on any one test and on all the other tests.

Bibliography

Which books students read as a follow-up to the present volume will be determined by the particular interests they have developed and the specific needs they have acquired. The list given below is intended to cover the range of assessment and testing discussed in this book without involving the reader in highly technical works.

BOOKS

GENERAL MEASUREMENT (Chapter 1)
Remmers, H. H., Gage, N. L. and Rummel, J. Francis, *A Practical Introduction to Measurement and Evaluation* (Harper International Student Reprint, 2nd ed., 1966).

TECHNIQUES OF TEST CONSTRUCTION (Chapter 2)
Green, J. A., *Teacher-made Tests* (Harper & Row, 1963).

OBJECTIVE TESTS (Chapter 3)
Macintosh, H. G. and Morrison, R. B., *Objective Testing* (Unibooks, 1968).

INTELLIGENCE AND ATTAINMENT TEST ITEMS (Chapters 4 & 5)
Vernon, P. E., *Intelligence and Attainment Tests* (U.L.P., 1960).

PERSONALITY: MOTIVATION AND PROJECTION TESTS (Chapters 6 & 7)
Anderson, H. H. and G. L., *An Introduction to Projective Techniques* (Prentice-Hall, 1951).
Cattell, R. B. and Warburton, F. W., *Objective Personality and Motivation Tests: A Theoretical Introduction and Practical Compendium* (University of Illinois Press, 1966).

SOCIOMETRIC MEASUREMENT (Chapter 8)
Gronlund, N. E., *Sociometry in the Classroom* (Harper & Row, 1959).
Northway, M. L., *A Primer of Sociometry* (University of Toronto Press, 1952).

SOCIOLOGICAL TECHNIQUES INCLUDING INTERVIEW AND QUESTIONNAIRE (Chapter 9)
Moser, C. A., *Survey Methods in Social Investigation* (Heinemann, 1958).

ARTICLES

A most important source of information on assessment and testing is the *British Journal of Educational Psychology* (*B.J.E.P.*). By reading this journal students can apprise themselves of past researches and keep abreast of current developments.

ARTICLES ON BASIC TERMS AND PRINCIPLES IN ASSESSMENT AND
TESTING (Part 1)

Reliability and Validity
Wiseman, Stephen, 'Reliability and Validity', XXVI, III, 172.

Bias
Farrell, M. J. and Gilbert, N., 'A type of bias in marking examination scripts',
XXX, I, 47.

Validation against External Criterion
Nisbet, J. and Buchan, J., 'The long-term follow-up of assessments at age
eleven', XXIX, I, 1.

Rating-scales: Norms
Kamat, V. V., 'A revision of the Binet scale for Indian children', IV, III, 296.
Sandon, F., 'Categories in rating scales – how many and how big?', XXIX, II,
155.
Vernon, P. E., 'A study of the norms and validity of certain mental tests at a
child guidance clinic', Part I: VII, I, 72; Part II: VII, II, 115.

ARTICLES DEALING WITH TYPES OF TESTS AND METHODS OF TESTING
(Part 2)

Subjective and Objective Tests and Marking
Edwards Penfold, D. M., *Symposium*: the use of essays in selection at eleven
plus; 'Essay marking experiments – shorter and longer essays', XXVI, II,
128.
Peel, E. A. and Armstrong, H. G., 'The predictive power of English composition in the eleven-plus examination', XXVI, III, 163.
Lawley, D. N. and Pilliner, A. E. G., 'A critical note on the above', XXVII, II,
142.
Pidgeon, D. A. and Yates, A., 'Experimental inquiries into the use of essay-
type English papers', XXVII, I, 37.

Bagley, D., 'A critical survey of objective estimates in the teaching of English',
Part I: VII, I, 57; Part II: VII, II, 138.
Cast, B. M. D., 'The efficiency of different methods of marking English
compositions', IX, III, 257; and X, I, 49.
Finlayson, D. S., 'The reliability of marking essays', XXI, II, 126.
Robertson, R. K. and Tryhorn, F. G., 'Objective test form in a School
Certificate examination', VII, II, 156.
Sandon, F., 'The basis of marking', I, III, 296.

Burt, C., 'Test Construction and the Scaling of Items', *British Journal of
Statistical Psychology*, IV (1951), pp. 95–129.

*Intelligence and Attainment Tests as Predictors (Prognostic Use of Tests) for
Secondary Education*
Hughes, A. G., 'Intelligence tests and entrance examinations to secondary
schools', IV, III, 221.

Thomson, G. H., 'The value of intelligence tests in an examination for selecting pupils for secondary education', VI, II, 174.

Wrigley, J., 'The relative efficiency of intelligence and attainments tests as predictors of success in grammar schools', XXV, II, 107.

Educational Abilities
Burt, C., 'The relation between educational abilities', IX, I, 45.

Ability and Attainment
Pidgeon, D. A., 'Ability and attainment of children at three age levels – a national survey', XXX, II, 124.

Sutherland, J., 'A comparison between pupils' arithmetical ability in the secondary school and their ability at the time of their transfer from primary school', XXI, I, 3.

Testing the Intelligence of Young Children
Cattell, R. B. and Bristol, H., 'Intelligence tests for mental ages of 4–8 years', III, II, 142.

Walekam, B. B., 'The application of a new intelligence test and the prediction of backwardness in an infant school', XIV, III, 142.

Personality and Personality Measurement
Astington, E., 'Personality assessment and academic performance in a boys' grammar school', XXX, III, 225.

Burt, C., 'The assessment of personality', XV, III, 107.

Chown, S. M., 'Personality factors in the formation of occupational choice', XXIX, I, 23.

Himmelweit, H. T. and Petrie, A., 'The measurement of personality in children', XXI, I, 9.

Maberley, A., 'Personality of the problem child', XVI, I, 5.

Maddox, H., 'A discussion of the measurement of personality in children', XXII, II, 205.

Articles on Personality from Other Sources
Cattell, R. B. and Drevdahl, J. E., 'A comparison of the personality profile of eminent researchers with that of eminent teachers and administrators', *British Journal of Psychology* (1955).

Northway, M. L., 'A study of personality patterns in children least acceptable to their age mates', *Sociometry* (February 1944).

Projective Technique
Bene, E., 'The objective use of projective technique illustrated by a study of the differences in attitude between pupils of grammar schools and of secondary modern schools', XXVII, II, 89.

Interviewing
Burroughs, G. E. R., 'A study of the interview in the selection of students for teacher training', XXVIII, I, 37.

Burt, C., 'The Psychology of the Interview', *Occupational Psychology*, XVI, pp. 38–41.

Statistical Calculations
Amos, J. R., Brown, F. L. and Mink, Oscar G., *Statistical Concepts* (Harper

& Row, 1965): one of the simplest introductions to the basic techniques and processes. It presents the information, step by step, in the form of a linear programme. After every step, the reader knows whether he has made the correct response.

Note

Students who eventually become interested in research, and who wish to obtain up-to-date information concerning research in the areas outlined in the present volume will find great assistance in *Educational Research in Great Britain*, ed. H. J. Butcher, University of London Press.

Index